Albanian Identities

Centre for South-East European Studies,
University College London
Nash Albanian Studies Programme

'Skanderbeg and the people', sculpture by Janaq Paço and Genc Hajdari in the National Museum, Kruje, Albania

STEPHANIE SCHWANDNER-SIEVERS
BERND J. FISCHER
editors

Albanian Identities

Myth and History

HURST & COMPANY, LONDON

First published in the United Kingdom by
C. Hurst & Co. (Publishers) Ltd,
38 King Street, London WC2E 8JZ

Printed in Scotland by Bell & Bain Ltd

A Cataloguing in Publication data record for this book is available from the British Library.

ISBNs
1-85065-571-5 *casebound*
1-85065-572-3 *paperback*

A Coat*

I made my song a coat
Covered with embroideries
Out of old mythologies
From heel to throat;
But the fools caught it,
Wore it in the world's eyes
As though they'd wrought it.
Song, let them take it,
For there's more enterprise
In walking naked.

WILLIAM BUTLER YEATS

*W.B. Yeats, *Collected Poems*, London: Macmillan, 2nd edn 1950, p. 142. Reprinted by permission of A.P. Watt Ltd on behalf of Michael B. Yeats.

CONTENTS

Part II. MYTHS IN COMMUNIST POLITICS, SOCIETY AND CULTURE

Part III. NATIONALIST HISTORIOGRAPHY— OR FRIENDS, FOES AND HEROES

Part IV. MYTHS AND CONTESTED BOUNDARIES

ACKNOWLEDGEMENTS

We are greatly indebted to many colleagues and friends without whom this work would be considerably more flawed than it is, and to the various institutions whose generous funding helped bring the contributors together at the London conference which made this book possible.

First, we thank the contributors for their wonderful work, and for coping with our occasional badgering. We appreciate, too, the encouragement, cooperation and inspiration kindly offered by the editorial advisory board which included Wendy Bracewell (London), Ger Duijzings (London), Michael Dwyer (of C. Hurst & Co., Publishers, London), Fatos Lubonja (Tirana), Piro Misha (Tirana), and George Schöpflin (London).

We also thank H.E. Agim Fagu, Ambassador of Albania to the United Kingdom, and Professor Michael Branch, Director of the School of Slavonic and East European Studies (SSEES), University College London, for setting a most valuable frame in their introductions to the conference. We particularly acknowledge SSEES for providing the venues and facilities for the conference, and we are grateful to Kristin Molloy and Esther Williams for their invaluable administrative support. The following institutions have earned our gratitude for their generous sponsorship: the Nash Fund for Albanian Studies (London), the Open Society Foundation (Tirana), the British Association for Central and East Europe (London), the Anglo-Albanian Association (London) and the British-Albanian Legal Association (London). Mr Gëzim Qëndro, director of the National Gallery of

Arts, Tirana, kindly gave permission for the fine picture 'Diary of a Partisan' by Pandi Mele to be used on the cover.

But as usual in projects of this nature, it is those closest to us who always pay the greatest price. We would therefore like to mention in particular the patience, support and help of Garry Marvin, Nicola Schwandner and Debra Fischer.

London and Fort Wayne, October 2001 THE EDITORS

THE CO-AUTHORS

Roderick Bailey graduated with an MA in History from the University of Edinburgh and M.Phil in Historical Studies from the University of Cambridge before returning to Edinburgh where, for his PhD, he is researching the activities in wartime Albania of Britain's Special Operations Executive. He was the Alistair Horne Fellow at St Antony's College, Oxford, for 2000/1.

Isa Blumi graduated from the New School for Social Research. Previously a Fulbright fellow, he currently holds a Social Research Council/ International Dissertation Research Fund fellowship working towards a PhD for the joint History/Middle Eastern Studies program at New York University on late Ottoman History in North Albania and Yemen.

Nathalie Clayer, a researcher at the Centre Nationale de la Recherche Scientifique (CNRS), Paris, is known as a specialist of the history of Sufi orders in the Balkans, and of Islam and identity questions among the Albanians. She is the author of *L'Albanie, pays des derviches* (1990) and *Mystiques, Etat et Société. Les Halvetis dans l'aire balkanique de la fin du XVe siècle à nos jours* (1994).

Ger Duijzings is Lecturer in Serbian and Croatian Studies at the School of Slavonic and East European Studies, University College London. As a cultural anthropologist he did most of his fieldwork in Kosovo, Croatia and Bosnia. His latest publication is *Religion and the Politics of Identity in Kosovo* (2000).

Bernd J. Fischer is Professor of History at Indiana University, Fort Wayne. He is the author of *Albania at War, 1939–1945* (1999) and *King Zog and the Struggle for Stability in Albania* (1984). In addition he has contributed numerous chapters, articles and papers on Albanian history.

Denisa Kostovicova received her PhD from the Department of Geography, University of Cambridge. She has been looking at the parallel education system in Kosovo in 1992–8. She is co-editor of *Kosovo: Myths, Conflict and War* (1999) and author of *Parallel Worlds: Response of Kosovo Albanians to Loss of Autonomy in Serbia, 1989–1996,* (1997).

Annie Lafontaine is a PhD candidate in Social and Cultural Anthropology at the University of Montreal, and in the department's research team on Albania and Kosovo. Funded by the Canadian Research Support Fund (FCAR) she is currently conducting anthropological fieldwork in Kosovo to complete her thesis on Migration, Identity and Trauma: the Displacement in Kosovo and the North American Diaspora.

Fatos Lubonja is a writer, journalist and the chief editor of the quarterly review *Përpjekja* (Endeavour)—the endeavour is to introduce a critical spirit into Albanian culture. He is known as author of *Ploja e Mbrame* (The final slaughter), (1994), *Në Vitin e Shtatëmbëdhjetë* (In the seventeenth year), Tirana: (1994) *Ridënimi* (The second sentence), (1996) and *Liri e Kërcënuar* (Threatened freedom), the (1999), all published in Tirana, as well as numerous critical essays and articles published in Albanian and in the international press during 1991–2000.

Nicola Mai is a DPhil candidate in Media and Cultural Studies at the Graduate Research Centre in Culture and Communication, University of Sussex. He has conducted fieldwork in Albania and Macedonia, where he has also been involved in development work with young people and refugees. His work has focused on cross-cultural media consumption in relation to the emergence of transnational youth cultures, trauma, memory and identity, anthropology of development in relation to the phase of post-communist transformation in Albania and the rest of the Balkans.

Noel Malcolm received his PhD in History from Cambridge University, where he was a Fellow of Gonville and Caius College from 1981 to 1988. Since then he has been Foreign Editor of the *Spectator*, a Visiting Fellow of St Antony's College, Oxford, and a Visiting Lecturer at Harvard University. He recently gave the Carlyle Lectures at Oxford. His publications on south-east European subjects include biographies of Marc' Antonio de Dominis (1984) and George Enescu (1990), and histories of Bosnia (1994) and Kosovo (1998). His most recent work, co-edited with Quintin Hoare, is *Books on Bosnia: A Critical Bibliography* (1999).

Piro Misha is Programme Director of the Open Society Foundation for Albania. He has published several books, including *In Search of the Roots, or Albanians Return to History* (1998), published in Tirana. He is also member of the working group for the United Nations Development Programme's *Human Development Report for Albania.*

Mariella Pandolfi is Professor of Anthropology at the University of Montreal. As a psychoanalyst and anthropologist she previously worked and published on themes such as the political links between collective traumatic experiences and the body's narratives in southern Italy, as well as on internal ideological differentiation processes. In the late 1990s she investigated the humanitarian and international presence in Albania and Kosovo which she defined as 'supra-colonialism' in her book *Mobile Powers: the Humanitarian Industry in Albania and Kosovo* (Rome, 2000).

Gilles de Rapper, CNRS Paris, completed his doctoral research in Social Anthropology at the University of Paris X-Nanterre and studied International Relations at the University of Marne-la-Vallée. His work addresses the issues of borders and mobility in south-eastern Europe. He has published on the Greek-Albanian border and on Albanian communities in Greece, Turkey and former Yugoslavia.

Fabian Schmidt graduated from of the Free University of Berlin in 1994 before working and continuously publishing on Albanian political development and crises for the Open Media Research Institute in Prague and for the Radio Free Europe/Radio Liberty. From 1997 to 1998 he was director of the Albania Media Monitoring Project of the Institute for War and Peace Reporting in Tirana and London. He served as research analyst for political issues on former Yugoslavia and Albania at the Südost Institut, Munich before becoming director of the Bosnian section of Deutsche Welle.

George Schöpflin holds the Jean Monnet chair of East European Politics and heads the Centre for Studies in Nationalism at the School of Slavonic and East European Studies, University College London. His numerous publications include *Politics in Eastern Europe, 1945–1992* (1995), *Myths and Nationhood* of which he is co-editor (1997); and *Nations, Identity, Power: The New Politics of Europe* (2001).

Stephanie Schwandner-Sievers is the first Nash Fellow for Albanian Studies at the School of Slavonic and East European Studies in London. Since 1992 she has conducted anthropological research and published intensively on questions such as identity and social cohesion, politics of ethnicity and 'tradition' during the transition in Albania and, recently, Kosovo.

Elias G. Skoulidas received his PhD in History from the University of Ioannina, Greece, working on topics related to the Greek-Albanian relations especially in the second half of the 19th century.

Alex Standish is chairman of the Board of the British Centre for Research into Post-Communist Economies and editor of *Jane's Intelligence Digest*. A Balkan specialist, resident in Albania in 1992–4 and in 1997, he has produced television documentaries on Albania and Kosovo for the BBC.

Galia Valtchinova graduated in History at the University of Sofia in 1983. Currently she holds a senior research fellowship at the Institute of Thracology in Sofia, is an associate member of the Institut des Sciences et Techniques de l'Antiquité (ISTA), Université de Franche-Comté, Besançon; and is completing her second doctoral thesis in Anthropology at the EHESS-Paris. She is the author of two books and numerous articles (in Bulgarian), and teaches history and anthropology of the ancient and contemporary Balkans.

More information on these and other specialists on Albanian topics can be found in the Albanian Studies Registry of Scholars and Research in the Humanities and Social Sciences, www.ssees.ac.uk: *Centre for South East European Studies / Albanian Studies.*

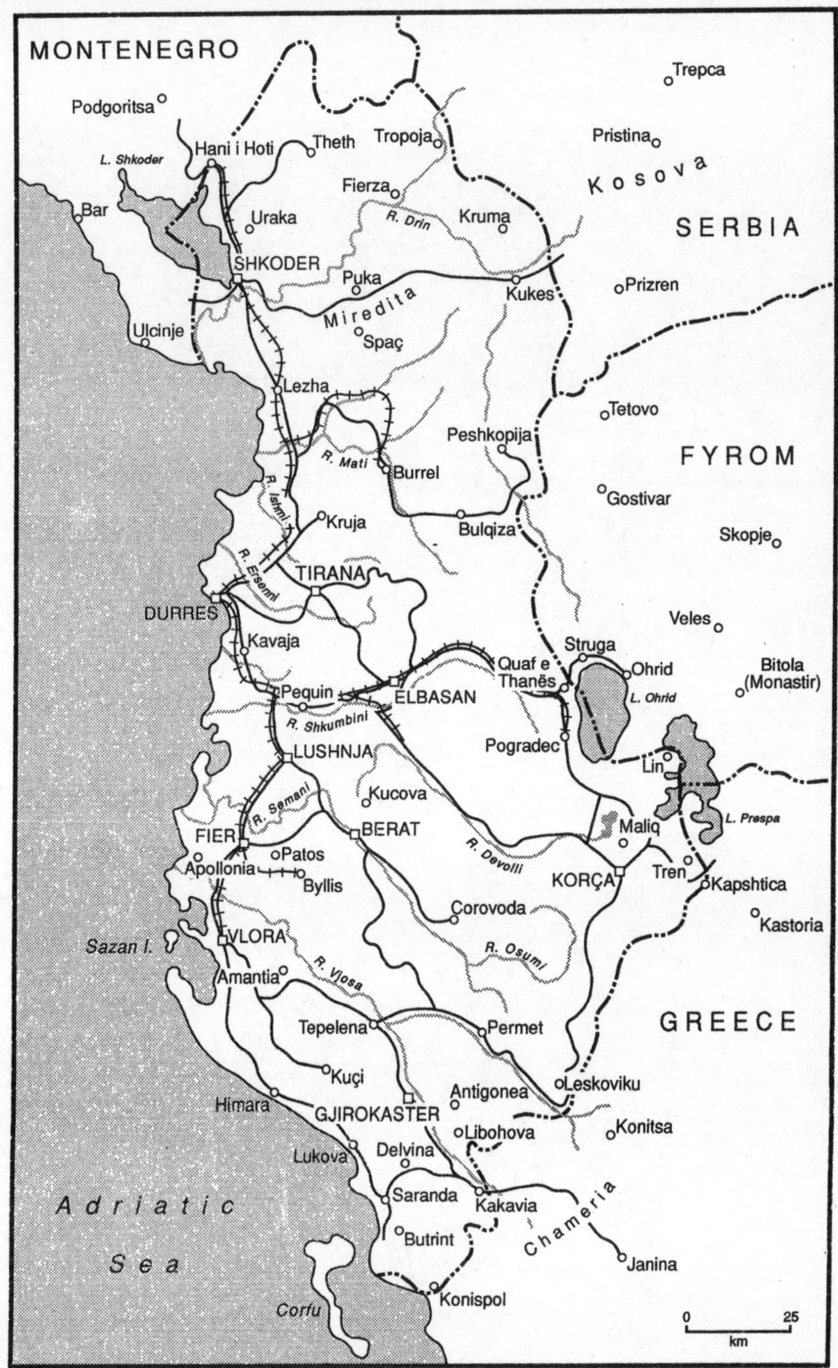
MONTENEGRO
Podgoritsa
Hani i Hoti
Theth
Tropoja
Trepca
Pristina
L. Shkoder
Bar
Uraka
Fierza
R. Drin
Kruma
Kosova
SERBIA
SHKODER
Puka
Kukes
Prizren
Miredita
Spaç
Ulcinje
Lezha
Tetovo
Peshkopija
R. Mati
Burrel
FYROM
R. Ishmi
Gostivar
Kruja
Bulqiza
Skopje
R. Ersenni
TIRANA
DURRES
Veles
Kavaja
Struga
Quaf e Thanës
Ohrid
Bitola (Monastir)
Pequin
ELBASAN
L. Ohrid
R. Shkumbini
Pogradec
LUSHNJA
Lin
Kucova
R. Semani
L. Prespa
FIER
BERAT
Maliq
Patos
R. Devolli
Apollonia
Byllis
KORÇA
Tren
Kapshtica
Corovoda
Kastoria
VLORA
Sazan I.
R. Osumi
Amantia
R. Vjosa
GREECE
Tepelena
Permet
Kuçi
Leskoviku
Himara
Antigonea
GJIROKASTER
Libohova
Konitsa
Lukova
Delvina
Saranda
Kakavia
Adriatic Sea
Chameria
Butrint
Janina
Konispol
Corfu
0
25
km

INTRODUCTION

NARRATIVES OF POWER

CAPACITIES OF MYTH IN ALBANIA[1]

Stephanie Schwandner-Sievers

In his recently published *Dictionary of Psycho-Errors* the psychologist Rolf Degen revisits the paradigms of his academic discipline and sharply deconstructs what he takes to be the myths on which contemporary psycho-analytic practices are based. For example, he dismisses the idea that 'it is a sign of spiritual health to seek—without any bias—the truth.' He claims, rather, that embedded universally in the human psyche is a healthy tendency to appropriate selectively only such information as confirms positive self-perceptions and world-views while less favourable ones are ignored. Such a tendency helps the psyche to avoid 'dissonances'. Yet, he continues, in experimental situations participants told to defend their opinions before a critical public suddenly opened up to counter-arguments in anticipation of the need to argue their case. Degen makes the point that 'political actors are well-advised to engage with the standpoints of dissidents if they do not want to be taken by surprise by their arguments.'[2]

If we shift the focus from the level of individual, personal psychology to that of the social and the collective (however defined)—in terms of deeply held opinions and beliefs—one might question the right of others, outsiders, to deconstruct such opinions and beliefs. In the specific context here, do others have the right to deconstruct another people's national myths? Can those so engaged be held responsible

[1]I thank Garry Marvin, Wendy Bracewell and Bernd Fischer for their invaluable comments on earlier drafts of this paper, and particularly for helping me polish my stilted 'Germanic' English.

[2]Rolf Degen, *Lexikon der Psycho-Irrtümer*, Frankfurt/Main: Eichborn Verlag 2000.

for the 'destruction' of a particular form of national integrity? Those who closely identify with their particular national myths will possibly feel offended. From the standpoint of those who employ myths, who live by them, for whom they have deep significance and meaning, myths may be recounted and interpreted but they are not meant to be deconstructed. Myths are, in part, constitutive of collective identity, symbolic narratives communicating individual membership of a group and the deconstruction of myths might be taken as an attack on the social and political capacities of a people and therefore interpreted as an aggressive or at least a political act.

In terms of this present collection of essays, what might be the effect of an academic enterprise which deconstructs a selected nation's myths? On what basis, and how, are we defining the term 'myth' and the qualities and power we ascribe to it? How can we approach terms such as 'truth,' 'fact,' 'history' and 'memory' in relation to 'myth'? Lastly, if we venture to identify 'myth' in the history and politics of a country, are we claiming that there is a dichotomy between the 'rational' and the 'irrational', or between 'critical' and 'passionate' ways of thought, in which our own approach represents the modern, developed forms? This introduction constitutes an attempt to clarify these sensitive issues and to locate the intent of writing *Albanian Identities: Myth and History* in the context of contemporary international academic debate.

This book engages with the field of tension arising between the homogenous thought of national ideology and a heterogeneous, diversified world within Albania itself and within which it finds itself internationally. Crisis-ridden Albania is a particularly interesting case in that it demonstrates how, during and after totalitarianism and international isolation, myths operate and how they underpin political and social processes. With political changes in the early nineties the 'dissonances' of a social and ideological pluralism have entered what was, arguably, the most closed society of all the former East European socialist states. Post-communist infusions of international recipes for development, themselves permeated by myth, have made it a test case for Karl Popper's dichotomies of 'closed' and 'open' societies, and the transition from one to the other. Equally, the repeated experience of violently contested territory and of international intervention in contemporary Albanian history (the last being the 1999 Kosovo War), as well as repeated processes of state-political disintegration in the 1990s, have given new significance to the issues of political consolidation and national integrity.

The contributions here represent selected papers from a conference held in London in June 1999, entitled *The Role of Myth in History and Development in Albania*. This conference set out to deconstruct prevalent political or historiographic Albanian myths. It sought to trace the context of their production and transformations, and to show how local and individual variations stand in contrast to the homogenous national claims of Albanian myths. The emphasis lay on the social and political environment, the reasons and rationales of the actors who select, invent and use myths in shaping national ideology, as well as on the messages embodied in given myths.

The contributors to this book are international scholars of history, anthropology, sociology, cultural and development studies, political sciences and international relations. Each present the results of recent research or apply the contemporary theoretical perspectives of their discipline to the Albanian case. Additionally, academically and journalistically trained experts of Albanian politics, some of them active political consultants, were invited to contribute to the intellectual adventure of the conference and this book.

For most contributors, although they are not Albanians, Albanian Studies is a central part of their professional specialisation. The authors neither share an essentialist nor organic notion of the nation which, in contemporary theory, has been replaced by Bendict Anderson's postulate of the 'imagined community' based on ideological construction. Yet no author denies the 'Albanianess' of shared experiences and perceptions, i. e. a shared culture, nor questions that there are reasons for pride in being Albanian. This book is not an attack on the Albanian nation but is rather an academic and intellectual exploration of the nationalist politics of ideology. Albania, respected as a cultural, political and social entity with a particular history, is here construed as offering an intellectual challenge—that of analysing, interpreting and understanding what makes Albania what it is.

Given the demands of space, only a selection from an abundance of highly interesting and original conference presentations will be presented in this volume. Here are assembled those papers which addressed the political context of myth creation, the political use and control of myths, and their social implications. For the reader interested in a fuller range of the conference papers, the majority of these can be found, as originally presented, but translated into Albanian, in the journal *Përpjekja* 15–16, 1999, edited by Fatos Lubonja. [3]

One of the contributions, not included in this present volume,

[3]For those interested in a collection of classic Albanian myths, see Robert Elsie's *Dictionary of Albanian Religion, Mythology and Folk Culture*, London: Hurst 2001.

raised a number of significant issues which will be addressed here. Artan Fuga's philosophically sophisticated view of one individual Albanian myth was not included because its narrow in-depth focus did not allow for political contextualisation. Luckily, space in this introduction gives us a chance to highlight the value of this contribution for the wider discussion.

Fuga unfolded the layers of meaning of the Rozafa legend and its propitiatory sacrifice in which one of three brothers' wives is walled alive into a castle under construction in order to ensure its solidity. Fuga's interpretation emphasised the dilemma encapsulated in the narrative, which could very well stand for dilemmas of contemporary Albanian ambiguities in respect to political, or public, morale. In the legend three brothers are employed in the construction of the walls of a castle which, after being built during the day, mysteriously fall at night. The brothers are advised by a stranger that they should make a sacrifice of the wife who comes the next day with their food. They swear an oath of secrecy—none of them are to warn their wives. Only the younger brother is faithful to the oath—the others warn their wives—and it is his wife who comes and is sacrificed. Here the brothers who do not conform to their *besa*, manage to keep their wives while, because of their betrayal, the castle is built on the basis of their faithful brother's wife's sacrifice. According to Fuga, the allegorical message of this story is that amorality secures solidity whereas the proper contractual relationship is followed by permanent destruction (in the legend: of the building). The narrative's conflict could, therefore, also be interpreted as a metaphor for the conflict between immediate (family) solidarity and obedience to overarching authority (the stranger, sacral prescriptions, and the state). In this it encapsulates the conflict of nation-state building processes themselves. How can national cohesion be secured when local mythology tells of the tragedy involved, i.e. sacrificing primordial affiliations? One way is to transfer local mythology onto the national stage, appropriating *besa* as the highest 'national value', and thereby 'domesticating' local tradition. Indeed, the history of *besa* is a history of changing authorities making use of local mythology in their appeals to this tradition whenever there was a need to win local loyalty beyond narrow village kin-group solidarity. Yet such unwritten contracts based on notions of 'honour' between alien state administrators and locals always eventually failed.[4] Repeatedly, however,

[4]For a discussion of the role of the concept of *besa* in Albanian national history see Ismet Elezi, *E Drejta zakonore Penale e Shqiptarëve dhe Lufta për Zhdukjen e Mbeturinave të saj në Shqipëri*, Tirana: 8 Nëntori 1983; and for more recent Kosovo issues: *ibid.*,

besa became a successful ritual device to ensure internal appeasement and solidary action for any Albanian bonds in the national movement (for example, the League of Prizren) and nation-state building processes. Where the local knowledge holds that 'those who talk so much of *besa* might also break it,'[5] *besa* when gloriously transformed for the sake of national ideology offered, at least temporarily, a screen on which to project aspired collective characteristics such as loyalty, faithfulness, cohesion, and sacrifice for the sake of honour.

The political use and politically motivated transformation of the content of *besa*, from a complex representation of group conflict to mere glorified national self-description, evokes questions concerning the capacity of content and context of myth. Fuga's contribution demands sensitivity to the different definitions of myth used by linguists, philosophers, sociologists, anthropologists, and historians and in this context by the conference participants.

Are there archetypes in modern myths? Interdisciplinary problems in defining myth

Arguably, there is a risk of 'mystification of myth' in some approaches to its definition. There are different approaches within any of the disciplines named, and yet there are also intersections. They differ in the extent to which significance is assigned more to 'content,' 'form' or 'context' or to the implications of production and narration. In other words, do 'archetypal structures,' and the 'truth' of content or the social and political functions and implications of myth matter most? Here the aim is to benefit from the insights offered by all the approaches considered and, further, to attempt a theoretical reconciliation of such approaches.

'Pajtimi i gjaqeve në Kosovë dhe rëndësia e tij politiko-shoqërore', *Zëri i Popullit*, December 19, 1990, p. 3.; a critical summary of the political use of *besa* in history as well as its social functions, cf. Stephanie Schwandner-Sievers, 'Humiliation and Reconciliation in Northern Albania: The Logics of Feuding in Symbolic and Diachronic Perspective' in Georg Elwert, Stephan Feuchtwang, Dieter Neubert (eds), *Dynamics of Violence: Processes of Escalation and De-Escalation in Violent Group Conflicts (Sociologus)*, supplement 1, Berlin: Duncker and Humblot 1999, pp. 133–52, here 146 n.

[5]The words cited stem from personal conversation with Ardian Klosi at a conference in 1993. Incidentally, Klosi studied Ismail Kadare's literary interpretation of the Rozafa legend in its 'demythologising aspects:' Ardian Klosi, *Mythologie am Werk. Kazantzakis, Andric, Kadare. Eine vergleichende Untersuchung des Bauopfermotivs*, Slavistische Beiträge, vol. 277, Munich: Otto Sagner 1991, pp. 107, 115.

Joanna Overing explains that 'a usual way of categorising modern anthropological approaches of myth is to distinguish between functionalist, symbolist and structuralist approaches.'[6] Many contributors of this book, particularly the anthropologists and sociologists, would recognise themselves as falling into the structural-functionalist orientation of British anthropology regarding questions of social identity and (political) power. Going back to Emile Durkheim and Bronislaw Malinowski, this approach, rather than focusing on its archetypal structure, highlights a myth's capacity to provide social cohesion through symbolic information on a group's social order and on its function as a symbolic reminder for an individual of group identity:

> The strength of the functionalist framing of myth is that it contextualizes myth within the daily social and political life of the community ... Functionalists also insist ... that the meaning of myth is located only in the arena of pragmatic socio-cultural interaction.[7]

Overing points to Malinowski who 'stressed the social power of myth, and the potency of its use in matters of political concern that have to do with the legitimation of the inequalities of privilege and status.'[8] Accordingly, the role of myth in a given social group includes the construction of a collective identity as well as the justification and sanctification of existing rules and leadership. However, she criticises Lévi-Strauss's universalist approach of seeking understanding of the subconscious, analogical processes of classification of the human mind in the comparative analyses of myths and mythologies. In particular she is critical of the structural schism of scientific (or rational) versus mythical (irrational) thought which underpins his theories. Overing welcomes the current emphasis in anthropological theory (however much this still might be based on structural judgmental dichotomies such as 'rational' versus 'irrational') on understanding 'the conscious use of myths through which basic (conscious) postulates of reality are also expressed, and as such made constitutive of every-day practice.'[9]

Along the same lines George Schöpflin offers a useful definition

[6]Joanna Overing, 'The Role of Myth: An Anthropological Perspective' in Geoffrey Hosking and George Schöpflin (eds), *Myths and Nationhood*, London: Hurst 1997, pp. 1–18, here p. 7.

[7]*Ibid.*, p. 8.

[8]*Ibid.* pp. 7–8, referring to Bronislaw Malinowski, *Magic, Science and Religion*, Garden City, NY: Doubleday 1954, p. 84.

[9]Overing, 'The Role of Myth ...,' p. 10, cf. also 7.

of myth by explicitly emphasising its social role. To paraphrase him:[10] 'myths' can be understood as often fictitious, highly metaphorical and symbolic, and always identity-constitutive narratives reproduced as a set of shared references by members of a group in order to define their group characteristics and to mark the group's boundaries. Content, truth or facts as well as belief or disbelief in such narratives are secondary to the actual employment of myth as a means of identity construction—though the resonance among the members of the group ensures the myth's internalisation. However the actual sharing of the narrative can be more identity-constitutive (and group representative) than the explanatory character of the myth's content, or the group members' belief of a particular myth.

Schöpflin, in his contribution to this book, again underlines the value of myths in ensuring social cohesion. He also, significantly, reminds us, and illustrates this, that myths permeate all societies, past and present, East or West. But, developing from his functionalist approach, one can ask about the fixity and fluidity of myth. Can myth be transformed, changed, even in structure, as part of political processes and is it legitimate to compare modern political myths with archetypal ancient myths? In short, are 'myths' or 'people' shaping social groups?

Lucian Boia's discipline-reconciling article 'Explorations into the Imaginary'[11] allows for recognition of 'archetypal structures' within social contexts. According to him, archetypes are not only part of structure but must also be acknowledged in their historicity. They should be understood as 'dynamic, precisely because [they] are open structures, which evolve, are combined among themselves, and whose contents is [sic] incessantly adjusted to the changing social environment.' He distinguishes between the popular use of the term 'myth' and the 'rather restrictive definitions ... formulated by the specialist of "classical mythologies".' With the former, 'fictions of any sort, prejudices, stereotypes, distortions, or exaggerations are covered, all but unscrupulously, by this concept with an imperialistic turn.' The latter, limits 'the domain ... actually ... to archaic, traditional societies; it is the myth in its original sense: a fabulous narrative, essentially bent on origins.' Boia agrees implicitly with assumptions of the universality of archetypal structures in human thought as generated by mythologists

[10]George Schöpflin, 'The Functions of Myth and a Taxonomy of Myths' in *Myths and Nationhood*, pp. 19–35, here 19–28.

[11]Lucian Boia, 'Explorations into the Imaginary' in *PLURAL*, Romanian Cultural Foundation, Culture and Civilization, 1, pp. 15–41.

such as Mircea Eliade or Claude Lévi-Strauss. Yet he specifies that 'forms and functions evolve, whereas *mythical sensibility* remains inseparable from human spirituality,' and continues to define myth as an 'imaginary construction: a narrative, representation, or idea purporting to grasp the gist of cosmic and social phenomena, based on the intrinsic values of the community and with the purposes of ensuring its cohesion [sic].'[12]

Modern political Albanian myth and mythical tropes do indeed exhibit familiar archetypal structures. Loosely following the typology of archetypes suggested by Boia,[13] contemporary Albanian myths, dressed in new clothes, would fall into categories of archetypal structures such as 'transcendent realities' of mythical leaders; emerge in the holy paraphernalia of old and new heroes and in hero worship; in expressions of 'otherness' in both prevalent fears of the outside world and the 'decipherment of future' (the latter incorporated both in Orientalist and Occidentalist idealisations); in archetypes of 'unity' as, for example, visible in the purported unifying principles of one common language, gender and social equality in Communism; they appear particularly clearly in 'reiterations of origins,' i. e. in myths of descent and in 'the fight of (complementary) opposites' evident in all ideologies organising the world into friend and foe, such as modern conspiracy theories;[14] and lastly, in attempts to 'evade destiny' or history in strategies such as deliberate forgetting and oblivion.

Neither this introduction nor the book itself will present a comprehensive list of all Albanian myths employed today, nor categorise them in a Boia-type Albanian 'history of the imaginary' according to categories of archetypes, nor will it analyse universal archetypal structures prevalent in Albanian myths. However, contemporary Albanian myths as discussed in this book may be seen to conform to 'a number of fairly standard myths [that] can be found, notably, in Central and Eastern Europe.'[15] Schöpflin, in his 'taxonomy' of these myths, lists them as 'myths of territory;' 'myths of redemption and suffering' including 'antemural myths,' in which the nation in question makes sacrifices in fighting to save Europe from the invasions of Barbarians (or from 'Orientals'); myths of unjust treatment; 'myths of [formerly divine, now profane] election' in terms of moral superi-

[12]*Ibid.*, pp. 20, 38.
[13]*Ibid.*, pp. 30–4.
[14]On conspiracy theories cf. Schöpflin, 'The Functions of Myth ...', pp. 25, 27.
[15]*Ibid.*, p. 28.

ority; 'myths of military valour' (particularly in guerrilla movements); 'myths of foundation;' 'myths of ethnogenesis and antiquity;' and 'myths of kinship and shared descent.'

Arguably, if we refrain from 'mystifying myth,' then both ancient and modern myths differ only in respect to their stage of evolution, i.e. in terms of their divergence from living memory and historical accountability. Modern myths, for example, are confronted by, but also have access to, written culture. On the one hand they can be more effectively and more quickly standardised and more widely distributed. But, on the other hand, they may fall prey to a weapon of the modern historian—the close critical and 'scientific' reading of written documents. It is, accordingly, less the historicity of myths themselves in processes of transformation, or as shaped by changing social and political context, but the question of historical 'truth' which motivated the historians in this book to investigate Albanian myths.

'Truth', myth and history

As with the political scientists, the contributing historians are aware of the political or social context in which particular myths were created, transformed, used or manipulated in order to establish the legitimacy of leadership or to tell a group of people, particularly members of the nation, about themselves. Through questioning the 'truth' in nationalist historiography the historian's capacity to have an impact on perceptions of the past and the present within a given society may be more immediate than the sociologist's or anthropologist's attempt to describe social context and processes 'from within'. Historians are therefore more at risk of the accusation of being normative and judgmental by those who feel their particular 'truth' to be challenged.

From the anthropological perspective, Overing argues that myth and academic histories are employed with different intents, and cannot, therefore, be judged by the same standards. History as a discipline seeking 'scientific,' 'rational' or 'linear' understanding of physicalities is, ontologically, incommensurable with the moral and social concerns of the guardians and experts, such as shamans, of a society's myths.[16] Does this still hold true when myths leave the local and enter the state-political arena, which is much more the realm of historians? Perhaps the study of the different understandings of the myths, the variation of myths and the intents in the appropriations of myths offers

[16]Overing, 'The Role of Myth ...', pp. 10–15.

the possibility of uniting academic interest beyond the boundaries of the disciplines.

Contemporary historians themselves have pointed to the multiplicity of perspectives on myth as well as questioned the existence of 'true facts' in historiography. Felipe Fernández-Armesto's philosophical distinction between different truths and the co-existence of multiple truths might well be applied to the multiplicity of perspectives on myth: there is 'the truth you feel,' 'the truth you are told,' 'the truth of reason'; 'the truth you think for yourself' and lastly, 'the truth you perceive through your senses.'[17] William H. McNeill reiterated the contemporary self-reflective historian's insight that 'one person's truth is another's myth.'[18] He summarised the growing critical awareness among historians that even scientific source criticism falls short of guaranteeing 'truth' given the selection and arrangement of 'facts' according to apparently sensible patterns. Such patterns simply provide for one possible representation of 'history' out of the chaos of the available primary 'facts'.[19] While 'common parlance reckons myth to be false while history is, or aspires to be, true' and 'liberal faith, of course, holds that in a free marketplace of ideas, Truth will eventually prevail,' only 'a more rigorous and reflective epistemology,' and when historians 'bend their minds as critically and carefully as well as intelligible to an audience that shares enough of their particular outlook and assumptions to accept what they say. The result might best be called mythistory perhaps. ...'[20]

There may be truth in every 'mythistory.' But what then makes passionate nationalist historiography different from the particular epistemological character of 'objective' history which would, in any case, seek to go beyond 'narrow in-group sympathies'? It has been argued that the main difference lies in the narrative technique: the first would not hesitate to use 'metaphors,' the second has often been

[17]Felipe Fernández-Armesto, *The Truth: A History and Guide for the Perplexed*, London: Moreland/Albany: Black Swan 1998, pp. 6–7.

[18]William H. McNeill, 'Mythistory, or Truth, Myth, History, and Historians', *American Historical Review*, 91/1, 1986, pp. 1–10, here p. 6.

[19]Cf. Wulf Kantsteiner, 'Hayden White's Critique of the Writing of History', *History and Theory*, vol. 32, 1993, pp. 273–95.

[20]McNeill, 'Mythistory ...', pp. 1, 4, 8. McNeill was president of the American Historical Association in 1985, and these citations stem from his published presidential address. His prominent position makes his remarks all the more indicative of the significance of the self-reflective approaches within 'Western' history from the 1980s.

dominated by 'the limitations of the ironic trope' in attempting to establish a dispassionate distance to the object.[21] Be that as it may, I would argue that these techniques of historiography, and ethnography as well, are expressions of particular cultures, and histories, of academic writing and national memory.

Wolfgang Höpken has given an interesting explanation as to why historiography in South Eastern Europe still allows for metaphors of heroism and for textual strategies of glorifying the past—which would seem extremely dated to the outsider belonging to the contemporary critical Western 'culture of writing.' What might, at first sight, appear as an atavism of pre-modern orientation in its 'narrow in-group sympathy,' Höpken suggests, should be in fact, understood as, part of 'pan-European modernity.' Cults of heroes were part of national mobilising strategies in Western Europe and the USA until the Second World War, and, indeed, they still can be found. However, contemporary 'post-modern writing', which he understands as a result of post-Holocaust processes, fundamentally changed the forms of national memory of war. Schools of history in the established nations, including defeated Germany as well as the victorious Western Allies, 'after Auschwitz' found themselves unable to commemorate war in the previously acceptable and usually 'heroic' ways.

> Only the USSR, in the euphoria of a revolutionary utopia after 1917 and unlike the European states, had not participated in the cult of war commemorations of the [earlier] inter-war period—now incorporated a cult of the 'Great Patriotic War' with all its monumental, heroising forms, [characterised by] plenty of those visual and narrative stylistic methods of war commemoration which were most usual after the First World War [in Germany and among the Second World War allies].[22]

In South Eastern Europe, in which most nations soon became part of the Soviet sphere of influence, the Second World War had only just given birth to, or led to the reconstruction of, political entities (such as Yugoslavia), to new political systems (socialism), or to civil war (as in the case of Greece). Following Höpken's argument, the fragile and factional character of the South East Euopean nation-states resulting from this situation, as well as their ideological dependency on the

[21]Kantsteiner, 'Hayden White's Critique ...', pp. 277–8.

[22]Wolfgang Höpken, 'Krieg und historische Erinnerung auf dem Balkan' in Eva Behring, Ludwig Richter and Wolfgang F. Schwartz (eds), *Geschichtliche Mythen in den Literaturen und Kulturen Ostmittel—und Südosteuropas*, Stuttgart: Franz Steiner 1999, pp. 371–9, here p. 373 (my translation).

USSR (in all cases but Greece), may explain the continuing need for ethnically and politically reconciling myths of national homogeneity. Other historians implicitly suggest a more general historical explanation. They show that the nature of South East European historiography can best be understood in the context of the specific origins, nature, and development of nationalism in the region, including the influence of Great Power politics, as opposed to the impact of any aspect of World War Two itself.[23] In other words, the prevalence of nationalism in any form (of which the particular 'national historiography' would be just one among others) is explained in terms of historic specificity, and commonality within the Balkans, and the circumstances of each particular historical movement. In any case, a 'modernist' style of nationalist historiography has been perpetuated in South East European countries up to the present; whereas, in contrast, perhaps because of the 'Holocaust shock,' Western 'post-modern' academic developments led much more to an abolishment of metaphors of 'heroism.'

Albania had certainly been in the sphere of influence of this 'modernist style' of writing. Contemporary Albanian high school history textbooks discuss the lessons of the Second World War in the nation-centred terms of an 'anti-fascist liberation war' rather than providing any material for critically debating universal lessons from the systematic mass extinction of humans on nationalist and racist grounds.[24] The plot of the Albanian historiographical narrative is motivated by a desire to 'prove' their national right to existence, and is, therefore, nation-centred, rather than a questioning of world history. The latter, of course, could be seen in context of the repeated experiences of the denial of the right to live, or the denial of territory and a national identity (see particularly Piro Misha's contribution for an in-depth debate on reasons for the persistence of nationalist ideology in Albania). Possibly, the recent international military engagement and attitude towards ethnicist driven violence in the Kosovo War

[23]Bernd Fischer, personal correspondence; examples include Edgar Hösch, *Geschichte der Balkanländer. Von der Frühzeit bis zur Gegenwart*, Munich: C. H. Beck 1988; Mark Mazower, *The Balkans*, London: Weidenfeld & Nicolson 2000; Misha Glenny, *The Balkans* 1804–1999: *Nationalism, War and the Great Powers*, London: Granta 1999.

[24]Cf. *Historia e popullit shqiptar për shkollat e mesme*, Tirana: Shtëpia botuese e librit shkollor 1996 (Albanian edition), pp. 194–218, particularly p. 208. *Historia e popullit shqiptar për shkollat e mesme*, Prishtina: Enti i teksteve dhe i mjeteve mësimore i Kosovës 1996 (Kosovar edition), pp. 296–332, particularly p. 317.

(1999) could foster an understanding of the relativity (or redundancy) of this issue on the international stage in Albania.

If the printed 'mythistory' of, for example, schoolbooks, represents the dominant and sanctified ideological discourse of a nation, there are also a multitude of voices which are not represented. There may be orally transmitted histories which are not as standardised and fixed as 'national history' and can, therefore, less easily be held up to scholarly scrutiny for an understanding of their adaptation to circumstances of time and space. While acknowledging that orally transmitted material of local or individual memory must also have been selective and subject to change, giving a voice to them helps challenge the validity of one national 'truth' only.

Contested 'truth' and memory

During the post-communist transition national history in Albania became visibly contested from within—as can be witnessed in anthropological research of local arenas. National myths resonate only with the subjects as a 'message from the ruler to the ruled and enhancing the solidarity, and thus the trust, between the two parties'[25] when they are built on some basis of previous experience. In the homogenisation project of national historiography a number of local or individual memories and experiences were excluded from historiographic representation. Does the new pluralism of thought, in which previously suppressed local 'mythistories' gain new significance, create new conflict, or does the multiplicity of mutually challenging myths guarantee a fairer balance in which political authority is negotiated more democratically? The Yugoslav case has shown that the re-emergence of previously suppressed and forcefully homogenised, distinct ethnic histories, in combination with a number of other factors (economic, political, personal etc.), can lead to new wars. Arguably, the content of a particular group's constitutive myths and self-descriptions could account for more or less belligerent attitudes.

Fatos Lubonja, in his chapter, points to the hypocrisy which developed within Albania where the dominant representation of history did 'not make sense' for recipients in terms of their individual memory, experiences and expectations. However, facing totalitarian means of coercion, they learnt to live with pretence. Today, emerging subgroups in contemporary society, which re-emphasise their own

[25]Schöpflin, 'The Functions of Myth ...', p. 23f.

particular group 'mythistories,' provide illustrative examples of ideological dilemmas emerging when national myths of homogeneity are in conflict with apparent diversity.

A particular example of this would be that of the Southern Albanian Aromanian (or 'Vlach') communities which, with political transition, have won rights as a special 'cultural group'. However, during my fieldwork with them in 1996[26] I found many who explicitly wished to identify with their Albanian nationality. There I understood how interpretations of a contemporary history-textbook[27] as well as politics provoked distress among them in relation to a part of their particular subgroup myth. In this historical work Sali Butka (1852–1938) is depicted as a patriot commander of the Albanian 'liberation war' in the Balkan Wars and the First World War against, particularly, Greek territorial military and brigand operations in southern Albania. In the context of these 'heroic' deeds, Butka executed a number of 'Greeks' at Voskopoja in southern Albanian (an early prosperous bourgeois Balkan trading city even more contested by Aromanian, Albanian, Romanian and Greek claims on its history). Unfortunately for my respondents, some of Butka's victims had been their fathers, uncles and grandfathers. Their internal inversion of national history included the view that their forefathers were not 'national traitors' but rather Aromanian 'martyrs', and the status of Sali Butka in national history was conceived as insensitive to Aromanian feelings. Even more upsetting though, was the fact that Butka's son had become a parliamentary deputy in government in Tirana at the time.

There was an aspect of subgroup self-control in the fact that these conflicting interpretations of history were not put on a public stage during times of repeated national crises in the 1990s. Despite their new collective rights, Aromanians learnt a bitter lesson after press reports made them national scapegoats for political failures and constructed them as the 'internal other' (see Fabian Schmidt's presentation of conspiracy theories in which southern Orthodox Albanians are seen as apt to be 'pro-Greek'). Luckily, the Aromanian self-image included reference to ideals such as education, tolerance, mobility, flexibility and peacefulness—which may have guided their conflict-avoidance strategies in times of crisis.

[26]Cf. Stephanie Schwandner-Sievers, *The Albanian Aromanian's Awakening: Identity Politics and Conflicts in Post-Communist Albania*, working paper no. 3, Flensburg: European Centre for Minority Issues (ECMI) 1999.

[27]*Historia e popullit* (Tirana), pp. 153–4.

It cannot be assumed that with socio-political changes from a totalitarian to a pluralist system a single dominating myth structure would completely disappear in favour of a variety of subgroup defining myths, nor that there were not segregative myths available in Albanian communist times (see particularly Nicola Mai's contribution on the early influence of Italian television in Albania). The detailed anthropological studies of Gilles de Rapper and Annie Lafontaine in this volume show how identities are negotiated when different myths are in competition. Generally, it can be suggested that in a society shifting from totalitarian control and forceful integration to pluralist fragmentation, international influences, and repeated state disintegration and crisis, myths—like any group ideologies—oscillate in a field of tension between local and national perceptions of the world, as well as between homogenous and heterogeneous interpretations of national history. There is scope and choice in when, or when not, to make an appeal to a particular myth as there is a rationale for the variety of ways in which distinct identities are more or less emphasised or understood as relevant at different times and in different circumstances.

The (fatal) capacities of myth, memory and history

The mutually challenging existence of sometimes contradictory myths does not inevitably guarantee that there is space for individual critical thought and contestation at a given time. In Albania today, it seems to me, it is precisely the political use of myths both in local and national realms that has the capacity to transfer ideological pressure for conformity from central settings to a plurality of new settings, and vice versa. Myth is the political *modus operandi*, the tool of choice, for those who want to simplify complex realities for the sake of making a group's action predictable in its conformist perception of the world.

During Albanian Communism, myth construction was part of the totalitarian project—and any contestation would have ended in denunciation as an 'enemy of the people.' As Klaus Lange already showed in detail in the late 1980s, both Albanian external isolation and internal totalitarianism under Enver Hoxha had to be understood as a political strategy to ideologically homogenise and socially reconcile (or rather, 'force together') internal divergent forces for the sake of national unity.[28] As many contributions here elaborate, nineteenth-

[28]Klaus Lange, 'Innenpolitische Aspekte der albanischen Sicherheitspolitik' in *Das Parlament*, Beiheft 6, 1988, pp. 34–8, here 35 ff.

century élite-created myths became standardised and transformed to serve the nationalist-communist purposes of Enverist Albania after 1945.

Similarly in those contemporary Albanian settings in which violence is understood as a legitimate tool to enforce coherence (in others it is simply public ostracism) the myth of *besa* with its central value of 'faithfulness' is again being successfully employed.[29] Kosovo provides the most recent illustration: *besa* was used to swear-in recruits for the Kosovo Liberation Army (KLA);[30] the early KLA became infamous for killing its own 'traitors' as well as Serb policemen, and journalists expressing critical opinions were under threat.[31]

A study of *Bota Sot*, a Kosovo daily newspaper produced in Switzerland, which clearly follows a nationalist line, provides ample evidence of newly developing myths of heroes, martyrs and traitors of the war and of the national cause. The public commemoration and heroisation of those who died in war is comforting to those who lost their loved ones. On the other hand, a combination of memory and myth construction constitutes a social contract in the case of repetition. In Kosovo, social care for war veterans is strikingly insufficient and their compensation is little more than symbolic capital. The hidden message for potential fighters in the future is that should they become victims—injured or killed in conflict—then only symbolic value rather than material support will ensure some sort of survival of handicapped fighters, of family dependants, or of their memory.

It is often pointed out in studies of myth, particularly in terms of the theme of 'eternal return', that myths are in an important sense ahistorical, with time being circular and repetitive rather than linear. Yet doesn't history also try to understand patterns of the past in order to, ideally, serve as 'a fount of practical wisdom upon which people may draw when making decisions and taking action'[32] and possibly to predict the re-emergence of old patterns? Myth and History, in my understanding, share with Memory the potentiality of repetition, i. e. the capacity to become a self-fulfilling prophecy.[33] Those, for example, who have experienced the reality and immediacy of war and suffered

[29]Cf. S. Schwandner-Sievers, 'Humiliation and Reconciliation ...', pp. 149 n.

[30]Tim Judah, *Kosovo: War and Revenge*, New Haven and London: Yale University Press 2000, p. 99.

[31]Veton Surroi, 'Kosovo Tributes,' in *Balkan Crisis Report* 172, ed. by Institute for War and Peace Reporting, http://www.iwpr.net, September 15, 2000.

[32]McNeill, 'Mythistory ...', p. 2.

[33]Schöpflin, 'The Role of Myth ...', pp. 26–7.

the trauma of its destructive power usually hope that this will never reoccur. In contrast, those who remember with nostalgia dear and joyful events will seek their re-enactment. This circular understanding of the past can include the memory of sharing myths, in which case it is the actual experience of narratives being shared that becomes the object of retrospective yearning. Myth (as part of individual memory as well as of formal historiography), through its sacred and idealising character, in providing an idealised representation of past collective deeds, can be a particularly powerful inspirational and aspirational model for contemporary actors. Schöpflin emphasises the dangerous potential for myths to become self-fulfilling prophecies in, for example, creating perceptions of friend and foe, and McNeill highlights how

> a nation or any other human group that knows how to behave in crisis situations because it has inherited a heroic historiographical tradition that tells how ancestors resisted their enemies successfully is more likely to act together effectively than a group lacking such a tradition.[34]

In their archetypal structure and in the textual content of their narrative, myths tell us a story about ourselves. They provide an ideal-type model for understanding how we came into being as a group, who we were then and who we are now, the exploits and ideals of past heroes, as well as justifying our leaders and telling us who to avoid as an enemy. The active presence of myths in the politics and society of a given country cannot be taken as proof that the country is either more or less developed. However, the allowance of contested perceptions of myths, memories and experiences tells us something about whether a state-system is stable enough to tolerate the expression of difference from within.[35]

The capacity of contestation

Katherine Verdery in her study on Romanian nation-building processes elaborated on the idea of ideologies as the products of social and political processes.[36] In cases where myths serve as instruments

[34]McNeill, 'Mythistory ...', p. 6.

[35]George Schöpflin, *Nations, Identity, Power: The New Politics of Europe*, London: Hurst 2000. In this volume, Schöpflin particularly addresses the question of weak and strong states in relation to myths justifying the foundations of nation-states in terms of ethnic principles.

[36]Katherine Verdery, 'The Production and Defense of "the Romanian Nation",

of power her work suggests that élites could have reasons to deliberately invent, select, promote and establish them and to take into account the shading of alternative 'truths' for the sake of power and for cohesion of the group they aim to lead. There may be even a struggle between actors within the same interest groups as to which myths to emphasise. Through myth one can control access to information and shape the validity of a normative system. Myths, in their capacity as sacred narratives embodying idealised representations of a collective past, present or future, can serve those who seek to pursue power. They unite the individual with the group through the power of emotional attachment—they create feelings of, as well as moral justification for, belonging, pride, followership—and, by the same token, define exclusion, the 'traitor,' the other. When myths become politically controlled there is little space for deviant thought. The intellectual enterprise of the analysis of myth, if not itself subject to political oppression and is, therefore, a tool for recognising, clarifying and deconstructing the ideologies central to the present political processes of homogenisation and for identifying the agents of such processes and their motivations.

The contributions in this volume constitute an original approach to Albanian histories and politics. They aim to shed new light on, and offer new insights into, selected aspects of existing academic and popular knowledge of Albanian 'mythistory'. Most speakers at the conference from which this book derives were driven by a scholarly desire for understanding why, when, and how Albanian myths came into being, and how they once operated, still operate or, rather, are still operated. Many would hope, with Lévi-Strauss, that 'for each scholar and each writer, the particular way he or she thinks and writes opens a new outlook on mankind'[37]–in this case new outlooks on Albania.

Summary presentation of the contributions

Following the introductory section, which includes a theoretical debate 'The Nature of Myths' by George Schöpflin, the contributions

1900 to World War II' in Richard G. Fox (ed.), *Nationalist Ideologies and the Production of National Cultures*, Washington, DC: American Anthropological Association 1990, pp. 81–111.

[37]Claude Lévi-Strauss, *Myth and Meaning*, University of Toronto Press 1978, repr. London: Kegan Paul International 1999, p. 4.

are assembled and ordered in five parts, indicative of the approach of the authors: (I) 'The History of Albanian Myth Production' (Piro Misha, Isa Blumi, Ger Duijzings, Noel Malcolm); (II) 'Myths in Communist—Politics, Society and Culture' (Fatos Lubonja, Galia Valtchinova, Alex Standish); (III) 'Nationalist Historiography, or Friends, Foes and Heroes' (Nathalie Clayer, Bernd Fischer, Roderick Bailey); (IV) 'Myths and Contested Boundaries' (Denisa Kostovicova, Elias Skoulidas, Annie Lafontaine, Gilles de Rapper); and (V) 'Myths of Democracy, Development and the Future' (Mariella Pandolfi, Nicola Mai, Fabian Schmidt).

It should be noted that in order to avoid being drawn into any controversy about separatist terminology the spelling 'Kosovo' rather than the Albanian 'Kosova' will be used throughout this book unless explicitly indicated otherwise (as, for example, in the case of Ottoman categories in Isa Blumi's study). This follows the rules of international usage of the English language. Equally, city names and other non-English language designations are adapted to English phonetics where appropriate. In this the guidelines are entirely pragmatic.

(I) 'The History of Albanian Myth Production'

The wish to understand the reasons for the contemporary permeation of Albanian society and politics by myth motivates Piro Misha to seek the historical reasons for their creation and establishment in the drama of the delay of the nation-state building process. In debating the differences and similarities of Balkan nation-state movements he suggests an Albanian nationalism which resulted from the need to defend an identity denied within the processes of disintegration of the late Ottoman empire and by the other evolving Balkan nation-states, and as a reaction to experiences of repeated, often violent encounters. Isa Blumi picks up a significant detail in this process by investigating the role of education during the early Albanian nation-building process. In fact, he deconstructs a historians' myth which assumes general Balkan similarities in the process and form of national movements, particularly in the role of schools, by offering evidence of the effective suppression of Albanian schools during that time. Ger Duijzings explores the dilemma the Albanian religious divide posed for the ideologists of a national coherent identity. In his piece he tests the capacities of Bektashism as a national religion (as it was proclaimed by Naim Frashëri) in the nineteenth century. All authors tackling pre-communist national history in this book trace the impact of a myth coined by Pashko Vasa in the late nineteenth century according to which 'the religion of Albanians is Albanianism.'[38] Noel Malcolm precisely pinpoints the production and reimport of Albanian key national myths among Albanian writers in the US diaspora at the beginning of the twentieth century. An examination of the publications of the influential Vatra Association of Boston shows how the international political climate, particularly the need for international recognition of statehood at home, shaped the construction, or re-production, of identity providing myths such as the myths of origin, homogeneity and cultural purity, of permanent national struggle and of indifference to religion. Once again we re-encounter the themes of Albanianism as well as that of the historical delay of the Albanian nation-building process in this study.

(II) 'Myths in Communist Politics, Society and Culture'

Relating disasters of contemporary politics, particularly those of internal and external conflict, to the continuous reproduction of myths of friend and foe, Fatos Lubonja, more explicitly than the international contributors, emphasises the deconstruction of Albanian myths as a 'necessity'[39] at a time when 'here in Albania we still are under the tyranny of the old nationalistic myths.'[40] In his contribution to this book he makes us understand how, during Communism, the experience of indoctrination of nationalist-communist myths through history taught in schools, propaganda, and literature (illustrated by the writings of Ismail Kadare) affected Albanian perceptions of themselves and the world—an experience and a process which continues to have an impact today. Galia Valchinova follows the theme of the impact of Kadare's writing. She traces how, with sophisticated literary skills, in the multi-layered novel *The H-File*, Kadare transforms the early hypotheses of two American scholars on the Hellenic roots of traditional Albanian society into an ideological recipe for perceiving the Albanian myth of origin. Both of these homages to Kadare in relation to Albanian national myths are ambivalent, displaying both

[38]This myth was also subject of a paper given by Arben Puto to the conference which can be found in the Albanian edition of the proceedings, see in *Përpjekja* 15/16, 1999.

[39]Fatos Lubonja, 'Roli i miteve në historinë e shqipërisë', *Përpjekja* 15–16, 1999; this is the introduction to the Albanian publication and collection of papers, as originally presented in the same conference.

[40]Lubonja in personal electronic mail correspondence August 2000.

criticism and respect. Finally in this section, Alex Standish describes how history was actually manipulated and transformed in order to fit the Enverist *Führerkult*. Arguably, the introduction of the messianic myths of Hoxha's heroism, sacrifice and his qualities as founding father of the nation, with their sacral character served as a substitute religion while, at the same time, atheism was imposed. Furthermore it could be argued that this substitute-religious function effectively rooted and integrated Enver Hoxha's leadership in most of his peoples' affection for a long time. Standish's theme leads perfectly to the theme of nationalist historiography.

(III) 'National Historiography, or Friends, Foes and Heroes'

This section investigates some contemporary standard myths of Albanian national historiography covering the times before, during, and after Communism in Albanian history.

Complementing Ger Duijzings' contribution on Bektashism, Nathalie Clayer, using new archival evidence, deconstructs the national historiographic myth which for reasons of national self-definition claimed Ali Pasha to have been a follower of Bektashism. Bernd Fischer revisits the Albanian myth of military valour in national 'wars of liberation' in the two World Wars. He presents findings from British and German archive material which sharply contradict the Albanian national image of these conflicts. He also points to the consequences (in this case the negative seems to outweigh the positive) of the development of military myths under Zog and Hoxha, and more specifically to the costs for the Albanians.

A number of contributions in this book shed light on how outside actions and perceptions fed back into Albanian worldviews. Roderick Bailey's re-examination of British-Albanian relations, based on the British role in the 'National Liberation War', is one of them. Such historical myths were informed by former participants' memories of responsibility for post Second World War political constellations in Albania. New archive material, which became available for research only recently after a fifty year barrier, allowed Bailey to revisit documents telling stories of treachery and support for both communist partisans and national royalists (fierce political opponents themselves) in their fight against the Germans.

(IV) 'Myths and Contested Boundaries'

Denisa Kostovicova, in contrast to Blumi's insights on the overestimated role of education during the nineteenth century national movement, shows how Kosovo's 'house-schools' during the 1990s not only served as a vehicle for the transmission of national-Albanian history but also became a symbol of national cohesion and resistance themselves in an evolving parallel society.

Elias Skoulidas investigates in detail the early construction of the image of Albanians as rebels, bandits (brigands) and cruel mercenaries in the early nineteenth–century Greek press. This contribution suggests that images created then still have an impact on mutual Greek-Albanian perceptions today. Focusing on contemporary phenomena, the diaspora theme recurs in Annie Lafontaine's anthropological presentation of how Albanian national myths of identity are transformed and adjusted to the United States or Canadian host country's dominant myths of nationhood. This is explored in a comparison between the different rationales of a Kosovo-Albanian and an Albanian from Tirana. Also anthropologically, Gilles de Rapper leads us back to Albania and its southern neighbours. He investigates local notions of 'culture' and religious identity in the border area of Bilisht where local, inter-community, and national myths are contested and where outside contacts and relations determine local options. The last two pieces give contemporary evidence of how internal Albanian differentiations, as with every nation, are alive and thriving. Shifts in appeals to different levels of group identity (the local, diaspora affiliations, the national etc.) allow for an individual's reference to often mutually exclusive myths in the judgement of a myth's propriety in a particular context.

(V) 'Myths of Democracy, Development and the Future'

With post-communist transition, Albanian society became subject to an international 'development industry' in which the transfer of models (or 'Western myths')[41] of democracy, civil society, pluralism of political parties and political opinions, independent institutions, and concepts such as self-determination and the inviolability of national borders, were seen as guarantees in the pursuit of happiness, prosperity and the eventual integration into the 'European family.' Mariella Pandolfi draws attention to the neo-colonialist 'Orientalism' and

[41]Cf. Steven Sampson, 'The social life of projects: Importing Civil Society to Albania' in Chris Hann and Elizabeth Dunn (eds), *Civil Society: Challenging Western Models*, London and New York: Routledge 1996, pp. 121–42, here particularly p. 125 f.; Maria Todorova, 'The Balkans: From Discovery to Invention' in *Slavic Review* 53, 1994, pp. 453–82, particularly in her critique on George F. Kennan p. 457 ff.

essentialising 'exotisation' of international actors in this business which, she warns, may be part of a self-congratulatory project rather than any help to Albanians. In fact, these mythical perceptions of Albanians could be seriously damaging in that they may provoke an increase in mutual alienation, thereby becoming a self-fulfilling prophecy.

Nicola Mai contrasts Pandolfi's approach with his experiences among young Albanians. These, according to his findings, seem to nurture what I would almost call a 'cargo-cult' in their visions and material expectations of the democratic future while at the same time reproducing patterns of homogenous thought[42] internalised earlier. To conclude this section Fabian Schmidt encounters the prevalence of conspiracy theories in politics and media as a zero-sum game in which there exists only total social inclusion or exclusion, friend or foe, the loyal or the treacherous, hiding under superficial labels of 'democracy,' freedom of opinion, or 'pluralism.'

Most contributions discussing contemporary society and politics suggest that Enverist totalitarian politics of ideological homogenisation, supported by the artificially secured and paranoid isolation of the country, have indeed reproduced archetypal mythical worldviews of a pre-state society in contemporary Albania. Lack of communication and small isolated, often tribally organised settlements, as both Piro Misha and Fatos Lubonja suggest, and later self-imposed isolation, saved people from having to negotiate different 'truths' but allowed for the comfort of shared homogenous beliefs, values, traditions and wisdom. However, Albania has become entwined in global processes and communications, and Albanians face, whether they want to or not, the challenge of an abundance of alternative knowledge. This book constitutes part of that challenge.

The editors will have achieved their objective of provoking debate and academic controversy if those readers who disagree with 'dissident' ideas on Albanian national myths presented here would take up the challenge to reshape their arguments along the lines of empirical research, theoretical awareness, dispassionate methodology and intellectual rigour which underpin in these contributions to Albanian Studies.

[42]Here Mai relies closely on Artan Fuga, *L'Albanie entre la pensée totalitaire et la raison fragmentaire*, Paris: L'Harmattan 1998.

THE NATURE OF MYTH

SOME THEORETICAL ASPECTS

George Schöpflin

There are two meanings of myth. Its popular meaning, the one that we see in the press, is a story, an invention, a fabulation, something in which we do not believe. This is not the sense in which I am using it. Rather, myth is a particular set of ideas with a moral content told as a narrative by a community about itself. In this sense, myth may or may not be related to historical truth, though those who rely on the narrative generally believe that it is. At most, myth is a way of organising history so as to make sense of it for that particular community. Furthermore, for myths to be energising, they must have both a positive and a negative polarity. The universal structure of myth is as a narrative recounting something evil being overcome by virtue. The actual content, the details of the myth-narrative, vary enormously from community to community.

Myths, therefore, are an ineluctable aspect of collective existence. Indeed, all collectivities have them—they cannot exist without them. From this perspective, as we shall see, attempts to demystify, or to deconstruct myth, to make its falsity evident, are misplaced. They will not be read as a well-intentioned attempt to make a community see the error of its ways. The community concerned will not amend its ways and promise to behave better in the future, in a myth-less way. Rather, when one of its myths is under attack, the community in question will feel itself assaulted, it will see these attacks as an assault on its most basic foundations, questioning its very existence. Hence it will defend itself by whatever means are to hand.

The attack on myth in its most recent variant can be dated back to the Enlightenment, which placed the slogan of 'cognitive growth' on its banner. Nothing was to be beyond questioning, there was to be no privileged or sacred knowledge. The twentieth century legatees of the Enlightenment—Liberalism and Marxism—are both deeply dismissive of myth and prefer to write it off as 'irrational'. The difficulty with this dismissal is that it leaves this kind of Enlightenment analysis without any explanation for the persistence of what it would regard as 'irrationality.' It can only account for the reproduction of such attitudes either by saying that some things are inexplicable or that some people are inherently irrational. Neither is very satisfactory. If one claims inexplicability, one weakens the credentials of 'cognitive growth;' alternatively, imputing irrationality to others presupposes what the German philosopher Ernst Cassirer described as the assumption of 'primeval stupidity', *Urdummheit.*

There is a very clear illustration of some of these processes in the death of Princess Diana. Well before her death, the mystique of the British Royal family was systematically stripped of its mythic elements—deliberately so, supposedly as a way of making the monarchy more democratic and accessible. What this process also did was to weaken the resonance of the myth of royalty, an important cement in the British political system, so that Diana, while she lived, emerged more and more as a rival, resonant figure. Her death completed the process and she was transformed into something wholly transcendental. The reaction to her death was correspondingly powerful. British society experienced an extraordinary outburst of collective grief—Diana's had become a global myth—for which the overwhelming majority of British observers could find no explanation, relying as they did on their rationalistic categories; they dismissed it as a silly and shameful explosion of grief. A myth had been born and could be understood only by analysing it as myth.

The upshot of all this is that we need an alternative, more persuasive explanation for the nature of myth and for the role that myth plays in collective action. The starting point for this exploration of myth has to be the nature of collectivities—communities—and their purposiveness. Here the central proposition is that once called into being, collectivities acquire qualities that transcend the cognitive and intellectual capacities of individual actors. Individual actors contribute to the founding and the functioning of communities, but communities need the collective response of their members to function collectively. This raises two more problems. One is that there can never be universal agreement among all the members of a community, hence something has to substitute for that agreement. This is solidarity and solidarity is generated not by explicit consent, but by the implicit processes of myth, symbol and ritual. Members of a community take part in ritual, accept myth and respond to symbols. Their individual responses will be different, as people are different, but they accept participation at this implicit level without further questioning. They do so, because belonging to a community is a key aspect of our humanity. Without sharing in collective meanings, we cannot make sense of the complexity of the world. We benefit from the coherence and order that myth imposes on otherwise very different perceptions and assessments. But that necessarily means that we must accept the limitations on how we view the world set by the community or communities to which we belong.

The second problem is that of dissent. If individuals or smaller groups within the community were constantly to engage in questioning its purposiveness, the community would fall apart. Hence, it must be taken for granted, it must be transformed into something that we see as 'normal and natural' and is thus never questioned. The role of myth and symbol is central in this connection. Those who accept the myths of a community may actually be aware at one level that what they are dealing with is not one hundred percent accurate, but they recognise it as theirs.

These two factors provide the clue to something else—the persistence of myth, the persistence of the reliance on myth on the part of communities. Myth gives collective existence a temporal dimension, it roots the members of a community in a shared past which may be imprecise, but is felt to be authentic; equally, it gives them a sense of a shared future. No community can exist without a sense of a shared past and a shared future. In this sense, collective existence creates its own rationality, that of cultural reproduction. This raises difficult issues of individual rationality as against organic definitions of the collectivity. My position on this is that communities do indeed generate collective norms and that it is rational for the individual to accept these, otherwise he or she would be condemned to total isolation and complete anomie. The moment that we accept this argument, much else falls into place—we can see how in certain circumstances individuals ignore their empirical experience in favour of a collectively dictated norm. We can see the reason behind cognitive closures, often severe closures, that block off what others see as clear and self-evident. An example: during the 1960s and 1970s, the Western left was firmly gripped by the myth of 'working class solidarity.' Many believed that the industrial working class was inherently moved by a sense of mutual solidarity and egalitarianism. The sociological reality of major internal cleavage lines within the working class, the patterns of working class authoritarianism and exclusion (against women, for example), the insistence on pay differentials—these were simply screened out.

The power of myth to structure analysis, to include and exclude ideas, to make some things appear legitimate and others unthinkable, to determine how we understand our interests, cannot be underestimated. And this points towards something else—the gaps in classical Enlightenment rationalist structural analysis, which would dismiss all this as mythic thinking. As a result, this analysis is caught in a cognitive trap of its own as it cannot provide an adequate account of the kind of cognitive closures that I have been discussing. We are free agents, but nothing like as free as we like to think.

Myth has other functions in addition to these. Myth exists in order to create and sustain coherence and thereby stability. It fills in the cognitive gaps that we all experience by providing what appear to be logical and coherent explanations and guidance on what to do when the institutional and procedural rules are silent. Myth generates shared patterns of experiencing time and space. Time and space are understood as 'normal and natural;' in reality, the way in which they are measured is man-made, but its manufactured quality is taken for granted. Myth establishes a causal relationship—and thus a purposiveness—between individual and collective experience.

One of the most controversial aspects of myth is its relationship to nationhood and nationalism. Much has been written in an attempt to 'expose' the mythic foundations of nationhood in the hope that once this had been satisfactorily achieved, nations would vanish, having been shown to be artificial, invented and imagined, and thus somehow not real. Of course nothing of the kind has happened and this is not because people are 'primeavally stupid' or ill-intentioned. I believe it follows from my argument that nations are partly held together by their myths of identity, origins, future or other experiences.

Crucially, as myth is an aspect of collective existence, it forms a part of the theories of collective action. Myths do help to sustain nations and nations rely on myth for that reason. So deeper insights into the nature of both myth and nationhood should be sought in their interactions. In this area, myths contribute to the creation of identity by establishing the boundaries of identity, by binding together the members of the nation, by excluding non-members through collective meanings by which individuals know themselves and their fellow members, recognising without further reflection the tacit limits of solidarity, obligation and trust and pursuing transactions with a minimum of negotiation. It goes without saying that myths can be abused as well as used, but that applies to every arena of human action.

I think it is evident that myth is a central aspect of collective experience. However the way in which communities respond to their own mythopoeias is not quite so straightforward. The density of myth is not the same in all communities. Some have a wide range of often contradictory mythic narratives; others have few. Paradoxically, the greater the density of myth, the easier it is for modern and post-modern communities to cope with challenges, because it becomes easier to legitimate change. Each shift, even quite radical ones, can be presented as sanctioned by the past, and legitimated by a mythic narrative. The real trouble arises when the palette of myth is more restricted than the complexity of society and when one myth can capture the cognitions of a community to crowd out all others. This is still one of the central problems of Serbia. It was too easy to legitimate violence in the Serbian case by reference to Kosovo, whereas it was near-impossible to argue in favour of moderation and compromise—there are not enough strong myth-narratives to support it.

My conclusions follow on from what I have been arguing. Myths have to be studied because they are real and an authentic part of every system of collective existence; myths affect the exercise of power; they structure our thinking and provide insight into collective motivations; they affect the nature of causation through their power to structure collective thinking and behaviour. Reliance on myth is not some kind of a pre-modern relic, but exists universally, with the same structure, although the content of myth may vary. Myth is a central and essential aspect of the collective experience and that is something that we all share.

Part I

THE HISTORY OF ALBANIAN MYTH PRODUCTION

INVENTION OF A NATIONALISM

MYTH AND AMNESIA

Piro Misha

The beginnings of the Albanian national awakening, better known as the 'Albanian National Renaissance' (*rilindja*), took place during the 1830s and '40s. A quick look at these origins shows that, at least in its beginnings, the Albanian national movement did not differ much from any other national movement in the region.

As elsewhere in southeastern Europe, nationalism in Albania began as an élite phenomenon: the very idea of an Albanian nation germinated first in the minds of a handful of intellectuals living outside the country, mostly in Europe, but also in some of the main political and economic centres of the Ottoman Empire. The initial impulse and inspiration came from the European Enlightenment, as well as from the influence of the writings of a number of Western scholars, travellers, poets, ethnographers and philologists who were discovering this forgotten part of Europe, which for a long time had constituted a 'forbidden' land, generally referred to as 'European Turkey' or as 'the Near East', as if hinting at something already lost. Many of these scholars noted the fact that the Albanians had a distinctive language and culture, consequently making up a distinctive linguistic and ethnographic community in the Balkans. A number of them tried as well to reconstruct pieces of the puzzle of the Albanians' past.

Common with the other nationalisms is also the timing when the seed of the Albanian national movement sprouted. It was the period when the Ottoman Empire was witnessing the transition from the administrative system of *millets*, which divided the population according to religion, to a new uncertain reality, where the main criteria of self-identification became linguistic and cultural. It was a process which in the long run brought about fundamental change by devaluing the very concept that for centuries had constituted the essence of Ottoman rule, as well as the bases of Islamic or Orthodox unity which had characterised the multinational empire. In this the Albanian Muslims were part of the same *millet* as the Bosnians and the Turks, while their Orthodox compatriots belonged to the same *millet* as the Greeks and the Serbs. In ground ploughed by a series of reforms undertaken by the Sublime Porte in the first decades of the nineteenth century the seeds of Balkan nationalism, including the Albanian national movement, sprouted.

The process of Albanian nation-building cannot be fully understood unless we put it in the context of the nineteenth-century Balkans, characterised by severe conflicts and confrontations among the newly-created Balkan nation-states which, seeking to define their national territories, were constructing their national myths, codes, symbols, and histories to legitimise their policy of territorial expansion as well as to achieve the necessary national homogenisation. The Albanians were among the last to enter into this scene of seething nationalistic passions and ambitions, combined with the intrigues and interest politics of the European Great Powers. A number of factors contributed to keeping the Albanian national movement embryonic at a time when most of their neighbours (after succeeding in creating their own national states) strove to extend their national territories. This historical delay not only conditions the whole process of Albanian nation building, but should also be considered as one of the major factors affecting the history of the Albanians throughout the nineteenth and twentieth centuries.

Numerous parallels exist between the Albanian national movement and the other nineteenth-century Balkan national movements, but there are also important differences, resulting from Albanian history and its geography. The process of nation-building and self-definition of Albanians as a community conscious of its own distinct identity in linguistic, ethnographic and cultural terms first began as a result of an outside threat. The Empire they had inhabited for centuries was quickly collapsing, and their neighbours, trying to legitimise their expansionist claims, denied the very existence of an Albanian people. Under such circumstances Albanians needed not only to compete with their neighbours for contested territories, but were also forced to make their own case for nationhood in order to win the acknowledgement of the influential European powers. Similar confrontations existed at the time all over the Balkans and many of these conflicts are not yet fully resolved. Out of twenty-three existing state borders in the region nineteen continue to be contested. If one considered all territorial claims in the region, the surface of the Balkan peninsula would need to be at least doubled. This helps explain why so many of the nineteenth-century romantic nationalistic myths, stereotypes and symbols remain an organic part of the national consciousness of the Balkan peoples of today.[1]

When considering Albanian nineteenth-century history a question comes naturally to mind: what caused their historical delay? It is not enough simply to observe their late departure along the road to modernity, one should also explain why. What prevented the Albanians from moving in step with most of the peoples of the region? This leads to a number of other questions requiring a critical examination of the past and questioning much of what is taken for granted by the national narrative.

An answer should be found to the question why the Albanians were among the last to liberate themselves since they initially resisted the Ottoman invasion more vigorously and for longer than most of their neighbours, and during the first centuries of Ottoman rule revolted perhaps more often than any other people in the region.[2] This is particularly perplexing since geography (in terms of the distance to the centre of the Empire and the proximity to Western Europe) was on their side.

What brought about the change of the name the Albanians had identified themselves with for centuries? Normally a change of name is related to an identity crisis: is this the case with the Albanians? This well-documented change took place during the seventeenth and eighteenth centuries, two of the darkest centuries in the modern history of Albania. During this period a number of other important transformations with long-term consequences took place in Albanian society, causing the change not only of name but also of religion. It was principally during these two centuries that the conversion of a majority of Albanians to Islam took place. What does this change mean, and what are its implications for the identification patterns of Albanians? What is its impact on their subsequent history? Clearly, it would be impossible really to understand the turbulent history of

[1]Paul Garde, *Les Balkans*, Paris: Flammarion 1994, p. 12.

[2]See Fernand Braudel, *La Méditerranée et le monde méditerranéen a l'époque de Philippe II*, Paris: A. Colin 1949, p. 1217.

Albania of the last two centuries without taking into consideration a number of historical, social, cultural and economic processes underway before the century when the national idea originated.

The nineteenth century found the Albanians as one of the most backward and isolated peoples, with a number of disadvantages compared to their immediate neighbours. They had to overcome obstacles which most of their neighbours had either surmounted or had never known on their road towards the affirmation of a distinctive national identity. Albanians were cut off from contacts with the rest of the world even if judged according to the standards of the Ottoman Empire. Albania continued to remain a mysterious country, an image that pursued it for a very long time. Even as late as 1913 the French journalist Delaisi wrote: 'I don't know of any other country which is so closed to civilisation: even the Sahara is better known to us, even Tibet I cannot say is more mysterious.'[3]

In addition to isolation from the outside, there was also internal isolation. During a trip he made through Albania in 1854 the Austrian diplomat and scholar Johann Georg von Hahn pointed out that there existed no organic connection and no communication whatever between the Albanian provinces.[4] The country was divided administratively into four *vilayets*, which constituted *de facto* autonomous units. To move from one *vilayet* to another required special safe-conduct-passes. But even without these administrative barriers, travelling was very difficult, which meant that networks of contacts, exchanges and interests, necessary for the creation of the awareness of a community, could hardly exist. There was no road connecting Durres to Shkodra or to Vlora. The Albanian poet Asdreni, who lived in Bucharest, travelling in Albania in 1903, wrote that a journey from the port of Durres, where he landed, to Tirana, which is situated not more than 40 kilometres away, took him 'a long, tiring trip of two days', fraught with many dangers in a country plunged into the most complete anarchy. 'There is no passable road whatsoever,' he wrote. 'Only a horse or a mule accustomed to these most narrow paths can travel here. The life of a man here has so little value that if a traveller comes out alive, this happens more because the man who shoots does not feel like wasting a bullet just for a passer-by.'[5] A report written by the Intelli-

[3]M. Delaisi, *Les aspirations autonomistes en Europe*, Paris: Alcan 1913, p. 23.

[4]Johann Georg von Hahn, *Albanesische Studien*, Jena: Friedrich Mauke 1854, p. 4.

[5]Asdren [Aleksander Stravre Drenova], *Nga Durresi nde Tirane*, Brussels 1903, p. 138.

gence Division of the British Admiralty Staff in 1916, during the First World War came to the conclusion that one of the main factors causing the extreme stagnation of Albania was the geographical environment:

La première cause de la stagnation du peuple albanais est le milieu géographique dans lequel il vit ... Il n'y a aucune route carrosable, et même les sentiers muletiers sont difficiles à entretenir. En fait, lorsqu'un Albanais parle de route, il parle habituellement d'un sentier ou de pistes, tout à plus praticables aux animaux de bat. Souvent même, l'Albanais, en parlant de route, veut exprimer simplement une direction, parce que les itinéraires à suivre entre deux points dépendent de circonstances qu'il ne peut contrôler.[6]

Another major obstacle (although strangely enough it is rarely mentioned) which the Albanians faced was their lack of a single administrative, economic, cultural, or even religious centre, which could serve as a cohesive national factor. On the contrary, there were a number of regional centres which, because of competition with one another, often became factors of discord.

Examining the nineteenth-century history of Albania it is easy to see how many of the major obstacles the Albanians faced in attempting to construct a national identity are to be attributed to Ottoman policy in the last centuries of their rule in Albania. Feeling themselves increasingly threatened from the outside as well as by internal centrifugal movements, the Ottomans (particularly after the peace treaty of Küchük Kajnarca of 1774 which, following the crushing defeat of the Ottomans by the Russians, marks the beginning of the territorial disintegration of the Empire) adopted a policy in Albania which was increasingly characterised by the instigation of internal regional and religious divisions and differences. This was thought to be the best way of controlling this distant and turbulent province of the Empire. Because of its strategic borderland position Albania was considered by the Sublime Porte not only as a borderland defensive belt, but also as an important source of cheap cannon-fodder. To this end the Ottomans did their best to keep the country isolated and uncontaminated by contacts with Europe. Paradoxically, the geographical proximity to the western part of the continent was therefore a factor that made the contacts between Albania and Europe much more difficult. The constant refusal of the Ottoman administration to

[6]Admirality War Staff—Intelligence Division-London, *Personnages—Albanie—Les clans et le peuple*, London 1916, p. 2.

recognise Albanians as such, considering them either simply as 'Turks' or as 'Orthodox' because of the practical implications, constituted one of the most serious obstacles the Albanians faced in building a national identity. The Porte had also carefully divided the territories inhabited by Albanians into four separate administrative *vilayets*, making it difficult for anyone to imagine or clearly define what that foggy geographical notion known by the name of Albania truly meant. They also took care that none of these four *vilayets* should be ethnically homogeneous.

Under such conditions, when most of the factors which normally help in constructing a national identity were, to say the least, problematic, the last remaining factor which did have the potential to become an element of national cohesion was the language. In this light it becomes clear why the Ottomans undertook severe coercive measures in order to prevent the teaching of the Albanian language. Albanians were not allowed to use their own language even when, after the reforms carried out in the mid nineteenth century, the use of mother tongues became possible for almost all other peoples living under Ottoman rule. In fact, the Ottoman policy which allowed Albanian Muslims to attend only Turkish schools, while the Albanian Orthodox students could go to Greek schools only, was also encouraged by the Orthodox Patriarchate. And the success of this policy was evident in the fact that it took until 1908 for the Albanians to compile a common alphabet. Faik Konica wrote that until 1877 very few Albanians could imagine that their language could or should be written.[7] By the end of the nineteenth century in the whole of Albania only two Albanian schools existed, while there were some 5,000 Turkish or Greek schools.

However, this does not mean that Albanians were educated. On the eve of the First World War in the whole region of Mirëdita, with a population of 18,000 people, only three people could write and read.[8] One of the few Europeans who visited Albania at the beginning of the twentieth century, an Italian named Guicciardini, explained in his book *Impressioni d'Albania*, some of the reasons for this Ottoman policy in Albania:

> Turkey treats Albanian Muslims even worse than it does Christians, because of the fear it has that the unity of Islam would suffer if national awareness

[7]Faik Konica, *Parashtrese mbi lëvizjen kombëtare shqiptare—Vepra*, vol. 2, Prishtina: Rilindja, p. 9.

[8]Report of the Commission of the Council of the League of Nations on Albania, 1923.

is created in a part of the Muslim world, prevailing over the religious solidarity. In Albania this inhibitory policy extends also to the Christian population (the only case), as the Turks are afraid that they would have a negative influence on Albanian Muslims.[9]

The fact that education was only available in a foreign language helps explain why Albanian culture remained principally popular and folkloric and why Albanian nationalism was disadvantaged compared to that of other nations.[10]

This is in short the general context in which the process of national formation and, later, of national integration, slowly advanced: a context characterised by strong local and regional awareness, while the national consciousness remained rather vague. Bernd Fischer described this situation as follows:

> A combination of indigenous Albanian circumstances and conscious Ottoman policy succeeded in burying any national sentiment until the late nineteenth century ... in a classic carrot and stick fashion, the Turkish authorities subverted Albanian nationalism through outright repression as well as by means which amounted to little more than bribery.[11]

For some time the very existence of a real nation-building movement inside the country was very difficult, if not impossible, to maintain.

A great qualitative change in the movement took place at the end of the 1870s. It was at this time that the romantic national movement, restricted until then to a handful of intellectuals living abroad with limited real impact inside the country, began its transformation into a political national movement. The direct cause of this transformation were events that happened far away, the Russian-Turkish war (1877–8) in which the Turks suffered a crushing defeat. In order to avoid a dangerous unbalancing of the precarious existing equilibrium in the Balkans, which was seriously threatened by the peace treaty of San Stefano (1878), the Great Powers called the Congress of Berlin. The goal of the Congress was a more prudent partition of the Empire among the newly created regional nation-states. Among many internationally relevant decisions, the Congress of Berlin decided to partition among

[9]F. Guicciardini, *Impressioni d'Albania. Nuova Antologia*, Rome 1901, p. 48.

[10]Stavro Skendi, *The Albanian National Awakening 1878–1912*, Princeton University Press 1967, p. 88.

[11]Bernd Fischer, *Mbreti Zog dhe perpjekja per stabilitet ne Shqiperi*, Tirana: Çabej MCM 1996, p. 54.

its direct neighbours a number of territories inhabited by Albanians. For the Albanians the Congress of Berlin sent another quite alarming signal, which went far beyond its practical decisions. It did not even recognise that there was an 'Albanian Question'. The German Chancellor Bismarck pronounced that Albania was nothing but a geographical expression. Two Albanian nationalist leaders, Abdyl Frashëri and Jani Vreto, who went to Berlin in the hope of influencing the decisions of the Congress returned home without even succeeding in meeting anyone of significance.

This situation, of general identity and territorial insecurity, brought about the creation of the League of Prizren, a political-military organisation, which marked the transformation of the hitherto romantic national movement into a real political national movement, with an Albanian nationalist ideology. Although the League of Prizren eventually failed, defeated militarily by the Turks, it constituted a turning point in the history of the Albanians. Until then the main preoccupation of Albanian patriots was to identify and collect evidence proving that Albanians were a culturally distinct nation; until then they tried to legitimize the historical right of the Albanians to be considered a nation, discovering or often inventing facts to justify their claims historically, a process that was increasingly taking on the features of the rediscovery of an 'ethno-history'. Now the creation of the League of Prizren transformed all this into a nationalistic ideology, which accelerated the process of cultural and political fermentation that would lead not only to the creation, a few decades later, of an Albanian independent state, but which helped bring the Albanian Question to the attention of the world.

If we exclude the immediate objective of preventing the partition of Albanian-inhabited territories among its neighbours, the Albanian national movement had more or less the same platform as any other national movement during its affirmation phase. In short, demands included the creation of an 'organic', culturally and linguistically homogenous nation; the transformation of the passive 'ethnie' into an active ethno-political community; the transformation of the spoken language into a vernacular one, codifying the alphabet, the grammar and the vocabulary; and assuring an internationally recognised country, with well-defined borders, demanding at the same time administrative autonomy. But there was a very important difference: the demands of the Albanians came with a delay of at least a few decades compared to their neighbours. This delay determines the generally defensive character of the Albanian national movement. For Albanian nineteenth-century nationalists national affirmation meant first of all a way of interrupting what they considered to be 'the already advanced process of erosion of the national sentiment and national language'.

Under such conditions the most reliable remaining unifying element for a people which otherwise suffered from a number of dangerously centrifugal forces was language. That is why the language question and that of education in the Albanian language became the basic demand of Albanian nationalism, a demand which was soon transformed from a simple question of enlightenment into a political one.

The recreation of the past is an indispensable part of any process which makes a people a nation. That is why history occupies an important place in the construction of an Albanian national identity. But history itself was not sufficient as this is where what has come to be known as the 'nationalisation of history' enters into play. For Albanian nationalists the reconstruction of the past was important to give evidence to the Albanians that they shared a common history. It was even more important, in the words of Ismail Kadare, to convince them that 'they had a splendid history and that the national calamities were not a reason to cool them down about the fatherland, but on the contrary, to stand closer to it'.[12]

It was also important to produce evidence of the Albanians' historical continuity (which in the Balkan context meant first of all to show not only that the Albanians were autochthonous in the Western Balkans, but that they had been living there if not for ever, at least longer than their neighbours). This became crucial for the Albanian national movement which was faced with a very intense propaganda campaign carried out by Greek and Serb nationalists, who in their nationalist zeal not only denied the existence of an Albanian nation, but went to extremes, such as in the case of a propaganda book published in French and German by a former Prime Minister of Serbia, Vladan Georgevitch, who tried in earnest to convince the world that Albanians were so underdeveloped that they still had tails.[13]

The approach to history was of course selective: just as it was important to awaken parts of the past, it was also important to leave other parts of it out or, if this was not possible, to remake them.

[12]Ismail Kadare, *Kombi shqiptar ne prag të mijëvjecarit të tretë*, Tirana: Onufri 1998, p. 12.

[13]Vladan Georgevitch, *Les Albanais et les grandes puissances*, Paris: Calmann Levy 1913 (German translation by Prince Alexis Kara-Georgevitch).

Consequently, the dividing line between myth and history was often blurred and not easily discernible.

As with any other people, the myth of origin, or ethnogenesis, was of special importance for Albanian nationalist writers. At first, these forefathers were the mythical Pelasgians. But gradually, while the Albanian national movement matured, the romantic Pelasgian theory and others were replaced by the theory of Illyrian descent, which was more convincing because it was supported by a number of scholars. The Illyrian descent theory soon became one of the principal pillars of Albanian nationalism because of its importance as evidence of Albanian historical continuity in Kosovo, as well as in the south of Albania, i.e. in the areas contested by Serbs or Greeks. At the same time the almost 700-year-long Byzantine patrimony, in spite of the fact that the Albanian national symbol itself, the fifteenth-century Kastrioti emblem,[14] derived from it, was almost never mentioned because of the associations it carried with Orthodoxy in a country where the majority of the population had become Muslim.

In common with most nineteenth-century nationalisms, Albanian nationalism perceived itself as a national awakener. Leafing through the writings of Albanian poets, ethnographers, folklorists and journalists, one finds numerous metaphors and images expressing the idea of a glorious past where a true but dormant identity of the Albanians was to be found. Naum Veqilarxhi,[15] one remarkable personality of the first period of the Albanian national movement, compared the situation of the Albanians with that of a larva that one day would become a butterfly. The Arbëreshi[16] sang full of homesickness about 'the great time of Arbëri', i. e. medieval Albania. Consequently, the primary task of the Albanian nationalist project was to create the appropriate conditions for such an 'awakening' (the national awakening, the national revival). Viewed in this perspective, as with any nationalism, Albanian nationalism was determinist in nature: all individuals were seen as predestined by their nationality, regardless of whether they were aware of this or not. But when it came to the practical implementation of this principle, things became much more complicated. After centuries of interethnic

[14]'Kastrioti' is the name of the medieval family of Georg Kastriot, known also as 'Skanderbeg'.

[15]Naum Veqilarxhi (1767–1846) was the first ideologue of the Albanian national movement.

[16]Arbëreshi is the name for the Italian-Albanian communities living in southern Italy. They are descendants of Albanian population groups that left Albania under the Ottomans.

coexistence in a multinational empire, it was almost impossible to define clearly the cultural and linguistic borders dividing peoples. The implementation of the principal demand of nationalism, that of national affirmation, faced the contradictions of subjectively experienced realities in which ethnic or linguistic boundaries were blurred, and assimilation had taken place. Almost every nationalism faced this conceptual ambiguity, and Albanian nationalism faced it as well.

As with almost every Balkan nationalist project, an episode taken from medieval history was central to Albanian national mythology. In the absence of a medieval kingdom or empire the Albanian nationalists chose as their symbol the figure of Skanderbeg, who in his heroic tragedy had all the necessary ingredients for building up a myth. Skanderbeg was a rather well-documented historical figure, whose memory was still alive in oral tradition, especially among the Arbëreshi. The nationalist writers needed to do nothing more than provide him with a national significance and some embellishment, subjecting him to that laboratory that serves to transform history into myth. As with most myths, his figure and his deeds became a mixture of historical facts, truths, half-truths, inventions and folklore. Skanderbeg was made a national hero although his action had never really involved all Albanians. Neither Kosovo nor most parts of the south were ever included. An attempt he made in 1455 to take the city of Berat in fact failed. Therefore, the figure of Skanderbeg needed some adjustment. In particular, his Christian orientation could damage the cause. In Arbëresh poems he was not only the defender of their home country, he was also the defender of Christianity. For nineteenth-century Albanians, a majority of whom had adhered to the faith of Skanderbeg's Muslim enemies, this religious dimension needed to be avoided. Consequently, Skanderbeg became simply the national hero of Albanians, the embodiment of the myth of 'continuous resistance' against their numerous foes over the centuries.

But the transformation of Skanderbeg into a national symbol did not just serve national cohesion. Initially claimed by the Arbëreshi at the turn of the twentieth century, Skanderbeg's myth became the national argument proving Albania's cultural affinity to Europe. This identity construction had a double function: on the one hand, it served to convince Albanians to turn their backs as soon as possible on their Ottoman past, where most nationalists saw the source of all evils that had beset the Albanians. On the other hand, it was meant to win the sympathy and support of the European Great Powers. Accordingly, in the national narrative Skanderbeg symbolised the sublime sacrifice of the Albanians in defending Europe from Asiatic hordes.

At this point it would be well to make a clarification to avoid any misunderstanding of what has been said so far, because nothing is simple when we speak of the relations between the Albanians and Europe. The Albanian collective imagery of these two entities (with the Orient close by adding a further complication) incarnates the numerous contradictions and ambiguities that characterise the Albanians' identity process. Europe is for Albanians the land of aspirations, the incarnation of civilisation, power, the dream of wellbeing, the shelter in which to feel secure and protected. Yet there are contrasting images of 'Europe the faithless', Europe the inimical cause of many wrongs done to Albanians including their partition, Europe the immoral, 'the old whore' etc. Both these conceptions of Europe are part of the same pattern. On the one hand, there is the notion of being part of Europe, of its civilisation, for which the Albanians sacrificed themselves centuries ago by defending it from the Ottoman hordes. On the other hand, Europe is projected as an abstract entity, detached, situated beyond the sea *vis-à-vis* Albania and often identified with the policy of one particular European country at a particular moment. Europe is both dreamed about and yearned for as well as conceived of as being threatening, slippery and not to be trusted but rather to be avoided.

Part of this pattern is the syndrome of 'historical victimisation' (created in the nineteenth century and reinforced by the events of 1913 when a major part of the Albanian-inhabited territories was partitioned among neighbouring Balkan states), which to this day constitutes an important element in the Albanians' vision of their relations with history. The use of history by nationalism to project the image of a people as permanent victims constitutes an obstacle to a critical confrontation with the past. A pre-political mentality, sustained by a belated independence as well as an ideal impression of an incomplete liberation, may have created for the Albanians the complex of being under threat. This explains many of the developments of recent Albanian history, including even some of the features of the autarkic Albanian version of Communism, as well as some of the most distressing manifestations of the post-communist period.

'What does being Muslim or being Christian have to do with Albanianism?' asked Faik Konica in 1897.[17] Albanian nationalism had

[17]Faik Konica, *Albania*, 25 April 1897, p. 18.

to develop in competition with religion, often even assuming an anticlerical character.[18] It is rather peculiar that Albanians, the majority of whom are Muslims, which gave them, at least theoretically, a privileged position in the Empire, proclaimed as their national hero someone who for a quarter of a century was the sworn enemy of the Ottomans. The Albanians were also the only Muslim people in European Turkey who made common cause with their Christian compatriots to fight against the government in Constantinople. In contrast to other countries of the region where religion did play an important role in the process of nation building, in Albania it was seen as a serious obstacle. Nationalists considered religious divisions not only as a factor of discord but also as a vehicle for foreign influence. This explains the particular secular character of Albanian nationalism which made it resemble West European types of nationalism rather than Balkan types.

The concern for religion as the potential seed of discord constitutes a constancy of Albanian recent history. What differs is only the way this issue was approached during the different periods of Albanian history in the last two centuries.

Nineteenth-century nationalists saw a solution to the problem in making nationalism an alternative to the existing religions, which explains the near deification of the concept of 'Albanianism', a term coined by Vaso Pasha ('the real religion of Albanians is Albanianism'). Additionally, there were proposals which, though different from each other, shared the goal of neutralising the possible negative impact of the religious factor. Some nationalists proposed to proclaim Bektashism as a pan-Albanian religion, or to convert the Albanian Orthodox community to Uniatism (which was seen as a way of avoiding Greek influence), or even to arrange a massive conversion to Protestantism.[19] With the creation of the Albanian state, Zogu faced the problem by employing another strategy, which might be called the 'nationalisation of religion', and meant imposing state control over all religious institutions and minimising their outside connections. The reform of Albanian Islam and the efforts to achieve an autocephalous Albanian Orthodox Church must be seen in this light. Attempts to impose state control on the Albanian Catholic Church proved more difficult. Lastly, Enver Hoxha, as in many other things, chose to handle the

[18]Robert Moroco dela Roka, *Kombi dhe feja në Shqiperi*, Tirana: Elena Gjika 1994.

[19]Stavro Skendi, *The Albanian National Awakening*, pp. 77, 175.

problem in the most radical way. After fighting at length against religion, considering it a dangerous competitor to the ruling ideology, he abolished its practice altogether in the mid 1960s. This could be considered a radical Enverist-style solution to an old problem of Albanian nationalism.

'So it was created, more from the current of events than consciously aspired,' writes Peter Bartl.[20] In 1912/13 there were many who seriously doubted the capacity of Albanians, if left alone, to build their own national state. 'No Albanian, if we exclude only a few hotheads that have no idea of what is the real situation inside the country, would dream of an independent Albania,' Eqrem Bej Vlora wrote at the time (despite these misgivings he became a member of the first Albanian parliament a few years later).[21] After almost 500 years of Ottoman rule and 300 years with a Muslim majority population, Albania was more influenced by Turko-Oriental culture than perhaps any other country in the region. As Bernd Fischer writes, 'although official ties with the Ottomans were severed in 1912, a strong rather negative Ottoman legacy remained ... A unique *Weltanschauung* was created and it included a strong distrust of government and of the city as well.'[22]

As late as 1922, that is ten years after the proclamation of independence, only 9 per cent of the land was arable at a time when almost 90 per cent of the population lived either from agriculture or from animal husbandry. These figures help us to imagine the extreme poverty in which Albanians lived. Inadequate infrastructure and the lack of transport facilities and communications in the early period of statehood continued to exist as described above. Albania remained a divided country after it had become a nation-state, in which few people identified themselves primarily as Albanian nationals.

With the creation of an Albanian state, the construction of a national ideology became more dynamic. Now it was no longer simply a question of forging a national identity as the creation of the state made it imperative to build a national community. This meant first of all developing a unified code of national values and symbols, thus creating the necessary normative framework which would make possible state control over society. It also meant minimising the many

[20]Peter Bartl, *Die Albanischen Muslime zur Zeit der Nationalen Unabhängigheitsbewegung (1878–1912)*, Wiesbaden: Otto Harrassowitz 1968, p. 282.

[21]*Ibid.*, p. 217.

[22]Fischer, *Mbreti Zog ...*, p. 55.

existing social and cultural cleavages inherited from the past through 'socialising' and integrating the Albanians into one homogeneous ideology of shared cultural and historical heritage. At the same time, the demarcation of borders had left almost half of all Albanians outside of the Albanian state, while their neighbours never really dropped further expansonist territorial claims.

In such a situation the doctrine of national unity, which must be seen as a reaction to prevalent insecurities, became central to national ideology not only during the reign of King Zog, but also during the communist period. This doctrine was articulated at several levels. First, at the social level, where emphasis was put on the domestic national unity. In a broader sense emphasis was put on the unity of the Albanian nation as a whole. On the historical plane the temporal unity of the nation was underlined, putting the emphasis on the historical continuity of Albanians in their territories. The fact that this doctrine was given such special importance is the clearest evidence of the problems encountered in the process of building national cohesion and national integration, and helps explain why the social and cultural homogenisation of Albanian society was considered a priority. This was sought through the centralisation of power, the dispersion of public administration, the destruction of existing local autonomies, education in the native language (where national propaganda constituted an important part of the curriculum), compulsory military service etc.

Beyond this, the selective use of history continued, but this was no longer done only to serve the purpose of social cohesion. History served to legitimise Albanian leaders and their policies. For example, both Zogu and Enver Hoxha tried their best to present themselves as the heirs of Skanderbeg. During the communist period this logic reached Orwellian dimensions in the faking of historical photographs and documents.

As elsewhere, Communism in Albania began as a complete rejection of the past. However, Enver Hoxha soon came to understand how the selective use of tradition could augment his power. His half-century-long experiment can be considered a failed attempt to reach the impossible syncretism between communist ideology and selected tradition. One need take only the example of the myth of resistance which was made a central element of the national narrative by communist propaganda. The upgrading of this nineteenth-century myth by Albanian Communism was not fortuitous. It meant giving legitimacy to the autarkic Albanian version of Communism. That is why in national narratives the communist-dominated armed partisan resistance of the Second World War, led by Enver Hoxha, became the glorious epilogue to a long tradition of fighting ('The Albanians have passed through history sword in hand'). Gradually, Albanian Communism carried the manipulation of history to the level of paranoia, almost schizophrenia, and made Albania one of the world's most isolated countries dominated by a climate of terror and suspicion.

THE ROLE OF EDUCATION IN THE FORMATION OF ALBANIAN IDENTITY AND ITS MYTHS[1]

Isa Blumi

Since the second half of the nineteenth century, the Ottoman *vilayets* of Kosova (Kosovo), Yanya (Ioannina), Manastir (Monastir), and Ishkodra (Shkodra),[2] populated by a large Albanian-speaking majority, bore the brunt of the Balkans' massive shifts in political economy, demography and power. In this context, these Albanian-speakers were at once vital components of the Ottoman state but also beginning to assert new forms of political and social identity that constituted a threat to it. The series of geopolitical and sociological currents external to this dispersed and fragmented polity in particular proved to be essential to this period of transition.

The factors that shaped the numerous policies in and around the question of local education take on imperial dimensions during the latter half of the nineteenth century. These factors have often been identified in terms of sectarian allegiances—Orthodox, Catholic, Muslim—which in turn inform notions of ethnicity based on geographically identifiable states. Within the simplistic constructs of the external observer, however, there lie important distinctions within these comfortable sectarian and ethnic categories, at the time identified in Ottoman bureaucratic terms as *millet*.[3] Slavic and 'Greek'

[1]The author thanks the organisers and those who participated in the conference from which this book has come, the staffs at the state archives in Albania (AQSH), Austria (HHStA), and the Prime Minister's Archives in Istanbul (BBA) as well as the American Research Institute in Turkey which has financed portions of this research.

[2]The Ottoman spellings will be used throughout this text for Ottoman administrative units such as *vilayets* and *kazas*.

[3]See Isa Blumi, 'The Commodification of Otherness and the Ethnic Unit in

expansion into Ottoman territories was often carried out by spiritual and educational institutions. Their presence, however, and in the case of 'Greek'-financed schools, their near monopoly, must be carefully explored before we can draw conclusions concerning their impact.[4]

In an attempt to share a perspective of human life along the lines celebrated most recently by the likes of Robert Kaplan and Samuel Huntington, the dominance of 'Greek'-financed schools in the *vilayet* of Yanya for instance, could be read to render Greek sovereignty over many areas as self-evident. Indeed, there was widespread 'Greek' influence in the area. In 1909, an Istanbul newspaper exposed the staggering disparity between the number of Greek-language schools in operation, supposedly inculcating Greek nationalism, and Ottoman-funded schools. At both the primary (*Iptidai*) and intermediate levels (*Rüshdi*) Greek-language schools numbered 663 to the state's 135.[5] This disparity is a product of more than a century of foot-dragging and heavy lobbying on the part of the 'Greek' (henceforth *Rum*) Patriarchate which had seen its influence dwindle in Slavic territories situated further north. The marriage between the assumption of the old *Rum* monopoly on spirituality of the Orthodox *millet* and the expansionist claims of the *megali idea* find resonance in circles which wished to preserve the privileged place of the Church in the Balkans.[6] Such aspirations, however, did not result in an unmitigated victory over Albanian particularism. As early as twenty years before the publication of the article cited above, a number of prominent Albanian-speakers ignited Yanya by establishing Albanian-language schools, an act which directly pitted them against the power of the Patriarchate and their equally concerned partners, the Sublime Porte. Until the 1880s there did not exist a single officially recognised Albanian-language school in all of the Albanian-populated territories. To most scholars of

---

the Balkans: How to Think About Albanians', *East European Politics and Society*, 12, 1998, pp. 527–69.

[4]The Ottoman archives are filled with examples of local 'minority' communities winning educational and religious rights which often contradicted the same rationale behind denying Albanian Catholic and Orthodox Christians the same privileges. See for instance, BBA Irade-i Hususi 100/26.R.1315 (Serb school in Prizren) and Irade-i Hususi 53/21.N.1315 (Bulgarian school in Ohrid); both were built in 1897.

[5]Mustafa Suphi, 'Yanya vilayetinin ahval-ı umumiyesi', *Tanin*, 16 Temmuz 1325.

[6]For an example of how the *Rum* church blocked the construction of a Protestant church in Ohrid see BBA, Irade-ı Hususi 18/3.Z.1311.

nationalism, this constituted an important disadvantage since schools were central to the development of the intelligentsia that historically formed nation-states. After years of negotiation, the first secular school for boys (it was initially mixed) opened in Korça on March 7, 1887, and four years later, the first school for girls opened in the same town.[7]

This is the story of how educational institutions, and the more abstract construction of a national curriculum, were played in these territories. It does not assume to explain Albania's birth. While education became a vehicle to adjust to recognizable changes on the ground, it did not necessarily constitute a tool to inculcate notions of a nation-state among the people of the region. Using mechanisms that best mobilise both internal and external responses, local populations and various elements attempting to appropriate their cause are identified here in the institutionalised terms of a 'national' education but judging from archival evidence that is more a reflection of retrospective assumptions than realities on the ground.[8]

For Albanian-speakers in the late nineteenth century, the considerable tensions imposed on local communities during shifting political realities are key. With the expanding interest of neighbouring states and the related territorial dynamics involving questions of constituency and loyalties beyond, local politics became central to a number of people historically marginal to imperial life. Increased territorial pressures on a dispersed group of Albanian-speakers primarily in the Ishkodra, Kosova and Yanya *vilayets* constitutes an important area of focus but one that does not necessarily include education. As 'Greece' consolidated its status as a distinctive political (and to many ethnic) entity from the Ottoman Empire, and to a lesser extent the same for Montenegro and Serbia to the North, the politics of culture and ethnicity intensified on the ground, with the 'national' school being a main arena of such politics among some groups.[9]

For various reasons Albanians became the target of a number of external interests. As Muslims of Bektashi or Sunni extraction, Catholics

[7]See Faik Konitza, 'Mémoire sur le mouvement national albanais', Brussels, Jan. 1899, HHStA, PA XIV, 18, *Albanien* XII/2, pp. 11–12.

[8]See the important work by Eric Hobsbawm, *Nations and Nationalism since 1780*, Cambridge University Press 1990, and Benedict Anderson, *The Spectre of Comparisons: Nationalism, Southeast Asia and the World*, London: Verso 1998; both writers find institutionally inspired notions of nation key to manifested modern identity.

[9]See Theodor A. Ippen, *Skutari und die nordalbanische Küstenebene*, Sarajevo: Daniel A. Kajon 1907, pp. 38–40, and Stavro Skendi, *The Albanian National Awakening*, 1878–1912, Princeton University Press 1967, pp. 129–44.

and members of the Orthodox Church, their spiritual affiliations were deemed central to assimilating them into the rapidly changing Balkan environment. While far less capable powers such as Bulgaria and Serbia were still attempting to consolidate conceptual gains, established entities such as the Rum Patriarch, the Austrian-Hungarian, Italian, and no doubt the Ottoman empires from the 1850s onwards, began an aggressive campaign of establishing influence among a dispersed but important population in Albania through education. As targets for expansionist aspirations among competing imperial and spiritual entities, Albanians themselves manipulated this multiplicity of players.

As noted earlier, the *Rum* Orthodox Church aggressively sought to manipulate the claims to populations of the south-western Balkans, maintaining a near monopoly on schools, churches and other institutions, often competing directly with Abdül Hamid II's own efforts to develop an integrated educational system in the Empire's domains.[10] These factors speak of the highly charged political currency of education at the time. Under the banner of educational reform or the expansion of spiritual uniformity in all three sectarian entities, we find on the ground the realities of daily life dictated to a large extent by the organisational manifestations of such imperial projects.

It became clear to a number of well-established Albanian-born members of the Ottoman élite that related issues of imperial fragmentation and political intrigue in Istanbul had serious disruptive effects in areas throughout the Albanian-speaking world. Members of the social élite such as Sami Frashëri, his two brothers, Ibrahim Temo and Ismail Kemal, had much to lose in the social changes occurring due to the imperial dynamics of the region. The Berlin Congress of 1878 and the League of Prizren have been a watershed for most historians of the Albanian populations, representing significant manifestations of Albanian political consciousness in the face of rather ominous territorial changes between Serbia and Montenegro.[11] I would argue that what transpired in Albanian territories had little to do with creating educational programs for specific nationalists' goals but more with the reflection of regional lobbying on the part of those located within the inner circles of imperial power.

[10]A wide range of schools received extensive funding from the Porte during this period including a medical school which would prove key to twentieth century Ottoman social history. See BBA Irade-i Hususi, 133/22.S.1312.

[11]Among others Kristo Frashëri, *Lidhja Shqiptare e Prizrenit*, Tirana: Akademia e Shkencave e RPS të Shqipërisë 1989.

Through Ottoman rule, Albanian territories developed in separate, distinctive patterns. All tentative efforts to establish collective links beyond the most local of political and social spaces were ineffective, resulting in a diverse cultural field by the twentieth century. Not only did Istanbul consistently refuse to finance the existence of pedagogical institutions using the dominant local language, Albanian, but it was officially opposed to granting the local inhabitants' the minimal cultural rights which were enjoyed in their territories by non-Muslim, non-Albanian minority populations.[12]

The majority of the so-called Albanian élite who have historically been portrayed as the force behind Albanian national consciousness were Muslims who studied under an informative mix of 'traditional' curricula and were tutored, in their native districts, by *Hocas* and then later passed on to *medreses*. Some of the most prominent among them, the Frashëri brothers, Daut Boriçi, Hodo Sokoli, and Jusuf Tabaku had complemented such an education by then moving on to 'Zosima' in Yanya where they were able to formulate strong social bonds with others from the surrounding areas. The likes of Ismail Kemal studied under private European tutors before entering the same Greek-language school. A completely different strategy was to move to larger cities like Salonika and Istanbul to pursue one's educational and hence, political or military careers. Ibrahim Temo, one of the four founders of the Committee for Union and Progress (CUP), met his political partners while a student at the Imperial Medical School in Istanbul.[13] The CUP became an important incubator for prominent Albanian leaders during the last twenty years of Hamidian rule, many of whom followed Temo's educational path.[14] Not only did these figures become prominent (but often contradictory) forces in the articulation of one part of the Albanian national experience, they were able to articulate cultural, political and spiritual concepts of a nation despite using Turkısh, Arabic and Persian in clerical and secular schools of the Ottoman state, or studying under a decidedly hostile

[12]Even Vlachs in 1902 (the same year Istanbul banned all Albanian-language publications and schools) were given specific rights by the Sultan that came with a yearly stipend. See Henry N. Brailsford, *Macedonia: Its Races and their Future*, London: Methuen 1906, p. 188.

[13]This school was by far the most secular and important institute to Ottoman politics of the last fifty years, many of the CUP's leaders created firm links to ideas of constitutionalism while attending the school. See *Riza Tahsin, Mir'at-ı Mekteb-i Tıbbıye*, Istanbul: n.p. 1906.

[14]AQSH, Fondi 19, File 1 for Ibrahim Temo's autobiography.

'Greek' system.[15] This reality suggests that educational institutions and especially their curriculum and language of instruction did not constitute the key element in the development of the first generation of Albanian nationalists.

State-financed schools appeared in disproportionate numbers throughout the region in the 1850s. These schools—*iptidai*, *rüshdi* and *idadi* (gymnasium)—emerged alongside the religious institutions and military academies which received state funding. While the numbers are usually hard to come by, Bayram Kodaman's study demonstrates a clear geographical discrepancy in the construction of schools in Albania, favouring the south.[16] As noted, over 165 government schools existed in the southern provinces by 1908. Compare that to the *vilayet* of Kosova, where in Prishtina there were only seven primary schools and in Prizren there were sixteen *mekteb* with 655 students along with five schools with students of mixed faith. By 1900 these numbers grew to thirty primary schools in Prizren.[17]

This is a key period for Albanian politics. Therefore it is important to clarify that the rapid expansion of schools in these areas, particularly in the northern Gheg regions, only took place after the League of Prizren in 1878.[18] What this suggests is that nationalists' articulations of a sophisticated and geographically broad claim to a singular identity took place outside the context of an educational system that reinforced Albanian identities. The first generation of Albanian patriots in the age of the modern nation-state materialised from an educational environment specifically hostile to their Albanian identity. This suggests we should be looking for other factors which helped articulate one's identity and the myths surrounding them.

After 1870 the Greek-language church witnessed the rising power of the Bulgarian, Romanian, Serb and Russian churches which posed a direct threat to the Patriarch in the Balkans. 'Greek' schools began to concentrate their efforts on a smaller geographical area, mainly in Macedonia and all of southern Albania. These schools were widely

[15]Mirk Pirraku, 'Gjurmë të veprimtarisë letrare shqipe me alfabetin arab në Kosovë', *Gjurmime Albanologjike*, IX, 1978, pp. 203–16.

[16]Bayram Kodaman, *Abdülhamid Devri Egitim Sistemi*, Istanbul: Türk Kurumu Basimevi 1991, pp. 91–6.

[17]Hysni Myzyri, *Shkollat e para Kombëtare Shqipe*, Tirana: Institut i Historisë 1978 and Salname-i Prizren (Imperial Register of Prizren), 1904.

[18]Among others, see Jashar Rexhepagiq, *Zhvillimi i Arsimit dhe i Sistemit Shkollor të Kombësisë Shqiptare në Territorin e Jugosllavisë*, Prishtina: Enti i Historisë së Kosovës 1970, pp. 151–2.

seen as superior to other institutions in the area, attracting large numbers of Muslim students from throughout Albanian territories.[19]

The tenuous relationship between the church administrative hierarchy and the emerging Albanian intelligentsia put strains on communal relations. Growing resistance among Greek-educated Albanians included Papa Kristo Negovani, a priest who received his secondary education in Athens on a Greek scholarship. Negovani represented an important surge in efforts to institutionalise the Albanian language by teaching it in church-financed schools and providing the liturgy in the language, an act of defiance against Greek propaganda. On 12 February 1906, Papa Kristo Negovani was murdered for his efforts. Petro Nini Luarasi, also a graduate of Greek schooling and a teacher of the Greek language was also murdered for taking similar actions.[20] The list of Albanian intellectuals and clergy persecuted and murdered by the *Rum* church for their cultural activities is a long one. Gjerasim Qiriazi, Nuçi Naço, Baba Duda Karbunara, Hamdi Ohri, Siad Hoxha, Balil Tahiri, and Sotir Ollani all represent a southern movement that challenged the culturally hegemonic forces of Istanbul, ultimately leading to their murders or to exile.[21] The culmination of these efforts led to the declaration of an Albanian church in 1910, led by the Church Alliance of Korça's Orthodox Albanians.[22] These efforts, however, were far too isolated to have an impact on how local communities socialised and articulated their identities.

Albanian territories are not cleanly delineated cultural domains. Gheg regions in the north were exposed to a whole list of contradictory pressures which often led to their identification as distinctive political entities by all parties involved. Unfortunately, probably due to Enver Hoxha's persecution of Catholics after the Second World War, the role of Austrian and Italian schools in the preparation of an Albanian intelligentsia has yet to be fully explored. What we do know is that imperial interests, primarily Italian and Austrian, used their increasing strength to implement long-term imperial strategies, such as the *Kultusprotektorat,* to pursue a mission of civilisation and culture for Catholic areas in the Ottoman Balkans.[23] The Austrian intelligence

[19]See Robert Graves, *Storm Centers of the Near East*, London: Hutchinson 1933, p. 272.

[20]Myzyri, *Shkollat e para Kombëtare Shqipe*, pp. 114, 137.

[21]*Ibid.*, pp. 141, 161, 181, 218–20, 226

[22]This *Görice Arnavut Ortodokslarin Kilise Ittifaki* petitioned the Porte for recognition, which they failed to get. BBA Bab-i Ali Evrak Odasi, 265991, 2 Shubat 1325.

[23]See 'Das Kultusprotektorat Österreich-Ungarns in der Türkei' in *Politische Correspondenz*, 31/1913, p. 3

community was particularly interested in the development of education in northern Albania and the *vilayet* of Kosova for it solidified a second front that was meant to halt Slav expansion in the Balkans.[24] In 1856, Vienna opened the first European-funded school in the region in Shkodra (*Collegio Severiano*). By the end of the century there were nineteen Catholic schools in that city. By the beginning of the First World War, Austria had twenty-four schools scattered throughout Gheg Albania, marking an extensive interest in the propagation of pro-Austrian sentiments through actively suggesting the eventual use of Albanian as a language of instruction (along with Italian), as well as ceding increasing local autonomy to Albanian clergy, such as Prenk Doçi, who, paradoxically, were not necessarily loyal to their imperial patrons.[25]

Vienna sought to harness Albanian solidarity emerging against Serbian and Montenegrin expansion in some areas by co-opting political leaders, both Muslim and Catholic, to a 'programme of action' which, in the domain of cultural instruction meant the use of Albanian as a language of instruction. In accordance with resolutions drawn up in Vienna under the direction of an Albanian from Ohrid, Gjerg Pekmezi, they created a curriculum in Albanian which would adopt a single alphabet (a politically charged issue at the time) and set of goals.[26] It is important to stress that Albanians were brought in to develop local programs. The Prizren program prospered under the careful direction of Mati Logoreci who integrated Italian and Albanian into the curriculum.[27] The fact that it is too early to argue that these institutes fostered nationalist aspirations, exposes the crying need to explore the relationship Pekmezi and Logoreci had with Austrians for example with a more critical eye than was permissible during the height of Hoxha's regime, which was busy reconstituting the myths of the Albanians.

The Italians posed a serious threat to the Austrians in the struggle for influence in Albania. Italy enjoyed a solid presence in many parts of Albania due to important political and economic links established between Italo-Albanians from Calabria and the Balkans. Italian was

[24]'Memorandum', Szomolany, 4 Oct. 1907, HHStA, PA XIV, 28, Albanien XX/7–8.

[25]Ippen to Goluchowski, Scutari, 31 Jan. 1901, No. 2A-B, Beilage, PA XIV/7, Albanien V/1.

[26]'Mémoire über Albanien (Ende 1901 bis Anfang 1905), HHStA, PA XIV/28, Albanien XX/3, pp. 13–19.

[27]Musa Kraja, *Mati Logoreci*, Tirana: Shtëpia Botuese 8 Nëntor 1987, pp. 20–6.

spoken in the coastal areas and larger towns where Catholic schools existed, allowing Italian state-building efforts to reach this population. During the 1880s, and especially after the rise to power of Francesco Crispi (himself of Italo-Albanian origin) in 1888, Italy made a large-scale effort to create a solid political, economic and cultural hold on the area. In 1888–89, the Italian state opened schools in Ishkodra (Shkodra), Avlonya (Vlora), Preveza, and Yanya (Ioannina). There were schools for both boys and girls, including secondary schools which also functioned as night schools for adults.[28] These schools, modern and well financed, began to attract students from the Greek, Ottoman and Austrian schools which had until then monopolised the field. These realities caused a reaction from the Porte, under pressure from Vienna and the Patriarch, to harass Italian schools, leading to a momentary decline of these schools in Ishkodra around 1896–7 and their complete closure in the southern and Greek-dominated Yanya *vilayet*. The competition between Italian and Austrian schools led to a significant improvement in the quality of these schools as each sought influence amongst wealthy families wishing to educate their children. The principle distinction between these schools was that Italian institutions taught solely in Italian while Austrian schools allowed Albanian to be used. Despite this fact, many of the élite of the area sent their children to Italian schools.

It should be added that some members of the Italian policy-making community had some long term plans, such as allowing the Arbëresh in southern Italy to create a chair of the Albanian language in Calabria in 1899 and one in Naples in 1900.[29] They, like the Greek state, offered Albanians scholarships to come to Italy.[30] These factors put enormous and contradictory pressures on students, often contributing to the fragmentation of the élite as it negotiated within the treacherous Ottoman political environment, making the nationalist trajectory in Albania, and the myths which constituted it, just that much more inapplicable to classic theories of nation-state formation.

Clearly these summary observations indicate a vibrant cultural plane in which Albanian identity became a politicised concept. From these issues many individuals could derive local as well as regional influ-

[28]Bojka Sokol, 'Origine sociale de l'intelligentsia albanaise à l'époque de la Renaissance', *Etudes balkaniques*, I/1982, p. 117.

[29]'Mémoire über Albanien', p. 13.

[30]Both the painter Kolë Idromeno and photographer Mati Kodheli studied in Italy on government grants. AQSH Fondi 71, File 13 documents 1, 3, 7.

ence. The Porte understood the mechanisms at work and made every effort to stem the tide of Albanian-centered sentiments by forming alliances with those suiting their interests. The establishment of secular schools and the *Ashiret Mektebi* (Hamid's tribal school which was introduced to Gheg children in 1902)[31] show new ways of interacting with a local population which was not permitted to formulate its distinctive cultural identity (for long) in larger political arenas. Ultimately the wide gaps which separated Albanians, politically and culturally, manifested themselves in the fractured response to Serbian, Montenegrin and Greek expansion at the end of the Empire. The concerted efforts to add further division to already inherent differences allowed a number of imperial actors to solidify important spheres of influence in Albanian-speaking regions, ultimately resulting in the territorial dispersion which led to the recent débâcle in Kosovo.

While the near-legendary Frashëri brothers harboured complicated allegiances to Islamic, Ottoman and Albanian culture, they were also products of a social environment that had been confined to Greek-language schools for significant portions of their lives. Yanya as a social milieu is not alone in its linguistic and institutional 'contradictions.' But those contradictions carry little weight beyond the irony of Albanian nationalists gaining their formal education in an institution funded by a hegemonic Orthodox church which actively repressed Albanian expressions of distinctiveness. The fact that the Frashëri brothers and Ismail Kemal emerged out of such a seemingly hostile educational environment should inform our fixation on such socio-cultural sites as essential to nationalism. Indeed, in a social and political milieu that had little coherence at the time, the myth of nation–building along the grounds of collective indoctrination, fails to read into the contingent factors that led to the creation of the Albanian state in 1912. In the far north other, often incongruous advocates of educational and linguistic rights were firm believers of the Ottoman (or Imperial) project in the context of expanding Montenegro and Serbia. Independence was not a catch phrase to learn in secret lessons at Albanian-language schools, but one experienced with the realities of both domestic and external shifts.[32]

[31] Alishan Akpınar, *Osmanlı Devletinde Ashiret Mektebi*, Istanbul: Göçebe Yayınları 1997, pp. 43–6.

[32] This is not to deny that patriotic themes coloured the efforts by groups in Bucharest, Athens, Istanbul and throughout the Albanian territories, this only suggests our assumptions about the overwhelming sentiments behind education are not informative to those who propagated Albanian nationalism.

How did these deeply distinct regional tensions articulate themselves in these institutions which often sought to sustain local differences? There is a rich theoretical terrain here on which the relations between the institutionalisation of cultural expressions and the manifestation of national aspirations at the end of the nineteenth century need to be explored. I suggest the Albanian case exhibits just how complex these sociological domains are and certainly questions the value of rigid ethnic and sectarian categories in the study of the Abdül Hamid period in the southern Balkans. The questions raised here concerning the nature of an emerging notion of educational rights and the concerns over its institutional direction in Albanian-populated territories strategically identifies the interactive realities of local, regional and global factors. Underlying the study is a concern that as historians of the post-communist era, we begin to see events identified empirically as part of an interactive process, one which feeds off the mutually inclusive influences of external and internal political, cultural and economic dynamics in order to revisit contentious issues such as identity in the Balkans. It also suggests that our fixation on the power of ideas (in particular of 'European' origin) and the institutions supposedly central to such currents needs to be revisited when considering nation-building in the nineteenth century.

RELIGION AND THE POLITICS OF 'ALBANIANISM'

NAIM FRASHËRI'S BEKTASHI WRITINGS

Ger Duijzings

At least since the time of Turkish rule—when religious divisions were given primary political importance in the Ottoman *millet* system—religion has been a major source of identity in the Balkans. During the modern age of nationalism, this has had a decisive influence on the ways the various nations of the region have 'imagined' themselves: religious myths, doctrines, images and symbols have been incorporated into Balkan nationalist discourse. Albanian nationalism forms, however, an exception to this common Balkan pattern of overlapping ethnic and religious identities and religiously inspired nationalism: even though Albanian national ideologists have tried to 'sacralise' the nation, as I will show later, the result was quite different than for most other Balkan nationalisms. Unlike, for instance, Serbian nationalism, where ethnic and religious identities have merged (especially through the centrality of the Kosovo myth), Albanian nationalism today lacks any strong religious attachments.

From the start the Albanian national movement was confronted with a situation of strong internal religious divisions, since the Albanians belong to three different faiths: Islam, Orthodoxy and Roman Catholicism. If we add the Bektashis as a separate religious community—which it *de facto* was—then we have a fourfold confessional divide. Although Albanian nationalist ideologists have always claimed that this divide was unimportant—'Albanianism' being the true faith of the Albanians—religious differences have nevertheless caused divisions within Albanian society, constituting a major obstacle to national unity at the end of the nineteenth century. The threat of internal cleavages along religious lines was reinforced by the fact that many higher ecclesiastics tended to define the ethnicity of their believers in terms other than Albanian, thus inhibiting the development of a national consciousness: during the late Ottoman period, for instance, Orthodox Albanians in the south were subjected to a process of Hellenisation, while Orthodox Sunni Muslims were being defined as 'Turks.'[1]

Therefore, since the end of the nineteenth century there have been continuous attempts to neutralise the cultural and political legacies of these religious cleavages. Since none of the faiths was in the position to bring all Albanians together on a religious platform, language became the main vehicle for national unity: the Albanian language—very distinct from the languages of its direct (Slav and Greek) neighbours—was the only element at hand that could bridge the differences between various religious and regional identities. Religion as a source of communal identity was continuously being played down. More recently this has also been the case for Kosovo where, even though more than 90 per cent of the Kosovo Albanians are Muslim (only a small minority being Catholic), Islam has played almost no role of importance in Albanian political life. Kosovo Albanian nationalism has not been clothed in religious terms, in striking contrast to Serbian, Croatian and Bosnian Muslim (or Bosniak) nationalisms which have had clear religious overtones.

From the beginning, national ideologists have propagated a kind of 'civil religion' of Albanianism, which was epitomised in Pashko Vasa's famous and influential nationalist poem *O moj Shqypni* ('Oh poor Albania'): 'Awaken, Albanians, wake from your slumber. Let us all, as brothers, swear an oath not to mind church or mosque. The faith of the Albanians is Albanianism!'[2] The need to bury religious differences is a recurring theme in the literature of the Albanian *rilindja* period, and many patriots of different religious backgrounds expressed this idea in some way or another.[3] For instance after the annexation of Kosovo by the Serbs in 1912, in his poem *The Voice of the Flag*, the

[1]Max Demeter Peyfuss, 'Religious confession and nationality in the case of the Albanians' in Donal A. Kerr (ed.), *Religion, State and Ethnic Groups. Comparative Studies on Governments and Non-Dominant Ethnic Groups in Europe, 1850–1940*, New York University Press, vol. II, 1992, pp. 125–38.

[2]Robert Elsie, *History of Albanian Literature*, 2 vols, East European Monographs, New York: Columbia University Press 1995, pp. 263–7.

[3]Shkëlzen Maliqi, 'Albanians between East and West' in Ger Duijzings, Dusan Janjic and Shkëlzen Maliqi (eds), *Kosovo—Kosova: Confrontation or Coexistence*, Peace Research Centre, University of Nijmegen, 1997, pp. 115–22, here p. 122.

well-known Albanian poet Asdreni called upon the Albanians 'to end their religious quarrels and unite in order to save what remained of the country.'[4] This obsession with religious discord shows that confessional differences certainly mattered in Albania: for several centuries, under the Ottomans, religion had been the primary source of identification, and although nationalist rhetoric declared it to be unimportant (and religious fanaticism to be alien to the Albanian soul), reality on the ground was sometimes quite different. In travel writing and other (proto-)ethnographic sources, there are many instances of religiously inspired animosities, which present-day Albanian historiography tends to ignore. Well-known examples are the Sunni hostility towards the Bektashis in southern Albania, and the conflicts between Catholics and Muslims in the north, as in the towns of Gjakova and Shkodra.[5]

It is, however, also clear that due to the activities of the national movement the national issue slowly began to supersede religious differences. Now instead of religious divisions ethnic cleavages emerged, visible for instance *within* the religious communities, as in the Greek-Orthodox community in southern Albania: growing tensions between the Greek hierarchy and nationally minded Orthodox Albanian priests led to violent incidents there.[6] As a corollary, the religious differences among the Albanians lost some of their importance. In Shkodra for instance, the rift between Catholic and Muslim Albanians proved not to be as deep as the one between Albanians and Slavs, and during the period of the League of Prizren (1878–81), Muslims and Catholics worked closely together in the Shkodra committee.[7] The most radical attempt to eradicate religion from the political arena occurred under Communism. Enver Hoxha took Pashko Vasa's motto literally and made Albania the first 'atheist' state in the world. Under his regime, the struggle against religious divisions evolved into a fight against

[4]Stuart E. Mann, *Albanian Literature: An Outline of Prose, Poetry, and Drama*, London: Bernard Quaritch 1955, p. 58.

[5]For Shkodra see for instance Hyacinthe Hecquard, *Histoire et description de la Haute Albanie ou Guégarie*, Paris: Bertrand, 1858. Hecquard, French consul in Shkodra in the mid-nineteenth century, provides a vivid picture of the tensions that existed between conservative Muslims and Catholics (see pp. 327–28; 337, 340). See also Peter Bartl, *Die albanische Muslime zur Zeit der nationalen Unabhängigkeitsbewegung (1878–1912),* Wiesbaden: Otto Harrassowitz 1968, pp. 39–40. For Gjakova see Edith Durham, *High Albania*, London: Virago, 1985 (1909), pp. 246.

[6]Sabrina Ramet, *Nihil Obstat. Religion, Politics, and Social Change in East-Central Europe and Russia*, Durham, NC: Duke University Press, 1998, pp. 205–6.

[7]Bartl, *Die albanische Muslime*, p. 118.

religion *per se*, which aimed to replace the diverging allegiances to religious communities with one undivided loyalty to the Communist Party. In spite of Enver Hoxha's radical Stalinist outlook, it was nationalism which provided the backbone of his policies: his harsh treatment of the religious communities should be seen primarily in this light.[8]

After the demise of Communism, however, faith has regained some of its importance in the lives of ordinary Albanians, to some extent reviving the old religious divisions. Since the early 1990s, intellectuals and politicians have been debating whether post-communist Albania should find its allies in the 'Muslim' Middle East or in the 'Catholic' or 'Christian' West, and in this context former president Sali Berisha's move to make Albania a member of the Organisation of the Islamic Conference in December 1992 sparked much controversy. Also the fact that the country's (Orthodox) neighbours tend to perceive the Albanians primarily as a 'Muslim' nation has put the secular character of Albanian identity under pressure.[9] Liberal Albanian intellectuals have tried to counteract these tendencies, propagating Albanian 'ecumenism' as the only remedy against internal religious divisions or against attempts of one particular religion (Islam) to gain political predominance. Shkëlzen Maliqi writes that 'If the emptiness that Communism left behind can be replaced by something, by some kind of national faith or conviction, then it is the creed that Albanians are a nation of ecumenism, carrying on the tradition of people like Naim Frashëri, Fan Noli and Gjergj Fishta.'[10]

In spite of the continuous efforts to neutralise religion, it is interesting to note that there were nevertheless attempts to give Albanian 'ecumenism' a firm religious basis. I am thinking in particular of Albania's national poet Naim Frashëri (1846–1900) who tried to promote the Bektashi order as the religious pillar of an emerging Albanian national movement. He hoped that the heterodox and syncretist Bektashis could eventually supersede religious divisions in Albania and bridge the differences between Islam and Christianity. Naim Frashëri seemed to believe that only a bond of a religious nature could forge unity among the Albanians, an idea he shared with many

[8]Bernd J. Fischer, 'Albanian Nationalism in the Twentieth Century' in Peter F. Sugar (ed.), *Eastern European Nationalism in the Twentieth Century*, Washington, DC: University Press of America 1995, pp. 21–54 (see p. 45).

[9]Stark Draper, 'The Conceptualization of an Albanian Nation', *Ethnic and Racial Studies*, 20(1), 1997, pp. 123–144 (see p. 141).

[10]Maliqi, 'Albanians between East and West', p. 122.

other Balkan nationalists of his time.[11] For centuries religion had been the main repository of identity in the Balkans and the primary source of loyalty which could not just be obliterated. Consequently, many Balkan nationalists realised that new forms of identity and political loyalty required some sort of 'traditional' religious component in order to have popular appeal.

Naim Frashëri was above all a nationalist whose main aim was to unite the Albanians, and this dominant national orientation underlines most of his literary work. Nevertheless, his religious writings should not be unduly ignored, as has happened during most of the communist period.[12] In many of his works, especially in his pastoral poetry, he blended his passion for Albania's countryside and natural beauty (so characteristic for nineteenth-century romantic nationalism) with Bektashi pantheist ideas, adding a religious and mystical flavour to the former, and thus 'sacralising' Albania's landscape. Even more important, however, was that in some of his works he mobilised the anti-Sunni and Shi'ite orientation of the Bektashis to express opposition to Ottoman rule and to articulate a separate (Muslim) identity for the Albanians. He was thus trying to transmute the Bektashis' religious doctrine into a vehicle of national aspiration. This process took place against the background of Ottoman Islamic restoration under Sultan Abdül Hamid.

Naim Frashëri's Bektashi sympathies were evident throughout his life. He grew up in the village of Frashëri (in southern Albania), where he frequently visited the famous Bektashi monastery which later would become one of the main centres of the Albanian national movement.[13] Only after the suppression of the League of Prizren in

[11]'Without faith there is no fatherland' (*Pa fe nuk ka atdhe*), as a popular Albanian proverb says, or 'Blessed is the nation that professes one and the same faith' as a Greek nationalist exclaimed at the end of the nineteenth century: see resp. Qazim Qazimi, *Ndikime orientale në veprën letrare të Naim Frashërit*, Prishtinë: Këshilli i Bashkësisë Islame të Gjilanit 1996, p. 161; E. Arnakis, 'The Role of Religion in the Development of Balkan Nationalism' in Charles and Barbara Jelavich (eds), *The Balkans in Transition: Essays on the Development of Balkan Life and Politics since the Eighteenth Century*, Berkeley: University of California Press 1963, pp.115–44, here p. 115.

[12]See H.T. Norris, *Islam in the Balkans: Religion and Society between Europe and the Arab World*, London: Hurst, 1993, p. 168. The religious (Muslim) dimension in Frashëri's work has only recently become the subject of research again. See Qazimi, *Ndikime*.

[13]Nathalie Clayer, *L'Albanie, pays des derviches. Les ordres mystiques musulmans en Albanie à l'époque post-ottomane (1912–1967)*, Wiesbaden: Harrassowitz 1990, pp. 275–8.

1881 did he begin to play a role in the activities of the Albanian national movement, quickly becoming one of its key figures together with his younger brother Sami. Naim contributed to the nationalist cause by writing patriotic poems, historical epics and school textbooks. Most of his poetry, which was popular among the small minority of literate Albanians, was profoundly romantic in character, glorifying the natural beauties of Albania and the delights of rural existence, and expressing dislike for life in the city (a characteristic Naim Frashëri shared with many other nineteenth-century romanticists). As Arshi Pipa has noted, Naim was the first to introduce Albanian shepherds and peasants to the literary scene, describing their lives in idyllic terms and ignoring the hardships that were very much part and parcel of peasant life.[14]

As has been noted by several authors, Naim Frashëri's writings were primarily patriotic in scope, while the religious element served to strengthen and deepen his nationalist ideals. Nevertheless, as he was a devout and religious person, he hoped that Bektashism would one day become the national religion of all Albanians, bridging the religious differences between Islam and Christianity.[15] He tried to promote the Bektashi order in his *Fletore e Bektashinjet*, the 'Bektashi notebook' (1896), a 'sort of religious-cum-nationalist tract,'[16] which was his most direct testimony of Bektashi beliefs and primarily meant for non-Bektashi consumption.[17] From Naim Frashëri's account it is clear that the Albanian Bektashi order's allegiance was not with Orthodox Sunni Islam, which it saw as symbolising Ottoman domination over Albanian lands. Absent are references to the five pillars of Islam that are fundamental to Sunnite belief, and much of the prayer and almost all the fasting are centred around the Shi'ite Kerbela myth.[18] The Albanian Bektashis do not observe the fast of Ramadan.

[14]Arshi Pipa, *Albanian Literature: Social Perspectives*, Munich: Rudolf Trofenik 1978, pp. 105–8.

[15]Mann, *Albanian Literature*, p. 38; Elsie, *History* ..., p. 238.

[16]Anton Logoreci, *The Albanians—Europe's Forgotten Survivors*, London: Gollancz 1977, p. 44.

[17]The first part of the Bektashi notebook was published in a German translation by Norbert Jokl, 'Die Bektaschis von Naim Be Frashëri', *Balkan Archiv*, II, 1926, pp. 226–56. For an English translation see Frederic William Hasluck, *Christianity and Islam under the Sultans*, 2 vols, ed. Margaret. M. Hasluck, Oxford: Clarendon Press 1929. See also John Kingsley Birge, *The Bektashi Order of Dervishes*, London: Luzac 1937, p. 171.

[18]Norris, *Islam*, p. 170.

As Stuart Mann writes, the Bektashi Notebook 'was designed to attract Albanians to a liberal faith acceptable to Christians and Moslems alike, and so to remove one cause of national dissention.'[19] Naim Frashëri tried to capitalise on the non-sectarian and interfaith appeal of the order, and depicted it in most favourable terms. Apart from highlighting religious tolerance, he also stressed its national orientation as one of the central assets of the Bektashi doctrine:

> Not only among themselves but also with all men the Bektashi are spiritual brothers. They love as themselves their neighbours, both Mussulman and Christian, and they conduct themselves blamelessly towards all humanity. But more than all they love their country and their countrymen, because this is the fairest of all virtues.[20]

At the end of the text, his ideal of promoting the Bektashi order as the national church of Albania shines through in his wish for Bektashis to co-operate with eminent Albanians and local authorities and to work for the salvation of Albania, i.e. to guide the Albanians not only on their road to God, but also on their road to national unity.[21] It was Frashëri's ideal to establish an independent Bektashi order in Albania, and he seems to have put great effort into convincing Bektashi leaders of the need to form an Albanian Bektashi community, and to sever ties with the mother *teqe* in Turkey.[22] He also proposed purging Bektashi terminology of foreign loanwords; yet, as Norbert Jokl has noted, his purism was mainly targeted at Turkish loanwords, whereas he did not seem to mind much about loanwords from other languages.[23]

It seems that the Bektashi order was to some extent carried away by Naim Frashëri's designs, although there were some sheikhs who expressed reservations about too close an identification with the nationalist movement for fear of Ottoman repercussions.[24] On the whole, however, it is clear that the Bektashis accepted the national

[19]Mann, *Albanian Literature*, p. 40.

[20]Hasluck, *Christianity and Islam. ...*, vol. 2, p. 556.

[21]Nathalie Clayer, 'Bektachisme et nationalisme albanais' in Alexandre Popovic and Gilles Veinstein (eds), *Bektachiyya. Etudes sur l'ordre mystique des Bektachis et les groupes relevant de Hadji Bektach*, Istanbul: ISIS 1992, pp. 277–308, here p. 292.

[22]Stavro Skendi, *The Albanian National Awakening 1878–1912*, Princeton University Press 1976, pp. 123–4; see also Margaret M. Hasluck , 'The Nonconformist Moslems of Albania', *Contemporary review*, 127, 1925, pp. 599 -606, here p. 602.

[23]Jokl, 'Die Bektaschis', p. 229.

[24]Clayer, 'Bektachisme', p. 286.

role Naim Frashëri had in mind for them. In the final decades of the nineteenth century, Bektashi lodges (often places of worship for Muslims and Christians alike) were generally known to be centres of Albanian nationalist activity. In addition, the order played a very important role in the establishment of clandestine schools and the distribution of Albanian books, and it also provided active support to armed nationalist bands.[25] The prominent role of the Bektashis in the national movement led to an explosive growth of the order, though for historical reasons it never succeeded in extending its influence into the north. In the south of Albania, however, the number of lodges more than doubled between 1878 and 1912, from twenty to fifty.[26] This remarkable growth in strength and popularity enhanced the self-consciousness of the order, which increasingly began to differentiate itself from the Turkish Bektashis and Sunni Albanians, both of which opposed Albanian independence.[27]

The growing independence of the Albanian Bektashis and their support for Albanian national goals expressed themselves, for instance, in the composition of patriotic poems written in the traditional genre of Bektashi *nefes* (hymns), and in the cultivation of the Kerbela theme. In particular the Kerbela epics written by Dalip Frashëri (1842), and Shahin Bey Frashëri (1868) (both were no direct relatives of Naim) had a lasting influence. Both works described the events during the battle at Kerbela and their aftermath, and were recited during the *matem* ceremonies (the memorial services in honour of the main Kerbela martyr Husayn) in Albanian Bektashi lodges. These epics branded the established (Sunni) Islam as corrupt, and equated its representatives with the adversaries of Husayn during the Kerbela battle. Instead of stressing Muslim unity throughout the Ottoman Empire, greater importance was attached to good relations with other (Christian) Albanians. Through these epics, Kerbela had a certain impact, not only on literature, but also in the mindset of the Albanians, as H.T. Norris has argued. It generated a whole new genre of national epics, and served as a model for recounting other historical themes of national importance.[28]

[25]Clayer ('Bektachisme') gives a detailed picture of these nationalist activities, mainly using contemporary sources.

[26]There are parallels here with the rise of the Sanusi-order in Cyrenaica (in present-day Libya) which organized opposition against Italian colonial domination some years later. See the excellent account by E.E. Evans-Pritchard, *The Sanusi of Cyrenaica*, Oxford: Clarendon Press 1949.

[27]Clayer, 'Bektachisme', p. 296.

[28]Norris, *Islam*, pp. 180–1.

Naim Frashëri made his major contribution to this genre with his epics *Histora e Skënderbeut*, 'History of Skanderbeg,' and *Qerbelaja*, both published in 1898. Although the former work became much more famous (as the first epic account of Skanderbeg's fight against the Ottomans written by a Muslim), some Albanians consider his *Qerbelaja* to be more beautiful. The paramount theme of this epic, which contains twenty-five sections, is the lamentation of the martyrs of Kerbela, whose death is described in great detail.[29] Naim Frashëri describes the terrible thirst at the beginning of the battle, the heroism of its martyrs who are slaughtered one after another, Husayn's farewell to his womenfolk, his brave attack on his enemies, and his final death and decapitation. The tragic outcome of the battle is announced in vision-like dreams, which highlight the divinely pre-ordained nature of Husayn's defeat. Husayn accepts his martyrdom: of the two options offered to him—allegiance to Yazid which will make him a traitor, or resistance to Yazid which means he will be killed—he chooses the latter. There are many parallels here with the Serbian Kosovo myth: moral victory is achieved through actual defeat, suffering and martyrdom, and as in the Kosovo myth, the sacrifice of Husayn will lead to the redemption for the community of believers, whose sacred duty it is to avenge his death.

It is of particular interest that Naim Frashëri attempted to transform this theme of Shi'ite suffering and redemption into a national theme. He was not only describing a (lost) battle in the first century of Muslim history, a battle which became the founding myth in Shi'ism, he also used it as a symbolic tool for denouncing Ottoman (and Sunni) hegemony.[30] He was aiming at a national poem that would appeal to all sections of society and would provide a religious source of inspiration for the struggle against Ottoman domination.[31] As with the nineteenth-century Serbian efforts to put the Kosovo myth at the heart of Serbian nationalist ideology, Naim Frashëri seems to have tried to promote the Kerbela myth as one of the building stones of an emerging Albanian national ideology. It is evident that Naim Frashëri's Kerbela epic had a clear patriotic message (much like his Skanderbeg

[29]Naim Frashëri, *Qerbelaja* (*Naim Frashëri, Vepra*, 4), Prishtinë: Rilindja 1978 (1898). Norris (*Islam*, pp. 182 -5) gives a very useful section-by-section summary of Naim Frashëri's *Qerbelaja*.

[30]Dhimitër S. Shuteriqi *et al.* (eds), *Historia e letërsisë shqiptare që nga fillimet deri të lufta antifashiste nacional-çlirimtare*, Tiranë: Akademia e shkencave e RPS të Shqipërisë, Instituti i gjuhësisë dhe i letërsisë 1983, p. 186.

[31]Norris, *Islam*, p. 182.

epic): it was intended to offer an example for the Albanians' fight for independence. Throughout the work, Naim Frashëri appeals to the Albanians as a nation not to forget about Kerbela and to revere its heroes. At the very end of his epic, in sections XXIV and XXV, he turns his full attention on national issues, urging the Albanians to love their nation and country, to learn their own language which is given by God, and to become brothers and friends. He closes his epic in this undeniably nationalist fashion, linking the tragic events in Kerbela with the tribulations of the Albanians under Ottoman rule, cursing contemporary 'Yazids' for Albania's enslavement and suffering, and calling upon the Albanians to find inspiration in the events of Kerbela in their struggle against Turkish domination.

In spite of his efforts to bring Bektashism and its myths into the centre of Albanian national ideology and reframe Albanian national suffering in Shi'ite terms, Naim Frashëri's attempt had little impact. There are several reasons for this. Firstly, *Qerbelaja* had only a direct appeal to a small (Bektashi) minority of the population, and even there the Kerbela myth was not part of any longstanding folk tradition as was for instance the case with the Kosovo songs of the Serbs. *Qerbelaja* was much more the product of literary invention than the Kosovo myth. Secondly, the attempts by Naim Frashëri to promote the order as the national church of Albania also failed because the Bektashis were in a weak position as a religious minority group, even though they had a greater aura of nationalist respectability than any other religious community in Albania. Thirdly, one should bear in mind that it was not Naim Frashëri's first priority to promote the order as such, but rather to propagate religious tolerance. The Bektashi order offered the most appropriate vehicle to pursue such an aim. In spite of their popularity, however, neither Naim Frashëri nor the Bektashis were able to erase existing religious divisions and to counteract the resilience of other, more powerful, religious communities. Then during the Balkan Wars and the First World War, the Bektashis suffered heavily from the destruction of war, a shock which took the order much effort to overcome.[32] These factors contributed to the failure of the Bektashis to become a kind of national 'ecumenical' church. This failure helps to explain why Albania became one of the few states in the Balkans which fostered a strong secular and non-religious national identity.

[32]Between 1913 and 1916, the majority of Albanian lodges (about forty) were looted and burned by Greek troops, and many Bektashis fled from Albania. See Clayer, *Bektachisme ...*, p. 297.

MYTHS OF ALBANIAN NATIONAL IDENTITY

SOME KEY ELEMENTS, AS EXPRESSED IN THE WORKS OF ALBANIAN WRITERS IN AMERICA IN THE EARLY TWENTIETH CENTURY

Noel Malcolm

'ANCIENT ILLYRIANS IN ENTENTE: AFTER 2,000 YEARS OF SOLITARY STRUGGLE ALBANIANS JOIN FORCES WITH SOLDIERS OF DEMOCRACY—DUSK OF A PICTURESQUE NATION.' This was the headline that greeted readers of the *New York Evening Sun* one day in September 1918. One could hardly wish for a better example of the mythic mentality at work: two millennia of history are essentialised in a single phrase, and the 'ancient' and contemporary worlds are brought into immediate conjunction in a way that implies the existence of an almost timeless Albanian 'nation,' its identity standing behind or beyond history itself.

I found this *New York Evening Sun* article reproduced in the first issue of *The Adriatic Review*, a monthly journal produced by the Pan-Albanian Federation of America, 'Vatra.'[1] As the First World War drew to a close, the activists of Vatra—at that time, as much a lobbying organisation as a cultural body—were evidently pleased to see their homeland receiving such attention in the American press; indeed, the mythopoeic reference here to 'Ancient Illyrians' may have reflected the influence of Vatra's own publications, and those of other Albanian writers in America, whose activities in the first two decades of the century represented an extraordinary efflorescence of Albanian image-making and consciousness-raising.

Vatra had been formed in 1912 out of a number of Albanian associations in different American cities; its headquarters were in Boston, which possessed one of the oldest and largest Albanian communities

[1] *The Adriatic Review*, vol. 1, no. 1 (September 1918), pp. 11–14; I am very grateful to the staff of the Widener Library, Harvard University, where I consulted this and the other Albanian-American journals referred to in this chapter.

in the United States. Thanks partly to the proximity of Harvard University, Boston attracted some of the leading Albanian intellectuals in the first decades of the twentieth century—above all, Fan Noli and Faik Konica. Noli took his BA degree at Harvard, and Konica also studied there for some time; another Harvard graduate was Kostandin Çekrezi (Constantine Chekrezi), who published his own magazine *Illyria* in Boston during 1916, before taking over the editorship of *The Adriatic Review* from Noli in 1919. Also active in Boston during the same period was Kristo (Christo) Dako, who became editor of Vatra's weekly paper *Dielli* in 1913; Dako was also a major contributor to another semi-monthly magazine, *Ylli i Mengjezit*, published during the years 1917–20.[2] Although of lesser stature than Konica and Noli, these two writers and editors would also play an important part in presenting Albania to the world: Çekrezi's *Albania Past and Present* (New York, 1919) was the first book about Albania to be written in English by an Albanian, while Dako's *Zogu the First, King of the Albanians* (Tirana, 1937) would be the first work on Albanian history and politics to be published in English in Albania.

The writings of these four men, and other articles contained in the journals they edited, do not form an utterly homogeneous body of materials; even in the early years there were differences in emphasis and approach, and during the interwar period some strong political divisions would open up between them.[3] Nevertheless, their writings on the central issues of Albanian history and Albanian identity do exhibit a strong common stock of themes and arguments—particularly in the crucial period 1912–21. Those were the years in which the existence of an Albanian state was first accepted by the Great Powers, and then so thoroughly undermined by the war that the Albanians

[2]See Robert Elsie, *History of Albanian Literature*, 2 vols, Boulder, CO: Social Science Monographs, 1995, pp. 365–86; Blendi Fevziu, *Histori e shtypit shqiptar 1848–1996*, Tirana: Grupini 'brezi 22', 1996, pp. 46–9, 133.

[3]Noli remained for nearly a decade a bitter opponent of Zog after being driven from power in 1924, but underwent a quiet rapprochement with him in the 1930s. Konica, although well known to be critical of Zog, gave him his official support and was appointed minister plenipotentiary in Washington. Dako became a leading apologist for Zog, as his 1937 publication shows. Kostandin Çekrezi supported Zog in the 1920s but was imprisoned by him in 1932, later fleeing to America, where he led an anti-Zogist movement; his relations with Noli deteriorated to the point where the latter described him as 'an irresponsible, unprincipled, unscrupulous juggler' (letter of 18 December 1942, quoted in Bernd J. Fischer, *Albania at War 1939–1945*, London: Hurst, 1999, p. 243). For further details of Çekrezi's career see William Bland and Ian Price, *A Tangled Web: A History of Anglo-American Relations with Albania*, London: The Albanian Society, 1986, pp. 72–7, 133, 139.

and their spokesmen had to argue all over again to re-establish the principle of Albanian statehood in the post-war settlement.

As has often been observed, Albania came very late to national statehood, and had only a short space of time—essentially the period 1878–1921—in which to build the sort of national consciousness and national ideology that, in most other European countries, had been developing since at least the first stirrings of the Romantic movement. Also, more than in the case of any other country, Albania depended for the development of its national ideology on intellectuals who lived outside the Albanian lands. This was mainly a consequence of the Ottoman policy of hostility to Albanian-language education; but it was also a reflection of the fact that the crucial battle for Albania's independence had to be fought not in the mountains and plains of the Balkans, but in the hearts and minds of Western politicians, within whose gift it lay. Two activities which can sometimes be distinguished in the history of other countries—nurturing national self-consciousness among the home population, and presenting national claims to the outside world—were thus, in the Albanian case, virtually fused into one.

The writings of the Albanian-American publicists of the early twentieth century played, I believe, a significant part in that two-in-one process. I do not claim that the arguments they used were original to them: in virtually every case it is possible to trace their themes and motifs back to earlier writers, both Albanian (or Arbëresh) and non-Albanian. But, given the belated development of Albanian nationalist ideology and the crucial importance of the second decade of the twentieth century for the creation and survival of an Albanian state, this body of writings does take on a special importance. The purpose of this paper is to explore these writings, picking out some of the characteristic mythic arguments they contain. Like other contributors to this volume, I do not use the terms 'myth' and 'mythic' to imply that everything so labelled is false or absurd; some of these myths rested on serious historical arguments, elements of which are still accepted by modern scholars. Rather, the term 'myth' is used to suggest the symbolic, emotional and talismanic way in which such ideas have functioned, both as components of identity and as weapons in a war of conflicting political and historical claims.

Albanian myths of national identity—four categories

Myths of identity are usually historical myths: they make assertions about identity over time. But they are also ahistorical: they claim a kind of permanence and solidity outside time, in an attempt to establish an identity that is not vulnerable to flux, development or decay. (Those processes are presumed to apply to other people or peoples, who lack this special, myth-fortified identity.) Looking at the whole range of Albanian national myths, we can distinguish four major categories: the myth of origins and priority; the myth of ethnic homogeneity and cultural purity; the myth of permanent national struggle; and the myth of indifference to religion. Of these, the first is directly historical, concerned as it is with establishing a chronological priority over other peoples. But it also underlies the other myths: it provides the identity of the *Ur*-Albanian people whose unchanging characteristics (ethnic homogeneity, cultural purity, national struggle and religious indifference) are then exhibited throughout Albanian history.

The myth of origins and priority

'It is generally recognised today', wrote Kostandin Çekrezi in 1919,

> that the Albanians are the most ancient race in southeastern Europe. All indications point to the fact that they are the descendants of the earliest Aryan immigrants who were represented in historical times by the kindred Illyrians, Macedonians and Epirots.

Those 'earliest Aryan immigrants' were identifiable, he claimed, as 'Pelasgians'.[4] Kristo Dako agreed; two years earlier he had written that the Albanians were 'the result of the combination of the ancient Illyrians, Macedonians and Epirotes, who were all descendants of the more ancient Pelasgians. These Pelasgians were the first people who came into Europe. ...'[5] This 'Pelasgian' theory, which gave the Albanians a kind of racial seniority over every other people in southeastern Europe—or perhaps in Europe *tout court*—was the foundation stone on which rested all the other components of the myth-charged account of Albanian identity.

Questions about origins are perfectly valid historical questions, even if the full range of evidence needed to supply a conclusive answer may not always be available. In the case of the Albanians, modern scholarship recognises a strong balance of probabilities in favour of

[4]Kostandin Çekrezi, *Albania Past and Present*, New York: Macmillan 1919, pp. 4–5.

[5]Kristo Dako, 'The Albanians,' *Ylli i Mengjezit*, vol. 1, no. 3 (15 February 1917), pp. 67–73, here pp. 67–8.

the view that they are indeed descended from the ancient Illyrians. The evidence for this is primarily linguistic; its significance has become clear only with the development of the modern (twentieth-century) science of historical linguistics.[6] Long before that, however, versions of the 'Illyrian' theory of Albanian origins developed in competition with other hypotheses, of which the most influential was the one that identified the *Ur*-Albanians with the inhabitants of an area in the Caucasus also known (to classical geographers) as 'Albania,' and supposed that they had migrated from there to the western Balkans in the late classical or early medieval period.

This Caucasian theory was first expounded by Renaissance humanists (such as Aeneas Silvius Piccolomini) who were familiar with the works of the classical geographers and historians; it was developed in the 1820s by the French diplomat and influential writer on the Balkans François Pouqueville; and in 1855 it was presented in a polemical response to the work of Johann Georg von Hahn by a Greek doctoral student at Göttingen, Nikolaos Nikokles.[7] By the late nineteenth century this theory was in retreat, thanks to the work of linguists who had demonstrated that Albanian was definitely Indo-European, not Caucasian.[8] One last attempt to salvage the theory, however, was made by an Arbëresh writer, Francesco Tajani, who suggested that the *Ur*-Albanians were Scythians who spoke an Indian language but whose place of residence, before they moved to Albania, was in the Caucasus. With delightful ingenuity, Tajani derived the word *shqiptar* (Albanian) from the Sanskrit 'kship,' meaning 'to fight,' and 'tär,' meaning 'bow'—thus demonstrating, to his own satisfaction at least, that the original Albanians were Scythian archers.[9]

[6]For a summary of the key arguments see Noel Malcolm, *Kosovo: A Short History*, London: Macmillan 1998, pp. 28–40.

[7]Eneo Silvio Piccolomini (Pope Pius II), *Cosmographia Pii Papae in Asiae & Europae eleganti descriptione*, Paris: 1509, fo. 13r; François C. H. L. Pouqueville, *Voyage dans la Grèce*, 5 vols, Paris 1820–1, vol. 2, pp. 510–25; Nikolaos Nikokles, *De albanensium sive Schkipitar origine et prosapia*, Göttingen 1855; on Nikokles see Nelson R. Çabej, *Autoktonia e shqiptarëve në studimet gjermane*, Prishtina 1990, pp. 31–2. This Caucasian hypothesis was not the only rival to the Illyrian theory; some Renaissance writers supposed that the Albanians had migrated from Italy.

[8]The key breakthrough here was made by Joseph Ritter von Xylander, who, arguing against an even stranger hypothesis (that the Albanians were 'Tatars'), demonstrated that Albanian was an 'Indo-Germanic' language: Xylander, *Die Sprache der Albanesen oder Schkipetaren*, Frankfurt am Main: Andreaische Buchhandlung 1835, especially pp. 292–320.

[9]Francesco Tajani, *Le istorie albanesi*, Salerno 1886, part 1, pp. xxi–xxii.

In retrospect, it seems obvious that the proponents of the Caucasian theory were engaged in little more than wishful thinking, with their selective use of classical authors, their bizarrely fanciful etymologies and, in some cases (such as the work of Nikokles), their transparently political motivation. Yet it must be pointed out that even those writers who were developing the 'correct' (Illyrian) theory of Albanian origins were not always free of those same faults. Although the first major exposition of the Illyrian theory, published by the German scholar Johann Thunmann in 1774, was both tentative and based mainly on historical evidence, subsequent writers incorporated this theory into a much more mythopoeic frame of argument, identifying the *Ur-*Albanians with the Pelasgians—a quasi-mythical population, referred to by Herodotus, of non-Greek and pre-Greek inhabitants of the Balkan peninsula.[10]

The key move here seems to have been made by the French geographer Conrad Malte-Brun; his interest in the Albanians had been aroused by the Arbëresh scholar Angelo Masci (Engjëll Mashi), whose *Discorso sull' origine, costumi e stato attuale della nazione albanese* (Naples, 1807) he reissued, in French translation and with his own critical annotations, in his multi-volume compilation *Annales des voyages*.[11] Masci argued that the languages spoken by the Illyrians, Epirots and Macedonians in classical times were substantially the same, and that this was the source of the Albanian language; he did not, however, identify this *Ur*-language as Pelasgian. That step was taken by Malte-Brun himself in a later publication, albeit in a somewhat confused way. According to Malte-Brun the Albanians were descended from Illyrian tribesmen who had spoken a language 'affiliated' to that of the Pelasgians, Dardanians, Greeks and Macedonians. However, while identifying the Albanians as 'Illyrian' and their language as basically 'Pelasgian' ('the Albanian language is an ancient, important and distinct link in the great chain of Pelasgo-Hellenic languages'),

[10]Johann Thunmann's work was published as *Untersuchungen über die Geschichte der östlichen europäischen Völker* (Leipzig: 1774). One section of this work has been reprinted under the title *Über die Geschichte der Albaner und der Wlachen*, Hamburg: Helmut Buske Verlag 1976. Herodotus describes the Pelasgians as non-Greek and autochthonous (unlike the Dorian Greeks, who had migrated to their present location in the Peloponnese): Herodotus, *Histories* (translation by George Rawlinson in Herodotus, *The Histories*, London: Campbell 1997), I. 56–7, pp. 30–1.

[11]Angelo Masci, 'Essai sur l'origine, les moeurs et l'état actuel de la nation albanaise,' in Conrad Malte-Brun (ed.), *Annales des voyages, de la géographie et de l'histoire*, 24 vols, Paris: F. Buisson 1808–14, vol. 3, pp. 145–234.

Malte-Brun described Pelasgian as a primitive version of Greek, and distinguished it from Illyrian, which he regarded as a branch of the Thracian language.[12] These ambiguous invocations of a Pelasgian origin were repeated in turn by another influential Arbëresh writer, Giuseppe Crispi (Zef Krispi), in his *Memoria sulla lingua albanese.*[13]

The author who removed these confusions and finally established the Pelasgian theory in what was to become its classic form was the great Albanologist Johann Georg von Hahn, in his *Albanesische Studien* of 1854. Von Hahn reverted to Masci's original classification of Illyrians, Epirots and Macedonians as a single linguistic group (constituting the *Ur*-Albanian language), and added to this theory Malte-Brun's identification of the *Ur*-Albanians as Pelasgians: this meant that the language spoken by the Pelasgians was not a version of Greek, but something different and perhaps more ancient.[14] The theory quickly established itself among Albanian writers: one of the first Albanian weekly papers (printed in Albanian and Greek, and published in the Greek town of Lamia in 1860–1) was entitled *Pellazgu*; Pashko Vasa devoted the opening pages of his influential pamphlet *The Truth on Albania and the Albanians* (1878) to the Pelasgian story, and another magazine called *Pellazgu* was published by the Albanian community in Cairo in 1907.[15]

The primary function of this Pelasgian theory was, of course, to establish a claim of priority. In Kristo Dako's words, the Albanians were 'the autochthonous inhabitants of the Balkan Peninsula, which they have ruled for thousands of years before the Barbarians ever crossed the Danube.'[16] By identifying with Pelasgians, Albanians could claim that they were present in their Balkan homeland not only before

[12]Conrad Malte-Brun, *Précis de la géographie universelle, ou description de toutes les parties du monde*, 2nd edn, 8 vols, Paris: F. Buisson 1812–29, vol. 6, pp. 200–15 (quotation p. 204).

[13]Giuseppe Crispi, *Memoria sulla lingua albanese*, Palermo: L. Dato 1831, especially pp. 4–6, 33–4 (portraying Albanian as essentially a pre-Homeric version of Greek).

[14]Johann Georg von Hahn, *Albanesische Studien*, 3 vols, Jena: Friedrich Mauke 1854, vol. 1, pp. 214–19.

[15]Fevziu, *Histori e shtypit ...*, p. 127; Pashko Vasa ('Wassa Effendi'), *The Truth on Albania and the Albanians: Historical and Critical Issues*, translated by E. St J. Fairman, B. Destani, (ed.) London: LBTH Learning Design 1999 (1879), pp. 4–8. For details of some other expressions of the 'Pelasgian' theory see Xheladin Gosturani, *Historia e Albanologjisë*, Tirana: Albin 1999, pp. 105, 128–9, 132.

[16]Kristo Dako, *Zogu the First, King of the Albanians (A Sketch of His Life and Times)*, Tirana: Kristo Luarasi Printing Press 1937, p. 13.

the 'barbarian' invaders of late Roman times (such as the Slavs), not only before the Romans themselves, but also, even more importantly, before the Greeks. As Fan Noli put it in an article written in 1916, 'The Albanians are the only lawful owners of Albania. They have possessed that land from time immemorial, long before the Greeks and Slavs had come into the Balkan Peninsula.'[17] Dako too emphasised the theme of 'ownership': the Albanian, he wrote, 'is the descendant of the original owners of the soil.'[18] Albanian political leaders had felt territorially threatened by Greece ever since 1881, when a large part of the Ioannina *vilayet* was ceded to the Greek state. Their fears were strengthened by the transfer of Ioannina itself to Greece in 1913, and would be intensified in 1918 when news leaked out about the Allied powers' secret treaty of 1915, which had promised a large part of southern Albania to Greece. Although the idea of basing present-day geopolitical claims on theories about ancient Balkan tribes must strike the modern reader as bizarre, the emotional attraction of such theories for Albanians at that time is not hard to understand.

However, the implications of the Pelasgian theory went further than mere claims of 'historic right' to territory. It also enabled its proponents to claim that some of the most famous elements of ancient Greek culture and history had a Pelasgian, and therefore an 'Albanian', origin. 'Let it be known,' announced Kristo Dako, 'that Philip and his son Alexander the Great as well as all the Macedonians were not Greeks but the forefathers of the Albanians.'[19] Çekrezi, similarly, could refer confidently in passing to 'Alexander the Great, whose Illyrian-Albanian origin cannot be disputed.'[20] The greatest expansion of Hellenic civilisation and rule thus occurred thanks to an 'Albanian,' not a Hellene.

A similar but more subtle insinuation of an 'Albanian' element into Greek civilisation was prompted by Herodotus' comment that the Greeks had learned the names of many of their gods from the Pelasgians.[21] Taking up this hint, Malte-Brun and Crispi had devised Albanian origins for various ancient Greek names: Thetis (one of the

[17]Fan Noli, 'Mehmet Bey Konitza', *Illyria*, vol. 1, no. 8 (1 August 1916), pp. 4–6, here p. 6.

[18]Kristo Dako, 'The Independence of Albania a Necessity for International Peace', *Ylli i Mengjezit*, vol. 1, no. 6, (2 April 1917), pp. 161–9, here p. 163.

[19]Dako, 'The Albanians', p. 68.

[20]Kostandin Çekrezi, 'Past and Present Conditions of Albania,' in *Illyria*, vol. 1, no. 7 (1 July 1916), pp. 1–3, here p. 1.

[21]Herodotus, *Histories*, II. 50–3, pp. 149–51.

Nereids, mother of Achilles) was derived from *det*, 'sea,' the goddess Hera from *erë*, 'wind,' Deucalion (the man who repopulated the earth after the Flood) from *dhe ka lënë*, 'he has left the earth' (referring to his embarkation during the Flood), and so on.[22] This etymology game was also played by von Hahn (Chronos from *krujë*, 'source'; Deucalion from *dhe*, 'earth,' and *kalli*, 'ear of corn'), and by Pashko Vasa (Chronos from *kohë*, 'time'; Chaos from *has*, 'eater'; Mousai, the Muses, from *mësoj*, 'I teach').[23]

Such arguments were taken up enthusiastically by the Albanian publicists in America: Çekrezi referred to 'the Albanian Zeus, whose memory survives even today in the appellation of God as "Zot" by the modern Albanians,' while Dako reproduced almost the whole list of derivations, however dubious, proposed by Pashko Vasa.[24] As Dako explained, 'Until lately it was believed that the mythology taught in schools as "the Greek mythology" was of Hellenic conception. The Albanian furnishes enough material to prove that this is not so.'[25] Another, slightly more practical use to which this method of argument could be put was to derive the Greek names for Albanian-inhabited areas from Albanian words, in order to reinforce the claim about ancient ownership of the territory: thus, according to Çekrezi, 'the historical names of what we now call Southern Albania or Epirus were "Thesprotia", i.e. the land of the sack-bearers, as it is very plainly expressed in Albanian, or "Molossia", i.e., "the Land of the Mountains."'[26] Similarly, in a pamphlet published in England in 1918 and reproduced in *The Adriatic Review*, Mehmet bey Konica derived Emathia (an ancient Greek name for Macedonia) from *e madhe*, 'the great,' and Illyria from *liria*, 'freedom.'[27]

Such derivations, almost all of which would be rejected by modern

[22]Malte-Brun, *Précis de la géographie ...*, vol. 6, p. 205; Crispi, *Memoria sulla lingua albanese ...*, pp. 25, 33–4 (most of Crispi's examples are taken from Malte-Brun).

[23]Von Hahn, *Albanesische Studien*, vol. 1, pp. 249, 251; Vasa, *The Truth on Albania*, pp. 11–13.

[24]Çekrezi, *Albania Past and Present*, p. 4; Kristo Dako, 'The Religious Beliefs of the Albanians', *Ylli i Mengjezit*, vol. 1, no. 5 (15 March 1917), pp. 129–31.

[25]Kristo Dako, 'The Albanian Language', *Ylli i Mengjezit*, vol. 1, no. 4 (28 February 1917), pp. 97–9, here p. 99.

[26]Kostandin Çekrezi, 'Southern Albania or Northern Epirus?' (editorial), *Illyria*, vol. 1, no. 2 (1 April 1916), pp. 5–6, here p. 6.

[27]Mehmet bey Konica, 'The Albanian Question,' *The Adriatic Review*, vol. 1, no. 4 (December 1918), pp. 145–64, here p. 148. While modern scholars reject these derivations, they do accept similar claims in relation to the place-names 'Dalmatia' and 'Dardania.'

scholars, exhibit some of the classic features of a mythic style of thinking. They elide the difference between the ancestral past and the present, identifying the ancient Pelasgians as 'Albanian' (rather as if one were to refer to the ancient inhabitants of Britain as 'English', or to ancient Gauls as 'French'), and assuming that they spoke a version of the modern Albanian language. Etymology, instead of illuminating the nature of long processes of change over time, is thus used to imply an eternal present. What is more, a kind of intentionality is built into the past: classical names are treated not as products of chance and change, but as riddles and rebuses, cleverly devised by an Albanian-speaking, Albanian-thinking mind.[28] And, where the connections with the Greeks are concerned, these arguments do something very characteristic of mythic thinking: exploiting the ambiguous status first given to the Pelasgians by Malte-Brun, the Pelasgian theory implies, simultaneously, both that the Greeks were quite distinct from the Albanians (being mere alien immigrants to the Albanians' ancestral lands) and that they were somehow derived from the Albanians, culturally or even linguistically. (According to Dako, scholars were 'convinced that the Albanian language is the most ancient language of Europe, the mother of the Greek and the Latin.')[29]

The myth of ethnic homogeneity and cultural purity

Closely linked to the myth of origins was the myth of a pure, homogeneous ethnic identity: in addition to claiming that the Albanians had always lived in the same place, it was necessary to show that they had always remained pure Albanians, untouched by any intrusion, admixture or dilution by foreign elements. Although some of the other myths of Albanian identity may have contained an important element of historical truth, this one is hardly defensible at all: modern scholars know that no Balkan population has remained in a watertight

[28]The most extreme example of this tendency was a work by Bernardo Bilotta, *Gli enti sacri della Bibbia ne' numi mitologici venerati da' Pelasgi Albanesi del gentilesimo*, Castrovillari 1897, which treated not only classical names but Biblical ones too as riddles to be solved in Albanian: thus Semiramis was *s'e e mirë ëmë?*, 'isn't she a good mother?,' and the Hebrew Noemi [Naomi] was *njoh ema*, 'I know how to weave.' (This rare work, listed in E. Legrand, *Bibliographie albanaise*, Paris 1912, p. 183, is known to me only from the review of it by Faik Konica in *Albania: La Revue albanaise*, vol. 'A', 1897, pp. 100–1; even Konica, who was not lacking in a taste for whimsy, found Bilotta's theory hard to swallow.)

[29]Dako, 'The Albanian Language', p. 97.

compartment, and that all have undergone ethnic interminglings of many different kinds. In the case of the Albanians, the added ingredients would include Romans (themselves of various ethnic origins), Slavs (especially during the early middle ages, when Bulgarian Slav settlers penetrated much of Albania), Greeks and (in much smaller numbers) Turks. And, just as the gene-pool of the Albanians contains many different elements, so too their language, culture and way of life reflect the many influences they have absorbed, such as the linguistic legacy of Latin and Slavic vocabulary and the strong cultural imprint of the Ottomans.

The myth of ethnic homogeneity and cultural purity, however, dictated otherwise. As Kristo Dako explained in 1917, 'the Roman conquest seems to have wrought little change in the social condition of the Albanians. They still retained their language and their national manners and usages, and still remained a distinct and peculiar people.'[30] Two years later Kostandin Çekrezi wrote:

> In the course of her long history, Albania has been invaded by various civilised, half-civilised, and barbarian races. The Gauls, the Romans, the Goths, the Slavs, the Normans, the Venetians, and, finally, the Turks ... So many invasions and influences have left hardly any appreciable traces, least of all on the national characteristics, traditions, customs, and language of the Albanian people.[31]

That Albanian writers felt the need to argue in this way was easily understandable at a time when Greek propagandists were claiming that the Albanians were not a proper people at all, that their language was just a mish-mash of other languages and that any Albanian member of the Greek Orthodox Church was 'really' a Greek. At the same time, Slav publicists were insisting either that the Albanians of Kosova were 'really' Slavs, or that they were 'Turks' who could be 'sent back' to Turkey. It is not surprising, then, that Çekrezi argued with particular vehemence that the Turks had not made even the slightest cultural impression on the Albanians: 'the despised Turk has been utterly incapable of exercising any kind of influence on their national characteristics, language, customs and traditions.'[32]

It was Faik Konica, however, who extended this argument from

[30]Dako, 'The Albanians', p. 68.
[31]Çekrezi, *Albania Past and Present*, p. 10.
[32]*Ibid.*, p. 36.

the cultural level to the ethnic or genetic. In one of his posthumously published essays he defined the Albanian race as

> a group of men who, having lived together for many centuries, speaking the same language, having led a secluded life, constantly intermarried, and until now successfully fought large settlements of invaders, present certain unmistakable similarities in physical appearance and in temperament.[33]

Konica himself thought there were two physical types in Albania, 'the tall man with clear eyes and light hair, and the shorter man with brown eyes and dark hair.' Nevertheless, he went on to cite approvingly the findings of the German anthropologist Paul Traeger, who claimed that 'the Albanians on the whole were a homogeneous racial group,' and the French professor Eugène Pittard, who observed that 'It is difficult to find a population whose skull characteristics are more clear-cut.'[34] The explanation of this remarkable ethnic homogeneity was supplied by Kristo Dako, who imputed a kind of permanent 'national consciousness' and national pride to the *Ur*-Albanians and Albanians: 'While the Macedonians, Epirotes and Illyrians intermarried among themselves, they never did so with the Greeks.'[35] The fact of permanent identity was thus founded on the permanent consciousness of, or belief in, identity: in this way, the myth enlisted all the Albanians of past centuries as believers in the myth itself.

The myth of permanent national struggle

From the myth of permanent consciousness of national identity, it was only a short step to the myth of a permanent struggle to defend that identity against outsiders. Çekrezi referred to 'struggles with the Romans, the Galles, the Goths, the Slavs, the Turks and with all the powerful hordes of invaders who poured from time to time into the Balkan Peninsula,' concluding in his book that 'The Albanian has always been noteworthy for his dogged endurance in resisting the consummation of foreign conquest and occupation of his native soil.'[36]

[33] Faik Konica ('Konitza'), *Albania: The Rock Garden of Southeastern Europe*, ed. G. M. Panarity, Boston: Vatra 1957, p. 30.

[34] *Ibid.*, p. 33.

[35] Kristo Dako, 'The Strength of the National Consciousness of the Albanian People,' *Ylli i Mengjezit*, vol. 3, no. 5 (August 1918), pp. 129–32, here p. 130.

[36] Çekrezi, 'Past and Present Conditions,' p. 1; Çekrezi, *Albania Past and Present*, p. 39.

Here the myth had much genuine historical evidence to draw on: from Illyrians resisting Roman conquest to Albanians fighting under Skanderbeg, there were many examples of active resistance to invasion or foreign rule. However, modern scholars would be much less willing to assume that the thinking and motivation of the resisters were dominated in every case by a 'national consciousness' of the modern sort. Modern historians would also think it necessary to refer to the many examples of cooperation (sometimes to mutual advantage) between inhabitants of the Albanian lands and their foreign rulers—above all, in the case of the Ottomans, with their innumerable soldiers and officials of Albanian origin (including more than forty Grand Viziers).

For Albanian publicists in the late nineteenth and early twentieth centuries, however, the most important aspect of the myth of permanent national struggle was the struggle against the Ottomans. The reasons for this, in the political context of that period, were obvious: as the Ottoman Empire was eroded and finally broken up, there was a danger that the West would regard only the Christian states of the Balkans as the historic practitioners of a national anti-Ottoman struggle, and therefore as the sole legitimate claimants to ex-Ottoman territory. In addition, the status of Ottoman Turkey as an enemy power during the involvement of the United States in the First World War made it particularly necessary for the Albanian publicists in America to dissociate themselves from it. Thus we find Fan Noli and five other Orthodox Albanian priests submitting a 'Memorandum' to President Woodrow Wilson in November 1918, in which they declared:

> Of all the Balkan nations, they [the Albanians] were the last to surrender to the Turk but never acknowledged his rule and never bowed to him. While all the other Balkan races were utterly crushed, the Albanians ... still defied the Turk early in the nineteenth century.[37]

Interestingly, the picture of eternal enmity between Albanians and Turks supplied by these writers, who were active outside Albania, was considerably more extreme than that supplied by Albanians commenting from a viewpoint inside the Albanian lands. Ismail Qemal Vlora gave

[37]Fan Noli *et al.*, 'Memorandum on Albania', *The Adriatic Review*, vol. 1, no. 3 (November 1918), pp. 97–104, here p. 98. Later in the same text they referred to 'the unspeakable Turk' (p. 103); cf. Çekrezi's remark about 'the despised Turk': Çekrezi, *Albania Past and Present*, p. 36.

what was perhaps a more realistic account of the Albanians' relations with the Ottoman regime when he wrote:

> Since that time [the death of Skanderbeg], although the Albanians have never given up their passionate desire for independence, they have been the only Balkan people really attached to the Ottoman Empire, always ready to support it, always happy to help strengthen it and to profit by its strength. But whenever the Albanians have become aware that, instead of growing stronger, Turkey had weakened herself, and hurried to her ruin, they have risen in an effort of self-preservation with the unanimous cry, 'Let her commit suicide if she wishes; we intend to survive.'[38]

A similar picture could be derived from the writings of Eqrem bey Vlora, or indeed from the comments of Isa Boletin reported by Aubrey Herbert.[39]

One explanation of this divergence of views would simply be that the publicists stationed outside Albania had a much stronger sense of the political needs of the day, so far as the policy assumptions of the Great Powers were concerned. But the full explanation goes deeper, surely, than that. Writers such as Konica, Noli, Çekrezi and Dako were responding not just to immediate political requirements, but to the dictates of their whole mythical pattern of thinking itself. The underlying line of thought was most directly expressed by Faik Konica in the first issue of his journal *The Trumpet of Croya*, published in St Louis, Missouri, in 1911:

> I wish that I could break every connection between Albania and Turkey, obliterate as far as possible the results of the conquest, and connect the present with the past by making it possible for my country to resume her natural evolution just where it was interrupted by the alien invaders.[40]

One could hardly wish for a more explicit statement of the mythic approach to time: half a millennium of human history can simply be erased, and what remains on either side of it can be 'connected' as if nothing at all had happened in between. This is possible not in the

[38] Ismail Qemal Vlora, 'Albania and the Albanians', reprinted in *Ylli i Mengjezit* (from first publication in *The Quarterly Review*, 1917), vol. 2, no. 5 (29 September 1917), pp. 129–34, here p. 134.

[39] Eqrem bey Vlora, *Die Wahrheit über das Vorgehen der Jungtürken in Albanien*, Vienna: Karl Fromme 1911; Aubrey Herbert, *Ben Kendim: A Record of Eastern Travel*, D. MacCarthy, ed., London: Hutchinson 1924, pp. 200, 205.

[40] Quoted in Konica, *Albania: The Rock Garden*, p. xxix.

real world of human time, but in the timeless (mythical) world of essences, where identity is supposedly located.

The myth of indifference to religion

Among the essential and timeless characteristics imputed to the Albanians, one other deserves special mention: religious indifference. Once again, it should be emphasised that to call this a 'myth' is not to imply that there was no truth in it at all. By the early decades of the twentieth century, when these Albanian publicists in America were writing, it was quite common for even the leading 'Muslim' families of Albanian beys to be almost completely unconcerned with religion in their daily lives.[41] But, on the other hand, it is clear that the Albanians have produced many devoted believers, Muslim and Christian, over the centuries, and it would be absurd to suggest that these people were somehow less Albanian by virtue of possessing genuine religious beliefs.[42] When modern writers refer in general terms to the religious indifference of the Albanians, they are often mixing together various phenomena which need to be more carefully distinguished: these include the syncretism of folk-religious practices, the tolerance (and doctrinal syncretism) of the Bektashi, the much rarer phenomenon of crypto-Christianity (both Catholic and Orthodox), the social system of the northern Albanian clansmen (for whom loyalty to their *fis* would take priority over any division of that *fis* into Catholic and Muslim branches), and the perfectly normal practice of Muslim men taking Christian wives without requiring their conversion to Islam. These are all different factors, too easily blurred into a single syndrome of 'indifference' by casual outside observers.

One such observer was Lady Mary Wortley Montagu, whose comments in a letter from Istanbul in 1717 became the *locus classicus* for Western writers:

> These people [Albanian soldiers] ... declare that they are utterly unable to judge which religion is best; but, to be certain of not entirely rejecting the truth, they very prudently follow both, and go to the mosques on Fridays

[41] I am very grateful to Ihsan bey Toptani (born into one of the great landowning families of central Albania in 1908, and brought up with virtually no religious instruction) for a fascinating discussion of this point.

[42] For a valuable survey of Albanian Muslim writers and scholars, see Hasan Kaleshi, *Kontributi i shqiptarëve në diturite islame*, Prizren: 1991; for an important overview of Albanian Catholicism, see Zef Mirdita, *Krishtenizmi ndër shqiptarë*, Zagreb: 1998. Unfortunately there is no comparable study of the Orthodox Albanians.

and the church on Sundays, saying for their excuse, that at the day of judgment they are sure of protection from the true prophet; but which that is, they are not able to determine in this world.[43]

In his posthumously published work Faik Konica shrewdly analysed this passage, commenting that Lady Mary 'failed to perceive the dry humor of her informants. What those soldiers told her can still be heard daily in Albania: it is an ironical and nonchalant way, almost a cliché, with the Albanians when they want to keep out of a religious controversy.' He also unpicked the claims of the Rev. Thomas Hughes (in his *Travels in Greece and Albania* [London, 1830]), who had adduced as evidence of Albanian religious indifference the fact that Albanian Muslim men would marry Christian women: Konica noted the Western ignorance of Koranic law in these matters, and concluded that this was 'the key to the whole misunderstanding.'[44] Here at least Konica appeared as a dismantler, not a builder, of myths. Elsewhere, however, he quoted with approval Hobhouse's famous comment about the fellow-feeling of the Albanians being based on nationality, not religion—a comment which may be substantially true about the modern period, but which becomes more questionable the further back into the past the modern concept of 'nationality' is projected.[45]

Other writers of Konica's acquaintance were more willing to build up the popular image; nor is this surprising, given the political importance at that time of emphasising that the Albanians were a single nation with a claim to a single statehood. Thus Çekrezi wrote in 1919: 'The truth is that the Albanian is not fanatical; on the contrary, it may be said that, *au fonds* [sic], he is indifferent in religious matters.' While making this an essential characteristic of the Albanians, Çekrezi also attributed the climate of religious tolerance to the special influence of Bektashism. Cleverly adapting his language to his American readership, he described the Bektashi as 'the Protestant element of Islamism,' and declared that the rise of this sect had represented 'a liberal reaction against the fanaticism and rigorous rules of the faith of Mohammed.'[46] However, some confusion remained in Çekrezi's

[43]Lady Mary Wortley Montagu, *Letters and Works*, ed. Lord Wharncliffe and W. Moy Thomas, 2 vols, London: G. Bell and Sons 1893, vol. 1, p. 291.

[44]Konica, *Albania: The Rock Garden*, pp. 135–6.

[45]*Ibid.*, p. 50.

[46]Çekrezi, *Albania Past and Present*, pp. 201, 204. For an earlier version of these comments see Çekrezi, 'The Religious and Educational Question in Albania' (editorial) in *The Adriatic Review*, vol. 1, nos 5–6 (January-February 1919), pp. 187–91.

account; it was not altogether clear whether Albanian religious tolerance was the consequence of Bektashism, or whether the growth of Bektashism among the Albanians was a consequence of their own innate tolerationist tendencies.

Even more confusing was his deployment of another standard argument, using the evidence of syncretistic folk-religion to suggest that the Albanian commitment to Islam was only superficial: 'The Albanian Moslem has never forgotten ... his former religion to some of the saints of which he still pays tribute, such as St. George ... and ... St. Demeter.'[47] This argument (understandably popular among Catholic and Orthodox Albanians, but, in view of the use made of it by Slav and Greek propagandists, a dangerous one for Albanian interests) raised a potentially awkward question. If the Albanians had been so devoted to Christianity (which was at one stage their national religion), why had so many of them converted to Islam? This question becomes even harder to answer if one assumes that, as Çekrezi sometimes seemed to imply, the Albanians' religious tolerance or religious indifference was largely a consequence of Bektashism—in which case they must have been more committedly Christian before the Ottoman period.

The commonest way of answering this question was to invoke the most important element in the essentialised Albanian identity: the desire for freedom and independence. Kristo Dako put forward three main reasons for Albanian conversions to Islam. The first was that the Orthodox Church refused to preach the Gospel in the Albanian vernacular: this made the Albanians think of it as a foreign Church, to which they could feel little attachment. The second was the 'love of wearing a sword, symbolizing power, which is one of the greatest characteristics of the Albanian people.' And thirdly, 'Another reason why the Albanians embraced Islam was because this pledge gave special political rights for their country'—a somewhat dubious historical claim, but one which usefully brought the focus of the argument back to the central issue of national political rights.[48] Similarly, Çekrezi observed that

> Whenever life became intolerable under the Turkish regime, the Albanians found a way of escaping their miserable lot by an outward adoption of the religion of the conqueror. The Albanian is too zealous in the cause of liberty and independence to be a fanatic in religion.[49]

[47]Çekrezi, *Albania Past and Present*, p. 202.
[48]Dako, 'The Religious Beliefs of the Albanians,' p. 129.
[49]Çekrezi, *Albania Past and Present*, p. 202.

Of all the comments on this question, however, the most revealing of the mythic pattern of thought I have tried to describe in this chapter was the one made by Tajar Zavalani, a friend and at one stage political colleague of Çekrezi, whose explanation of the conversion of Albanians to Islam was as follows:

> Without wishing to minimize the importance of the historical factors which caused the spread of Islam among the Albanians, we must emphasise that their racial characteristics also played a part ... For it is evident that Albania developed under Ottoman rule in a completely contrary direction to the one taken by the other Balkan peoples. The reason may be that the Albanians were formed spiritually under the influence of Roman paganism, which was added to the pagan traditions of the Illyrians. For the Illyrians, the development of a national consciousness was not channelled through the acceptance of Christianity. Thus, from ancient times, the thinking and social activities of the Albanians were characterised by a clear separation between religion and nationality.[50]

With this argument, the mythic pattern becomes complete, its components mutually sustaining one another. According to this interlocking set of beliefs, the choice between Christianity and Islam did not greatly matter for the Albanians, because their national identity existed independently, rooted in its ancient Illyrian past. The Albanians had preserved the traditions and the 'racial characteristics' of the Illyrians, among which—as all Albanian writers were understandably keen to stress—a desire for freedom and independence, expressed through permanent national struggle, was the most important feature. It can easily be agreed that some elements of historical truth were woven into this mythic pattern of thought; but it is also one of the proper tasks of historians to enable present-day Albanians to understand the ways in which the pattern has operated, not as the product of historical science but as talisman, symbol and myth.

[50]Tajar Zavalani, *Historia e Shqipnis*, 2 vols, London: Drini Publications 1957–66, vol. 1, p. 218.

Part II

MYTHS IN COMMUNIST POLITICS, SOCIETY AND CULTURE

BETWEEN THE GLORY OF A VIRTUAL WORLD AND THE MISERY OF A REAL WORLD

Fatos Lubonja

Rilindja (Albanian 'renaissance')

Following Albania's independence in 1912, Mithat Frashëri, one of the fathers of Albanian nationalism writing about the country at the time, noted that Albanians were faced with the task of turning their country 'from a scattered array of clans into a nation.'[1] Albania in 1912 was inhabited by various tribes, north and south of the Shkumbin River, which were divided into four *vilayets*. The tribes identified themselves within the limits of their village, region or *bajrak* and recognised, to some extent, the central government in Constantinople, or its representatives in the provinces, but they had very few spiritual, economic or intellectual ties with one another. To speak of myths belonging to the romanticism of Albanian nationalism is to speak about the endeavour to unite this 'scattered array of clans' in order to transform the Albanians into a nation with a collective identity.

If we compare Albanian nationalism with that of its Greek and Serb neighbours, we see that it starts several decades later and in another historical context. Albanian nationalism does not originate principally as a necessary result of the desire for liberation from Turkish domination, as was the case for Greek and Serb nationalism. Rather, Albanian nationalism starts at the time of the Russian—Turkish war (1878) which brought independence to the Serbs. As the Turkish

[1]Mithat Frashëri, 'Çështje të indipendences,' *Përpjekja*, no. 2 (1995), pp. 95–103, and no. 3 (1995), pp. 89–101 (reprinted from 1912), here part 1, p. 95.

Empire began to rapidly disintegrate, it became necessary to save the regions inhabited by the Albanians from the threat of being partitioned by the Serbs and Greeks. At the same time, there was a perceived need to differentiate Albanians from the Turkish identity.

This historical context has very much influenced the development of the national romantic myths of Albanian nationalism. It is a key moment in the creation of that mythology which has since dominated Albanian collective memory and Albanian culture.

The main myths created by those who were the so-called 'men of the Albanian renaissance' (*rilindja*), who nourished Albanian national romanticism, are typical myths of European romanticism of the 19th century, creating the pride in Albanians of being a unique people. Among the main myths are those exalting the antiquity of the Albanian people and Albanian as one of the oldest languages. Since it was necessary to distinguish the Albanians from the Greeks and the Slavs—even to stress their superiority—the origin of the Albanian people was found to be in the Pelasgian people, which, according to mythology, were the inhabitants of the Balkans before the Greeks (later the Pelasgians were replaced by the Illyrians). Consequently, the myths of the great Albanian men of antiquity were created, among whom the most distinguished were Alexander the Great and Pirro of Epirus.

The central figure around whom the mythology of Albanian national romanticism was created is Skanderbeg. This hero, first mythologised by the Catholic church as a 'Champion of Christianity,' now became mythologised for the second time as a national hero of the Albanians—as the man who in 1443 liberated Albania from the Turkish occupation and who defended his country against the Turks for twenty-five years. He is a very ambivalent figure, having fought against the Turks but at the same time having a Turkish name and title. The fact that he changed religions (born a Christian, he became a Muslim and then a Christian again) fitted a very important historical construct created by one of the famous men of the Albanian renaissance, Vaso Pasha. With the intention of unifying the Albanian people who were divided into three religions, Vaso Pasha, a Catholic who had served the Turkish Empire, wrote in one of his most famous poems: 'The religion of the Albanians is Albanianism.'[2] In the collective memory of the Albanians, the figure of Skanderbeg (first treated in

[2]Vaso Pasha, see Vasa, Pashko (Wassa Effendi), *The Truth on Albania and the Albanians: Historical and Critical Issues*, translated by E. St J. Fairman (ed.) B. Destani, London: LBTH Learning Design 1999 (1879[1]).

a national romantic spirit by the Arbëresh, the Albanians of Italy) is removed from its religious content. Albanians find it difficult to decide which is his most important name, 'Gjergj Kastrioti,' his Christian name, or his Turkish name, 'Skanderbeg.'

The man who contributed most to the perpetuation of the mythology surrounding Skanderbeg is Naim Frashëri (1846–1900), who is considered to be the Albanian national poet. He wrote poems in Albanian praising the beauty of the country, '*Bagëti dhe Bujqësi*' (Cattle and Farming, 1886); and the beauty of the Albanian language, '*Gjuha shqipe*' (The Albanian Language, 1890); and telling the story of Skanderbeg, '*Historia e Skënderbeut*' (The History of Skanderbeg, 1898).[3] 'Kruja o blessed town/ wait o wait, for Skanderbeg/ he is coming as a golden dove/ to save the motherland'—these lines from his epic poem *The History of Skanderbeg* was to be memorised by every Albanian who finished elementary school after independence. To complete the mythology with an other side of the coin, i.e. forces of evil, the five centuries of the Turkish occupation were represented as a period of total obscurity. We thus have the myth of the Turkish obscurantism. Albania emerged into the light thanks to the heroes of its Renaissance who, inspired by Skanderbeg, fought 'with rifle and pen'. The culmination of that fight was in 1912, when the flag of Skanderbeg was once again raised in Albania. The choice of Skanderbeg as the national hero indicates another element of the nationalistic mythology. Due to their small territory and population, Albanians were constrained to seek another big brother who would replace Turkey in defending them from the Serbian and Greek threat. The 'Champion of Christianity' was a most appropriate hero because he was also a hero of the Christian Western world.

These are the basic myths that nourished Albanian nationalistic ideology. Every Albanian educated in the Albanian schools after 1912, if asked about the history of his country, would recount these fundamental myths without being able to distinguish legends from history. This was the mythology of the generation educated during the time of King Zog (1926–39)—the generation which during the Second World War participated in the resistance against Italian and German occupation. The war of resistance, led by the communists, could not

[3]Naim Frashëri, *Vepra letrare*, Tirana: Naim Frashëri 1995–8, for *ibid.*, *Bagëti dhe Bujqësi*, 'Cattle and Farming,' 1886; and *ibid.*, *Gjuha shqipe*, 'The Albanian Language', 1890; *Histori e Skënderbeut*, Vepra, vol. 2, Universiteti Shtetëror i Tiranës, Tirana 1967.

have been organised without the nationalistic spirit which campaigned for the unification of people and the liberation of the motherland, which is why it was called the National Liberation War. Gradually nationalistic ideology became intertwined with the communist ideology, reappearing in the form of a project for the construction of a New World. Since that time we have the symbiotic syncretism of these two ideologies under which the Albanians were kept unified and at the same time dominated by the Communist Party for fifty years. It is clear that the nourishment of that centaur needed the conjunction of the new communist myths with the old nationalistic myths.

The communist period

One of the most common compositions in Albanian social realist paintings is a scene in which one can see a communist commissar with a red star on his partisan cap or a communist secretary of the party with a proletarian cap, speaking with common people by a fireplace. We can see there the old man of the house who is listening with attention but with some suspicions, the open-mouthed young boy who is fascinated and the women staying behind the men, passively, knowing that they will do what the men will decide. What is this commissar speaking about? It goes without saying that he is not speaking about the old nationalist myths. He is speaking about Communism as the future of the world and about the Albanian Communist Party as the saviour—as the one which would realise that dream in Albania. He is saying that the past of the Albanian people, like that of all humanity, has been a continuous evil and that the only way to break free from it is to follow the teaching of the Communist Party. He is speaking of the big brother, the Soviet Union, as the country where the communist dream has become a reality, and who, as a defender and a powerful brother will help Albania to become the same paradise.

The poem of Ismail Kadare '*Përse mendohen këta male*' (What are these mountains thinking about?)[4] written in 1966 is perhaps the best expression in poetic form of this new mythology: The mountains

[4]Ismail Kadare, *Përse mendohen këto male*, vjersha dhe poema, Tirana: Naim Frashëri 1964; available also in English: *ibid.*, 'What are these Mountains thinking about?' in *An Elusive Eagles Soars: Anthology of Modern Albanian Poetry*, ed. and translated by Robert Elsie, London and Boston: Forest Books 1993, pp. 86–96.

of Albania are thinking about the suffering of the Albanian people throughout their history, about their resistance and their heroism throughout the centuries, which was not that successful because of the lack of a true leader. They are thinking about the long wait for that leader/saviour. Finally, he has arrived: it is the Communist Party. Now the caravan has a leader. The darkness we are leaving is our history and the capitalistic world, which is the actual expression of that evil. The Albanians must drive out all the evils that have infiltrated into their spirit from life in that world of evil.

It is obvious that we are facing a paradox: on the one hand Communism is represented as a saviour from the evils of the past, as a denial of the old world in the name of a new world; on the other hand, it is impossible to give away all of the past described in the nationalist mythology as it already has an important place in the collective memory of the Albanians. The new apostles were bringing a new faith, but, in order to stay in power, they needed to keep roots in the old faith on whose foundations Albania was created. Therefore, it was necessary to find a compromise. The compromise was found, like the compromise between the Old Testament and the New Testament, in glorious moments that had foreseen and prepared the way for the coming of the saviour. The glorious past had at least four major moments: the Illyrian battles, the time of Skanderbeg, the Albanian renaissance, and the partisan war. Each of these events had its heroes who became the principal characters in literary and artistic works created during the communist period. The two most exulted were Skanderbeg and Enver Hoxha. As in every mythology, the heroes of these epochs also had their anti-heroes: the Roman invaders, the Turks, the Serbs and the Greeks, the Nazi-Fascists and their Albanian collaborators. This dark world also included religion and its clerics, and in particular the Catholics. From the nationalistic perspective the three religions were interpreted as dividers of the Albanians ('The religion of the Albanians is Albanianism'), while from the communist perspective they were seen as representatives of an old conservative world, as Marx's 'opium of the people.' Some well-known clerics—like Gjon Buzuku (circa 1555), Pjetër Budi (1566–1622), Frang Bardhi (1606–43), Pjetër Bogdani (1630–89)—who were among the first to write and publish in the Albanian language,[5] were seen only as great patriots, not as people who had served their faith.

[5]On Bardhi, Bogdani, Budi, Buzuku cf., for example, Dhimitër Shuteriqi (ed.), *Historia e letërsisë shqiptare*, Tirana: Akademia e Shkencave e RPS të Shqipërisë 1983.

The need to combine communist and nationalist ideologies made necessary the elaboration and enlargement of the nationalist myths—sometimes even their modification—through a technique of syncretist combination with communist myths. In analysing this technique it is important to keep in mind that the nationalist-communist ideology was represented in two forms: in its religious form claiming that the doctrine of Marx was 'just, harmonious and complete' (Lenin); and in its theoretical form claiming that belief in this ideology was based on scientific knowledge, not on the unknown and the transcendental. In fact the ideology was neither a religion nor a theory, but a mutation of both. Acting as a belief, while asserting at the same time to be scholarly knowledge the national-communist ideology froze many truths (among them historical ones). There was thus a mutation of mythology into science and of science into mythology. For instance, the ethnogenesis of the Albanians was an open question among Albanian scholars during the 1950s, but when Enver Hoxha declared that their origin was Illyrian (without denying their Pelasgian roots) no one dared participate in further discussion of the question. During the communist era, literary and artistic activity as well as academic studies (especially historical and linguistic studies) all adhered to this pattern. By this means a virtual world was created in which Albanians lived within the propaganda framework of the party and of the literary, artistic and academic works which pervaded schools, libraries, cinemas, theatres and exhibitions.

During the 1950s the exaltation of the partisan war victory was accompanied by the promotion of Skanderbeg. This high point in national history was immortalised in the film 'Skanderbeg' produced in 1957.[6] The hero now had an actor's face (although in fact the face was not that of an Albanian but a Georgian from the Soviet Union). In the film, Skanderbeg's ties with the Christian world are ignored; there are no churches or crosses. The Republic of Venice is presented as a threat and the Turks as the force of evil. With Albania's break from the Soviet Union in 1961, the symbiotic syncretism of the nationalistic and the communist myths grew even stronger. Hoxha justified the break not only as a defence of Stalinist orthodoxy, but also as a defence of Albanian independence from the threat of Soviet social-imperialism. In this period the monument of Stalin was removed from the main

[6]'Skënderbeu', an Albanian-Soviet coproduction directed by Sergej Jutkevic, 1957.

square of Tirana, put in another minor place and replaced by the equestrian statue of Skanderbeg. Albania started to become more and more isolated.

National-communist syncretism in the works of Ismail Kadare

Innumerable literary creations of this period nourished the national—communist ideology and almost all authors worked in that direction. One of the most eloquent aspects of this symbiotic creativity was the elaboration of old folksongs. The music remained the same, while the old texts were replaced with new texts that glorified the new socialist life. But the strongest influence was that of literature and film-making. In order to illustrate the syncretist national-communist creativity I will take the example of the work of novelist Ismail Kadare not only because he is the best-known Albanian author inside and outside the country, but also because he is the one who developed that syncretism with the most fantasy and talent. The greater part of his work nourishes all the main moments of the Albanian national-communist mythology. The history of Albania can be reviewed as narrated in Kadare's work. From novels describing antiquity we can mention *Eskili, ky humbës i madh*, (Aeschylus, the great loser, 1990) and *Dosja H.* (Dossier H, 1989).[7] Both of them are inspired by the idea that the ancestors of the Albanians were as civilised as the ancient Greeks and that they contributed mutually to each other's cultures. Some of the myths and customs described in the *Iliad* and the *Odyssey* or in the tragedies of Aeschylus, are demonstrated in these works to be current among the Albanian mountain people of today as proof that their origin lay there. In these books the author does not mention ancient Greeks and Illyrians, but simply Greeks and Albanians.

Through a series of works such as *Ura me tri harqe* (The bridge with three arches, 1978) and *Kush e soli Doruntinën* (Who brought Doruntina back?, 1980)[8] the period before the Turkish invasion is

[7]Kadare, Ismail, *Dosja H.*, Tirana: Naim Frashëri 1990 (Engl.: *The File on H*, London: Harvill 1997); *ibid.*, *Eskili, ky humbës i madh*, Tirana: 8 Nëntori 1990 (*Eschyle ou l'éternel perdant*, translated by Alexandre Zotos, Paris: Fayard 1988).

[8]*Ibid.*, *Ura me tri harqe: triptik me një intermexo*, Tirana: Naim Frashëri 1978 (Engl.: *The Three-Arched Bridge*, London: Harvill 1998; in French Paris: Fayard 1981 and 1993); *ibid.*, *Kush e soli Doruntinën, triptik me një intermexo*, Tirana: Naim Frashëri 1978 (reprinted Prishtina: Rilindja 1980; Kadare, *Qui a ramené Doruntine?*, translated by Jusuf Vrioni, Paris: Fayard 1986; Kadare, *Doruntine*, London: Saqi 1988).

described. Albania is represented as a flourishing civilisation, whereas the Slavs and Turks are presented as barbarians who came to destroy the flourishing Albanian civilisation. The most eloquent expression of this can be found in the novel *Doruntine*. The myth of Costandin and Doruntina—a Byzantine myth which was originally a moral tale against the practice of exogamy, or marrying members of a different tribe or clan—is interpreted rather differently by Kadare. The rise of Costandin from the grave, in order to return Doruntina to her mother, is presented as an institutionalisation of the *besa* (the 'promise' or 'oath'), and the creation of a superior institution that Albanians needed in order to keep themselves united against invaders. The *besa* is a basic element in the Canon of Lekë Dukagjini, the Albanian form of Medieval Canons which were collections of guidelines for a tribal society preceding the legal structures of a modern state. In Kadare's work, the *besa* is represented as an institution superior to the state.

Skanderbeg's reign is described in the novel *Kështjella* (The castle, 1970) which glorifies the resistance of the Albanians against invaders.[9] In this novel we can see clearly the technique of knitting together nationalist and communist mythology. The novel was written in the 1960s when communist propaganda glorified on a daily basis the resistance of Albania to imperialism and revisionism in the name of the defence of true Marxism-Leninism and the independence of the country. In the novel *Përbindëshi* (The monster, 1965),[10] written during the same period, the Albanian castle was compared with Troy: the author is warning us that we should be vigilant of 'wooden horse revisionism'. The image of Albania as a strong castle withstanding attack had a strong influence on the creation of the myth of isolation and later of the bunkerisation of the country. Kadare has written several works describing the period of the Ottoman Empire. In nearly all these works we find the myth of Turkish obscurantism, which often alludes to other eastern enemies of socialist Albania such as the Soviet Union and China (these works were written after the break with the Soviet Union and China). In '*Fehrexhe fermani*' (The sender of the veil, 1984) we find the most explicit expression of the myth of Turkish obscurantism.[11] Civilised Albania begins to be covered with the veils

[9] *Ibid.*, *Kështjella, roman*, Tirana: Naim Frashëri 1970 (reprinted Prishtina: Rilindja 1976; Engl.: *The Castle*, New York: Gamma 1980; French: *Les tambours de la pluie*, Paris: Fayard 1972)

[10] *Ibid.*, 'Përbindëshi', in *Nëntori* 12, 1965 (*Le monstre*, translated by Jusuf Vrioni, Paris: Fayard 1991).

[11] Originally entitled *Sjellësi i fatkeqësisë—Islamo nox* ('The Bearer of Ill-tidings—

sent by the Ottoman invasion. Meanwhile, in almost all of these works there are glorious Albanian figures who led the Turkish Empire and are always represented as more civilised than their Turkish oppressors.

Like most Albanian writers and artists of the communist period Kadare also wrote works glorifying the partisan resistance. *Gjeneral i ushtrisë së vdekur*, (The General of the Dead Army, 1963), *Nëntori i një kryeqyteti* (November of a Capital City, 1975) etc.; glorifying the construction of a new world by the communists: *Dasma* (The Wedding, 1968), *Ëndërr Industriale* (Industrial dream, 1967) etc.[12] These two themes have an important place in Albanian socialist-realist literature and are often intermingled as the heroes of the resistance become, in the second or third volumes of the novels, the heroes who build the new Albania. A very important element of Kadare's œuvre is *Dimri i Madh* (The Great Winter, 1973),[13] a novel in which we find once again the close linking of the national and communist ideologies. The break with the Soviet Union is represented as a combination of two motives: the defence of the independence of Albania against Soviet socio-imperialism; and the defence of Stalinism. It is difficult to say which is more important. The same thing can be said for the novel *Koncert në fund të dimrit* (Concert at the End of the Winter, 1988) which deals with Albania's break with China.[14]

These themes and these ways of treating them formed the basis of all creativity during the fifty years of Communism. During these years the myths nourishing nationalism and Communism grew together in a symbiosis as a combination of the glorious past with the happy future and the great brother. That propaganda pushed Albanians to escape into a strange virtual world and thus impeded their

---

Islamo nox'), known in English as 'The Caravan of Veils', see Robert Elsie, *Studies in Modern Albanian Literature and Culture*, Boulder, CO, East European Monographs, 1996, p. 48 (relating to the German edition: Kadare, *Die Schleierkarawane: Erzählungen*, Berlin: Volk und Welt 1987).

[12]Kadare, *Gjenerali i Ushtrisë së Vdekur,* Tirana: Naim Frashëri 1963 (*Le Général de l'armée morte*, Paris: Albin Michel 1970; in English: *The General of the Dead Army*, London: W.H. Allen 1971; *ibid., Nëntori i një kryeqyteti*, Tirana: Naim Frashëri 1975; *ibid., Dasma,* Tirana: Naim Frashëri 1968 (*The Wedding*, translated into English by Ali Cungu); *ibid., Ëndërr Industriale, poemë, Motive me diell (vjersha dhe poema)*, Tirana: Naim Frashëri 1968 (reprinted Prishtina 1978).

[13]*Ibid., Dimri i madh*, Tirana: Naim Frashëri 1981 (*Le grand hiver*, Paris: Fayard 1978, 1982).

[14]Kadare, *Koncert në fund të dimrit*, Tirana: Naim Frashëri 1988 (in Engl. *The Concert*, London: Harvill 1994).

comprehension of the misery of their everyday lives. If Albanians educated during the communist time were asked what was, for them, the most important thing in life, their answers invariably included: 'the fatherland,' 'its freedom and independence,' 'the Party,' 'Enver Hoxha,' 'the Soviet Union' (or later China) and 'the construction of Socialism.' Things such as love or individual freedom were never mentioned. Here, however, it is very important to note that with time these affirmations became more and more hypocritical. The national-communist ideology increasingly became a 'belief not believed,' a 'general lie imposed' as Alexander Solzhenitsyn puts it. It was growing oppression which forced people to behave as if they believed in it. As time went by, the perversion caused to the human spirit by that 'belief not believed' became an increasingly conscious mechanism of the system of repression. Meanwhile, the spirit of people who, in the name of that ideology, had undergone so much suffering and poverty, began to open up to other myths—those of the enemies of that virtual world and the heroes they had been forced to adore.

The post-communist period and the myth of the west

In 1990, when the communist regime started to open its doors, Albania was visited for the first time by Mother Teresa. She came as one of the first visitors who landed in an Albania isolated for decades. It is obvious that in her speech she could not avoid speaking of Jesus Christ and of religion. A young Albanian female journalist, born and educated in the communist period, never having heard a positive word about religion or Christ, could not resist saying to her: 'Yes, but the religion of the Albanians is Albanianism'. Mother Teresa gave an answer which predicted all the crises Albania would face with the withdrawal of the national-communist mythology: 'You will love your country more when you love each other more.'

The biblical images of the exodus of Albanians fleeing their country in the beginning of the 1990s were the most eloquent indicator of the failure of national-Communism. They showed that it had neither helped the Albanians to feel closer to each other nor cultivated in them a love for their country and for Communism, but merely served to oppress and isolate them. The Albanians overthrew the communist heroes with rage from their pedestals. They did, however, leave the national heroes on the pedestals built by the communists, but without believing in them and without being inspired by them. Generally, we can say that with the withdrawal of the national-communist myths and symbols, Albanians found themselves in a severe identity crisis. For good or for bad, the lack of strong historical roots and the heavy abuse of the nationalist ideology by the communists, strongly influenced Albanians not to have the same experience as other Balkan countries such as Serbia or Croatia, or even the Albanians of Kosovo. While other Balkan countries filled the post-communist vacuum with a collective identity based on nationalist myths, the Albanians somehow fell back to where they had started their history of the formation of the nation: into a scattered array of clans trying to survive.

If we can speak of one myth dominating the post-communist period, it is the myth of the West. It appears as the strongest drive for the creation of a new identity and a new inspiration and, at the same time, the finding of a new big brother to provide support. 'We want Albania to be like the rest of Europe'—was the strongest slogan of the students at the beginning of the democratic movement. 'We rule and the (western) world helps us' was the slogan of the Democratic Party. One of the climactic points of the exaltation of that myth was the visit to Albania of US Secretary of State, James Baker, in 1991. A vast crowd of people, reminiscent of the masses of people in Mecca, surrounded his car kissing it.

In the name of the myth of the West, the separation from Communism was treated as a separation from an accidental event in the history of Albania. It was the betrayal of the communists that made Albania a part of a world in which it did not belong: the eastern world. The myth of the West even had continuity with the old nationalist myth of the prosperity and civilisation of Albania before the Turkish period. The Christianity of the Albanians before the Turkish invasion was treated as a Western identity. During this period one could even hear and read about some audacious idea that the suppression of religion by Enver Hoxha had its good side, because the Albanians could now return to their original faith. Kadare reissued the novel *The Castle* filling the book with churches and crosses that were absent in the version published during the communist period. Skanderbeg was presented not only as a liberator and defender of the independence of the country, but also as a defender of Christianity.

In the transition years the myth of the West gradually began to wane. There are several reasons for this: first, the myth of the West appeared more in the form of a distant promised land rather than in the form of the coming of the saviour. That is why, rather than serving to keep the Albanians together and motivated in their own country, the myth served to attract Albanians to the Western world. Secondly, the West itself did not bring a culture based on the belief of an ideology or religion but rather a culture based on the fragmentation of the society and of power grounded in the values of pluralism and diversity. Thirdly, direct contact with the West rapidly disillusioned Albanians who, for the most part, found themselves treated in the West as second-class citizens. Finally, a more realistic knowledge of the West caused the monolithic god of Albanians' imagination to fragment.

The religious appendix of the Western myth proved itself to be unsuccessful. The first reason is that, whereas 70 per cent of the Albanians were Muslims and 20 per cent were Orthodox (in Kosovo more than 90 per cent were Muslims), the religion of the West was identified with Catholicism and Protestantism. Secondly, religion clashed with the myth that 'the religion of the Albanians is Albanianism'—this myth retained its strength based on feelings of identity of race and blood. Thirdly, the West was not, in the minds of most people, identified with Christianity but with wealth and a hedonistic lifestyle. In the minds of the Albanian élite, who could elaborate it, the West was identified with the non-religious elements dating from the renaissance.

As an endeavour to raise new myths based on religion we could mention the anti-Western myth: there was an attempt in some circles to exalt Albanians' Muslim identity on the grounds that those Albanians who became Muslim were the only true Albanians—arguing that the Islamic religion was the strongest factor in the salvation of Albanians from their traditional enemies, the Serbs and the Greeks, whose ally was the West. Some even put forward the idea that Skanderbeg should not be the national hero because he betrayed the Turks by serving the Christians.

Nevertheless, the myth of the West, combined with the old myths of national romanticism like that of Skanderbeg and 'the religion of the Albanians is Albanianism' remain the dominant mythologies in Albanian cultural and political life today. On 2 March 1999, the 555th anniversary of the League of Lezha was celebrated in that town. According to the mythological history learned by Albanians, the Albanian princes were united in Lezha 555 years earlier under Skanderbeg's leadership and gave the *besa* to be united and to fight against the Turkish invader. The present-day government of Albania attributed this celebration considerable importance because it came at the time when Albanians (from Kosovo) needed to sign the Rambouillet agreement. The invitation to the event, distributed by the Ministry of Culture, was entitled '555

Years of the National League.' The president of the republic in his speech said: 'We Albanians had the honour to be the first ones who defended West European values.' In essence this is treating history as mythology—as a need for identity, hope and support from a big brother. Moreover, the NATO bombardment of Serbia is interpreted by the majority of the population in the same spirit. Many people, even politicians, argue that the main reason for the war against Serbia is that the West realised that its natural ally, Albania, was wronged in 1913 by the division of its land.

Meanwhile, a strong sense of reality (or betrayal), due to the lack of deep roots of these myths and the disillusion arising from their manipulation, has been very influential in making Albanians sceptical toward their myths. This is a very important element in the relationship of the Albanians to their myths: 'The Albanians, when disappointed by God, could very easily light a candle to the devil,' said Fan Noli (1882–1965), one of the later figures of the Albanian renaissance. That duality and the lack of critical spirit towards their mythology has made Albanians continue to live divided between the glory of their virtual world and the misery of their real world, even though not in the dramatic form of the communist time. One of the most eloquent expressions of that separation is the paradox in which on the one hand Albanians express their pride in being Albanians, considering themselves to be natural superiors while on the other hand, they regularly defame their country and try to escape from it in the search of a better life.

Albania remains today a fascinating example from which some very existential questions can be derived about both the necessity and the harm of myths for the creation of a community in transition towards a civil society—a society in which some of the most important values are the acceptance of diversity, a critical spirit, and the consciousness that to err is an essential part of being human.

ISMAIL KADARE'S *THE H-FILE* AND THE MAKING OF THE HOMERIC VERSE

VARIATIONS ON THE WORKS AND LIVES OF MILMAN PARRY AND ALBERT LORD

Galia Valtchinova

This chapter deals with the ways in which fiction can vehicle academic research, and at the same time, reflect current political events. The literature in question is Ismail Kadare's work, among the best of contemporary Albanian literature, in which, according to its admirers and critics, one can find interpretations of all major Albanian myths. Since 1990 Kadare has been living and working in France, and French translations of his books are generally taken as the editions of reference. I therefore refer to the French version of the work in question.[1]

Despite its title, which is worthy of a thriller, *The H-File* is rather a speculative novel. It tells the story of two Irish-American scholars who pursue research on Albanian rhapsodists. Behind the characters and the circumstances displayed in this novel, one can discern an account of the achievements of Milman Parry and Albert Lord, the two classicists who promoted a new methodology of research on oral poetry with a special reference to the Homeric epic. My initial intention was to examine closely the fictional story in order to demonstrate that *The H-File* is an inverted account of the research that Milman Parry and Albert Lord carried out together in Yugoslavia in the 1930s.[2] In the meanime, however, I became aware that Ismail Kadare himself mentioned this parallelism in his exchanges with

[1]Ismail Kadare, *Le Dossier* H, Paris: Gallimard 1989, Coll. Folio 2237.

[2]A. Lord, *The Singer of Tales*, Harvard Studies in Comparative Literature, 24, Cambridge, MA: Harvard University Press 1960, 1981; M. Parry, *The Making of the Homeric Verse: The Collected Papers of Milman Parry*, ed. by Adam Parry, Oxford: Clarendon Press, 1971.

French intellectuals.[3] I shall therefore delineate the relationship between the achievement of Parry and Lord and the context in which the 'prototypes' worked, and the way Kadare echoes their theory in the 1980s.

Two young Irish scholars working at a prestigious American university conceived the idea of resolving 'the Homeric enigma' through fieldwork. They decide to test the possibility of an oral transmission of the Homeric verses in the 'last laboratory of oral poetry' which, after careful inquiry, they locate in the mountains of northern Albania. After many episodes and a series of puzzling meetings with Albanian people, they settle on the spot of their choice, in an old inn near a crossroad, where they regularly meet the last local rhapsodists and record their songs on tape. Despite initial difficulties, the first results are promising. Their work makes progress and the hypothesis is pieced together in an original theory about oral tradition and epics, when a terrible event abruptly puts an end to the whole enterprise: at the instigation of a Serbian monk, ignorant local people attack the inn and destroy the recorder and the tapes. When the two scholars leave Albania for America in despair they realise they have themselves become heroes of the epic they have studied.

At the end of the 1920s Milman Parry, a Harvard graduate and disciple of the French linguist Antoine Meillet[4], 'had already made a name for himself in classical scholarship by his masterly analysis of the technique of the formulaic epithets in the Iliad and the Odyssey'.[5] In 1933 he did fieldwork in Yugoslavia where he found 'singers of epic songs'—illiterate performers of oral poetry whose capacity to memorise and reproduce many thousands of verses closely paralleled his ideas about Homer. After an initial stay of several months in the region of the Sandjak of Novi Pazar, he returned accompanied by his best student and disciple, Albert Lord. Until his death in late 1935 he regularly did fieldwork in Yugoslavia, above all in the summer months, establishing a residence for himself and his family in Dubrovnik.[6] Although he employed native assistants (among them Nikola Vujnovic is the best known), he was able to speak the local dialects and knew

[3]My thanks to Pierre Vidal-Naquet for bringing this to my attention; cf. also François Maspéro, *Balkans-Transit*, Paris: Seuil 1997, pp. 108, 110.

[4]In Paris, Milman Parry first came in contact with theories about the 'antiquity' and archaic nature of Yugoslav oral poetry.

[5]Lord, *The Singer of Tales*; Tales, p. 3.

[6]Parry, *Homeric verse*, pp. xxxv–xxxvii.

the behavioural codes of the local society. There are indications that he particularly loved the mixture of South-Slavic and Muslim/Ottoman spirituality; his photographs in native costume reveal some fascination with the 'oriental' look. At the beginning of 1935 he turned to the study of the Yugoslav epics themselves, which became the dominant orientation of Albert Lord. The latter's first and most famous book, *The Singer of Tales*, borrows the title of his teacher's work which was never written.

Besides the numerous similarities existing between the two main characters and the life histories of the actual American scholars, the main analogy resides in the nature of the research itself, related to the type of society represented as the reservoir of Homeric cultural traits. Without any doubt, Milman Parry's great scientific innovation is the theory of the 'formulaic' mechanism of the oral transmission of epics. This theory, and above all the field approach he had adopted, had challenged the radical distinction between history and anthropology, introducing a kind of anthropological practice explaining what has been considered to be the first great literary achievement of ancient Greek culture: the Homeric epic. To record the text had been the prime concern in Parry's fieldwork, but he was also concerned with the social characteristics of the people who shared their knowledge with him, and with the life-story of his main informants.[7]

This concern with living conditions and with what a modern anthropologist would label the life-history method characterises both Parry and Lord, who went beyond merely descriptive ethnography. They were conscious of the impact of life experience on the training of singers, on their aptitude to memorise and perform oral poetry, and even more on the particular themes in their songs. Both of them sought to catch those occasions when the best singers performed outside their own local societies, and carefully to delineate under what circumstances those 'events' had taken place. Thus, war experience or military service appear to be crucial points in the singer's experience: this is true for the case of '*çor* [blind]' Huso and for the *guslar* Avdo Medjedovic.[8] The latter embodied the very 'Homeric' type of singer: he is described as moving permanently 'from town to town, from

[7]Parry, *ibid.*, p. 437.; Lord, *The Singer of Tales*, *passim*, and A. Lord, 'Avdo Mededovic, Guslar', *Journal of American Folklore*, 69 (1956), pp. 320–30.

[8]Lord, 'Avdo Mededovic, Guslar', pp. 320–30; and Lord, *The Singer of Tales*. This issue is discussed also in J. Goody, *The Interface between the Written and the Oral*, Cambridge University Press, 1987 pp. 86–91.

kingdom to kingdom', including the Habsburg court, and performing his songs.[9]

All these particularities of the original Parry-Lord approach are masterly interwoven in the intrigue of *The H-File* which consists, precisely, of the substitution of the original field and culture studied in the 1930s, with an Albanian 'field' and culture exactly at the same time. Kadare's novel embodies a vast enterprise of what can be termed the 'reversal of status' and of the basic features of the theory it draws upon. What in Parry-Lord's research had been 'Yugoslav' or 'South-Slavic' reality is withdrawn from the 'Slavic' domain and made a purely Albanian reality. Some of the common themes and the 'inverted' features will now be described.

(1) After the general setting, Kadare marks the entry into matters by delineating the 'cultural geography of epic tradition.'[10] It is centred on north Albania, the area of 'most authentic oral performance' and also comprises Montenegro and parts of Bosnia, both 'in Yugoslav territory.' Thus, this is an Albania where one could find the best-preserved 'laboratory.' Instead of being in the periphery for oral performances of the *aedic* type (following Parry and Lord), in Kadare's novel Albania becomes its centre. References to geographic and political maps of the Balkans, and especially ones of the limitroph Albanian-Yugoslav area, are frequent throughout the book.[11] This exercise echoes the real preoccupations with geographical distribution of the phenomenon studied by Parry and Lord, which from the beginning proved to be a delicate question. Parry himself had never extended his research outside the 'core' area; so he always referred to it as the 'South-Slavic epics.' After the death of his teacher, Lord engaged in short-term investigations in Albania (in 1937) without developing particular insights from this field. In the 1950s, he did fieldwork in two other South-Slavic countries: Macedonia (1950 and 1951), and Bulgaria (1958 and 1959).[12] He also knew Byzantine and modern Greek oral poetry, and produced some papers on the common themes in ancient and modern Greek oral poetry, as well as on themes and features shared by Greeks and South-Slavs.[13] Nevertheless he always

[9]Parry, *Homeric verse*, 439 ff.

[10]Kadare, *Le Dossier H*, pp. 55–6.

[11]cf. *ibid.*, pp. 99–101.

[12]For the dates cf. Lord, *The Singer of Tales*, pp. i–ii, 125.

[13]A. Lord, 'Parallel Culture Traits in Ancient and Modern Greece', *Byzantine and Modern Greek Studies*, 3 (1977), pp. 71–80, with ref.

preferred the term 'South-Slavic' for the singers he studied with Parry, and later by himself within the initial area. For him these were the main references.

(2) In Kadare's view, 'fieldwork' is comparable to a scientific 'laboratory' in which one could study, in ways closely resembling the analytical procedures of biologists, 'the mechanism which produced, throughout several thousands of years, this magical substance,' the epic.[14] At first glance, this representation is analogous to Parry's own concept of the 'mechanism' of transmission[15] as well as to the fact that he saw fieldwork to be the touchstone of theory. Nevertheless Kadare's speculations on their theory are marked by two modes of alteration of the meaning that things have in Parry and Lord: on the one hand, this is what I label 'organicism;'[16] on the other hand, a claim of direct continuity 'from Homer to our day and time.' These features are fundamental in Kadare's approach, while they remain either insignificant, or entirely absent from the theoretical constructs of Parry and Lord. They constitute the main weapon for essentialising oral poetry as a particular expression of a nation's 'spirituality,' and, finally, of the nation itself. In particular, the first one is a perfect example of the relationship between organicity and essentialism, and—at another level—of the "dangers of metaphor" recently discussed by Michael Herzfeld.[17]

(3) The attention paid to the performance itself is perhaps the only feature in which Kadare does not alter the spirit of Parry-Lord's research. As Lord puts it, 'an oral poem is not composed for but in performance,' and singing, performing, composing are facets of the same act.[18] This point is one of the most fascinating for Kadare who develops it and gives many illustrations. Let us examine just one element of the performance, the role of the rhapsodists who closely parallel the ancient Greek *aoidos*.

In Parry and Lord, the 'singers of song' are exclusively Muslim

[14]Expressions like 'observe under microscope' or 'catch through a stethoscope' are frequent in the book. In a more general manner, one can note the profusion of biologic metaphors and simile for oral poetry, as well as for the process of verse-making itself.

[15]Parry, *Homeric verse, passim.*

[16]i. e. to indicate the usage of vocabulary of the body and metaphors of human organism to describe and to represent such a complex social phenomenon like poiesis.

[17]Michael Herzfeld, *Cultural Intimacy. Social Poetics in the Nation-State*, London and New York: Routledge 1997, pp. 54, 74 ff.

[18]Lord, *The Singer of Tales*, p. 13.

'Slavophones.' Despite the examples of Christian 'Slav' performers of oral epic, the best representatives of the Homeric-style *aed* are of Slavic 'blood' and language and of Muslim faith. Both the Homerists saw the two characteristics as essential in producing the specific context which made possible the survival of an epic tradition. The contents of their songs are strongly influenced by the Ottoman context, and they seem to be the very last 'remnants' of this cultural mixture which is recreated by and in their performances. Lord's portrayal of the *guslar* Avdo Medjedovic, 'our present-day Balkan singer of tales',[19] is suggestive in this respect.

Avdo was Moslem; but by blood he was Slavic. In centuries past his family has been Serbian Orthodox and had come from Central Montenegro ... His pride in tales of the glories of the Turkish Empire in the days of Sulejman ... was poignantly sincere without ever being militant or chauvinistic. That empire was dead. But it had once been great. ... Avdo believed with conviction in the tradition that he exemplified.[20]

Despite the structural similarities such as the blindness or weak vision of the singer, and the particular musical performance of the poetry, Kadare's actors lack any explicit characterisation as being Muslim or Christian. One cannot discern any allusion to some 'imperial' (either Ottoman or Habsburg) context. They move back and forth through the chain of mountains which mark the border of Montenegro, but are firmly implanted in the Albanian national soil and, of course, speak Albanian. They are presented as competing with the 'Slavs' over the authorship of this epic tradition which 'is the only artistic creation throughout the world to exist in two languages, to be shared by two mutually hostile nations.'[21] After stating the existence of this'bilingual epic,' Kadare goes on considering it as 'a program of an absolute term-to-term opposition'.

In the political context of the 1980s it is hardly surprising that the author cannot associate 'Slav' (Serbian) with 'Muslim.' Curiously, he closes his eyes to the Bosnian formula of 'Slavic and Muslim' which existed at the same time. This is his first step in dissociating the 'original unity' of the ethnic and religious elements of Parry's 'singers of song.' This procedure allows Kadare to operate the second, more radical one: to distinguish the Serb/'Slav', generally speaking, from the Albanian

[19] *Ibid.*, p. i.
[20] Lord, 'Avdo Mededovic, Guslar', pp. 320–1.
[21] Kadare, *Le Dossier H*, pp.135–6.

precisely in his quality as a 'singer of song.'[22] The 'Slav' is presented as the radical other, and this 'otherness' is expressed even in racial terms (put into the mouth of 'German scholars'[23]). By another *tour de force* the author eliminates the Ottoman context which, according to Parry and Lord, had been decisive in producing the circumstances that made possible the oral performance of long epic texts. This allows him space for a deliberate search of antiquity and themes known from Greek tragedy.[24] No wonder, then, that we see him playing the Illyrian card,[25] one of the most powerful myths in the Albanian national construction.

As scholars, Parry and Lord were deeply aware of the importance of their research for local people and, by extension, for Balkan national ideologies. The 'Homeric question' is not only an integral part of the 'Greek miracle;' it is, in a sense, the key to it. The view professed both by classic scholars and historiographers over the centuries is that Homer's epic represents a kind of watershed between one 'archaic', 'barbarous' or 'primitive' state of society (all these characteristics being rooted in oral culture) and the 'civilized' one, identified as the triumph of literacy.[26] With the progress of Renaissance ideas and even more the ideas of the Enlightenment, the 'Greek heritage' came to be considered the centre of the eminently euro-centric concept of 'civilisation' and 'democracy' and as the very basis of modernity. The tremendous and ambiguous impact of the love of ancient Greece on the modern one is too well known to recall.[27] It is understandable that conducting research in order to discover pre-existing 'cultural traits' of this remote and most prestigious past known as the 'Homeric Age,' appealed to Balkan national élites.[28] Given the rivalries over geographical space in terms of 'national territory,' while, at the same time, living on, or in near proximity to, historic lands referred to by

[22] *Ibid.*, pp. 99–101 and passim.

[23] *Ibid.*, p.102.

[24] *Ibid.*, p. 158.

[25] *Ibid.*, pp. 117, 156.

[26] Despite the existence of an enormous body of literature on this issue, the critical approaches of John M. Foley, *Traditional Oral Epic: The Odyssey, Beowulf, and the Serbo-Croatian Return Song*, Berkeley and Los Angeles: University of California Press 1990, and Goody, *The Interface Between the Written and the Oral*, deserve special attention.

[27] Michael Herzfeld, *Anthropology through the Looking-Glass: Critical Ethnography in the Margins of Europe*, Cambridge University Press, 1987.

[28] Ernest Gellner, *Nations and Nationalism*, London: Basil Blackwell 1983, pointed this out earlier.

Homer, this appeal became even more powerful for Balkan élites. The supposedly visible persistence of 'ancient cultural traits' in traditional ways of life during the interwar period, when Parry and Lord conducted their research, proved significant for arguments concerning a continuity from Homeric to modern times.

Thus the type of (South-Slavic) rhapsodists studied by Parry and Lord came to represent more than a cultural artefact, a mould which could be used and manipulated in various constructions of identity. It seems that in Yugoslavia itself, the appeal to Greek Antiquity has had little impact; there is rather a tendency to 'nationalise' the pre-national phenomenon of South-Slavic oral poetry, to put ethnic or national labels on it. Writing in the late 1950s, Lord warned:

> The fever of nationalism in the XIXth century led to the use of oral epic for nationalist propaganda ... Hence the hero emerged as a 'national' hero, and the poems themselves were labelled 'national' epics ... To designate oral epic 'national' is woefully inadequate and an insidious imposter.[29]

To my knowledge, the disappearing species of Bosnian or Serbian-Muslim[30] *guslar* has never been seen, locally, as a 'national' figure of the Homeric *aed*. The research of Parry and Lord could have and has provided grounds for the pride of local people, aware of the interest that some Westerners have in their culture, but in Yugoslavia it did not serve claims of autochthony going back to Homeric times.

In the final analysis, the *H-File* is fiction which manipulates real events as well as a real theory which still has considerable impact on social and historical academic studies. Basing himself on the 'formulaic' theory of oral transmission and, partly, on the biographies of Parry and Lord, the author dissociates the real time from the real place and the real place from the real people. The result is a complete inversion of the initial situation in a highly nationalist opus, an ideological 'correction' of the original, which, nevertheless, perfectly follows the logic of the two scholars' research.

Kadare 'nationalises' as Albanian not only the performers, the 'singers of songs,' but the epic itself which is defined as 'a great national testament,'[31] a kind of Albanian 'national' private property legitimated by the Illyrian roots. In 'deconstructing' the unity of epic tradition

[29]Lord, *The Singer of Tales ...*, p. 7.

[30]Both Parry and Lord stress this combination which, in the light of later developments, appears as an impossible expression.

[31]Kadare, *Le Dossier H*, p.156.

common to both Slavs and Albanians, as well as to Greeks themselves, Kadare proceeds, at the same time, to 'reconstruct' the initial Greek-Illyrian unity.[32] The exclusivity of persisting traditions of epics in the contemporary Albanian cultural space, possibly shared only with Homeric Greeks, appears to be essential to Kadare's text. In a dramatic way, Kadare denies that one epic tradition can be vehicled in two cultures simultaneously, for example in Serbia and in Albania. He believes that one must have 'stolen' it from the other, perverting the themes, making the heroes traitors and *vice versa.* Clearly, the Albanian one is first, given that Illyrians predated Slavs. Beyond the claims of Illyrian descent and continuity a more powerful myth emerges here: that the Albanians are 'more Greek than the Greeks' themselves, because Albanians are closer to Homeric society and Homeric ideals.

In exploring the motivations behind Kadare's transformation of Lord and Parry's work it seems sensible to look at his *The H-File* as a key novel. It is well known that behind all the historical themes with which Kadare deals the subject matter relates to his own time, to Albanian life under Communism, and often reflects major events of recent history. In *The H-File* the action takes place in interwar Albania, and apart from the vividly written account of the construction of an academic theory, the intrigue consists mainly in Kadare's capacity to include the all encompassing spy-mania which must have characterized the regime of Enver Hoxha as well as, although to a lesser extent, that of King Zog. The narrative goes through vicissitudes of various kinds, and through national history as viewed by two American scholars. In this the author lends credence to his suggestions that history belongs to the realm of 'scientific research' rather than 'fiction.'

Additionally, the story of the two scholars is embedded within a scenario of 'catastrophe' and 'surveillance', a feature largely exploited in pseudo-scientific thrillers. Of course, this genre does not apply to Kadare's novel but such elements become evident in the literary technique Kadare uses. He shapes the story as a police report made by a 'spy' (the 'ear') and uses terminology of threatening secrecy and intrigue, as well as the word 'catastrophe' in the crucial episodes, thereby making the reader sensitive to this string. Why is the narrative—which appeared to primarily relate, purely and simply, to philology and oral literature, underpinned by this theme of threat and catastrophe? Tentatively I would suggest that this is rooted in the Kosovo crisis of 1981. If this suggestion holds true, Kadare's novel could be seen as

[32] *Ibid.*, p.117.

one of the first reactions to the crisis: Kadare finished it in 'Tirana, December 1981'.[33] There is a clear allusion to the Kosovo crisis, to the violation of 'the Albanian Kosovo house' when Kadare's figures, the scholars, speak about the fate of Albanian oral tradition. One remarks that 'the others [the Slavs] have taken, too, their epics.' 'Naturally,' the other replies, 'when one appropriates somebody else's house, one takes the most precious things in it.'

I will conclude with some comments on the Serb monk 'Dusan,' responsible for the destruction of the most precious part of the Albanian cultural patrimony. The Orthodox monk and the wandering Albanian rhapsodist incarnate a juxtaposition of two types of memory: the written and the orally transmitted. Yet there are similarities between both the 'Serb monk' and the 'Albanian rhapsodist.' Both are specialists of collective memory whose permanent mobility preserves group ties. As with all Balkan rhapsodists,[34] Kadare's rhapsodists are constantly travelling, and despite the author's rhetoric on the reasons for this in modern times, he is aware that wandering is the basis of the rhapsodist's social function. From Ottoman history it can be assumed that a Serb Orthodox monk may be associated with travelling as well. The French geographer Jacques Ancel observed in the 1920s that, for the inhabitant of the central Balkan area (Macedonia), the merchant was a 'Greek,' the shepherd was a 'Vlach,' the ploughman—a 'Bulgarian,' and the *intellectual* was a 'Serbian'.[35] In an attempt to explain this latter attribution, Ancel recalls 'the memory of the monks of past times.' This association of the 'intellectual' with 'Serb' and with 'monk' includes a reference to the relationship between Slav literacy and clergy. Some members of Orthodox clergy as the *taxidiotes*—the professional beggar-monks, were constantly on the move. Such clergy travelled across the Orthodox provinces of the Ottoman Empire, on the fringes of the Habsburg Empire and in Russia, in order to collect money for their monasteries

[33] *Le cortège de la noce s'est figé dans la glace* (Paris, 1986) which, as Kadare recognises, is directly inspired by the 1981 crisis: I. Kadare, 'Un crime annoncé' (propos recueillis par M.-F. Allain) in A. Garapon, and O. Mongin (eds), *Kosovo, un drame annoncé*, Paris: Michalon 1993, 1999, pp. 100–14, here pp. 101–2. In *The H-File* the same expressions, particularly metaphors of freezing (as applied to oral poetry), occur three times in a similar context of perdition and death. Kadare, *The H-File*, p. 157, 160 ff.

[34] Demonstrated by Parry and Lord in the beautiful description at the beginning of 'Çor Huso' (Parry, *Homeric verse*, p. 438): 'He has no trade, only his horse and his arms, and he wandered about the world. He wandered from town to town and sang to people to the gusle. He went from kingdom to kingdom and learned, and sang.'

[35] Jacques Ancel, *Peuples en nations dans les Balkans. Géographie politique*, Paris: Éditions du CTHS, 1939, 1992.

and to perform life-cycle rites.[36] Given the meagre presence of secular clergy in most South-Slav orthodox communities, the monks represented the principal type of intellectuals available to the rural population. They contributed to the preservation of the collective memory of frustrated collective identities and, in the Serb case, of the very sense of a quasi-national genealogy.

In turning the Serbian monk into the terminator of Albanian oral memory, Kadare's plot completes the full circle of ideological transformation of Parry and Lord's academic research. Kadare implicitly juxtaposes two types of 'memory-holders', both representatives of Balkan society. Kadare himself, however, acts as a myth-maker in the vein of Gellner's theory on the intellectual's role in the construction of the national self-consciousness.[37] Kadare creates, shapes and explores configurations which are relevant for our analytical research on the interaction between memory, history and politics in the Balkans.

[36]Anthony Bryer, 'The Late Byzantine Monastery in Town and Countryside,' in Derek Baker (ed.), *The Church in Town and Countryside*, Oxford: Basil Blackwell 1979, pp. 219–41, here: 233, 239.

[37]Gellner, *Nations and Nationalism*.

ENVER HOXHA'S ROLE IN THE DEVELOPMENT OF SOCIALIST ALBANIAN MYTHS

M.J. Alex Standish

Given the high priority that the socialist Albanian authorities assigned to the dissemination and study of written texts, I consider textual analysis to be key for a non-partisan attempt to analyse the genesis, evolution and role of particular myths of Albanian society during the era from 1944 to 1991. For an impoverished country where 80 per cent of the population was functionally illiterate in 1920,[1] the rapid spread of literacy in the post-war period opened up ever-wider opportunities for state-sponsored and subsidised propaganda and the dissemination of political texts. Through the spread of popular literacy and the production of texts designed to aid in the development of what was considered to be the 'New Man' within the 'New Albania,' we have at our disposal much valuable source material which may be subjected to critical text analysis. Moreover, for the purpose of demythologising, we are in a position to compare critically later editions of published texts with their earlier versions. This enables us to identify the dates of origin, the development and evolution of specific myths, which became essential to socialist Albania's official understanding of itself and its place within the international sphere. Additionally, such comparison allows us to situate these myths within their particular political and cultural context and to approach the dominant *Weltanschauung* of Albanian society at any given time.

With reference to the methodological approach and the concept of demythologising developed by the German theologian Rudolf

[1]D. Hall, *Albania and the Albanians*, London: Pinter 1994, p. 73.

Bultmann (1884–1976),[2] who applied this concept to the study of the Christian New Testament, I will focus on the central figure around whom the myths were developed. In Bultmann's study the central character is of course Jesus of Nazareth, while in the case considered here it is Enver Hoxha. It is perhaps ironic that we should apply a methodology drawn from academic theology to the analysis of socialist Albanian myths, given the militant atheism which characterised much of that era. However, there is, arguably, a sacral character to Albanian political patronage under Enver Hoxha as there are to the myths which underpinned its political foundation.

Yet clearly the roles played by these two different, but pivotal figures, in the genesis and evolution of what I term 'keystone myths', are quite different. In contrast to Jesus, Enver Hoxha was both the principal subject of socialist Albanian myth-making—as well as being himself the principal myth-maker and author (or at least the main guiding spirit) of the essential texts of Albanian Marxism-Leninism. Whereas demythologising the New Testament requires various scientific approaches to ancient and often corrupted texts from over many centuries, our text sources derive from, and evolved in, a period of approximately only half a century. Additionally, there are other advantages in studying recent Albanian mythology. A significant number of living eyewitnesses remain with us so there is an abundance of audio-visual material surviving in archives, and we have access to an expanding body of critical research.

This chapter pursues a textual 'archaeology' of various strata of political and cultural development during the socialist period in Albania reflected in significant texts of various kinds, and in this follows the evolutionary development of the keystone myths. As an example I have chosen to explore the role played by Enver Hoxha in the National Liberation War, and in particular, the liberation of Tirana in November 1944.

Enver Hoxha as liberator of Tirana

According to the myth developed during Enver Hoxha's own lifetime and consolidated and enriched in the years immediately following his death in April 1985, he had been the guiding political genius of the anti-fascist resistance to the Italian—and later Nazi—occupying

[2] R. Bultmann, *New Testament and Mythology: and Other Basic Writings* (selected and ed.), London: SCM 1985.

forces. Moreover, in addition to his political pre-eminence, he was also a brilliant military strategist; the indefatigable founder and organiser of the Albanian Communist Party, and so on.

The evolution of these keystone myths can be charted by investigating perceptions of Hoxha's wartime role in official Albanian historiographies. These include the monumental official histories comprised of the two volume *Historia e Shqipërisë* of 1959 and 1965, the four-volume *Historia e Shqipërisë* of 1983–4, the *Historia e PPSH* (History of the Party of Labour of Albania) published in its first edition of 1968 and then 'completely reworked' (to use the official euphemism) for the second edition of 1981, as well as the *Historia e Luftës Antifashiste Nacionalçlirimtare të Popullit Shqiptar* (The History of the Anti-fascist National Liberation War of the Albanian people) published in four volumes beginning in 1984, and, of course, Hoxha's own Collected Works (*Vepra*)[3], publication of which began in that form in 1968.

Comparing early official historiography and their later revisions, such as *Historia e Shqipërisë* vol II (1965), and its mid-1980s revision, it becomes clear that mythologies had some way to evolve. Although from the beginning it is made clear that Enver had—to use the British phrase—'a good war', other parts of the narratives had to be changed. Such revision became necessary because of the mysterious death and subsequent demonisation of Hoxha's closest political collaborator, chairman of the Council of Ministers (i.e. Prime Minister), Mehmet Shehu. Shehu's death—regardless of whether it was murder or suicide—amounted to a cataclysmic disruption in the evolution of the mythology of socialist Albania. The fall from power of lesser stars within the political firmament—such as Koçi Xoxe (the Interior Minister purged in 1948), or Beqir Balluku (the Minister of Defence who was toppled in 1974) had had a much more limited impact upon the keystone myths of Hoxha's role in the National Liberation War.

In the case of Xoxe, the key elements of the myth were still in their infancy, the role played in the foundation and organisation of the Albanian Communist Party by the recently demonised Yugoslav Communist Party was only then being subjected to the process of revision as a consequence of political expediency in the wake of Tito's breach with Stalin in 1948. However, the Tito-Stalin rift laid the foundations on which successive layers of mythology were to be built,

[3]E. Hoxha, *Vepra* (Works), Tirana Naim Frashëri/ 8 Nëntori, 1968–85.

all of which bear in some degree upon Hoxha's own wartime record as a partisan commander.

But Mehmet Shehu's untimely death in December 1981 threatened the very substance of the myth that Enver and his wartime paladins were responsible not only for Albania's liberation as a nation from foreign occupation, but that those who continued to occupy key positions in the state and party—Haxhi Lleshi, Adil Çarçani, Ramiz Alia and, until his death in 1979, Hysni Kapo—were living and visible symbols of that achievement. Shehu's shabby end had to be explained and worked into the myth as a matter of urgency.

That this was a far from simple process is clear from the contradictory and disjointed manner in which various accounts of the Shehu affair emerged. From suicide due to a nervous breakdown in the hours following the death, through to suicide following exposure of his high treason as a 'multiple agent of all years and all foreign patrons'[4], to use Hoxha's own description of his former right-hand man, we can discern an evolutionary process as the requirements of the key myths were evaluated and refined.

However, once the subordinate myth of Shehu's treason had developed into a form which could—with some effort and not a little 'suspension of disbelief', if we may borrow a phrase from the Shakespearian critics—merge into the renewed myth, the former prime minister soon assumed a place in socialist Albanian mythology akin to that assigned to Judas Iscariot in the Christian texts.

Consequently, we can observe the results of this evolutionary process over a relatively short period of time. The sacred texts of the Albanian Party of Labour soon became 'Before Shehu' and 'After Shehu' as the commander of the wartime partisan 1st Division was systematically erased as hero and repackaged as traitor. It soon became apparent that the most recent and traumatic phase of myth making would necessitate the production of new texts with the old elements of the myth purged and replaced in the light of the latest revelation of truth.

Not only were Shehu's own written works, such as *The Battle for the Liberation of Tirana*[5] removed from circulation, but all favourable references to him had to be erased from the key Party texts. This required prolonged editing and reprinting of many documents essential to the maintenance and propagation of Party myths.

[4]E. Hoxha, *Laying the Foundations of the New Albania*, Tirana: 8 Nëntori (2nd English edn) 1984, p. 581.

[5]Mehmet Shehu, *La Bataille pour la Liberation de Tirana*, Tirane n.d.

In many respects, the task facing the Albanian myth-makers was far more profound than that which had accompanied the disgrace of key political figures during the Stalin era, since there was often a considerable time lapse between a Soviet politician losing office and his or her physical—and literary—liquidation. One such example is that of Grigory Zinoviev who lingered in the twilight for a full decade between his expulsion from the Central Committee following the Fourteenth Congress of December 1925, and his execution in August 1936.

Stalin's editors had the benefit of years to expunge all favourable references to Zinoviev from official party texts and inevitably there was extensive self-censorship throughout private book collections within the Soviet Union. During the Great Terror of the mid-1930s, the mere possession of a book mentioning an 'enemy of the people' was more than sufficient evidence of counter-revolutionary activity. So perhaps we should be surprised that so much textual evidence has actually survived. In part, as is true to a lesser extent in the case of Albania, texts and other evidential materials have often survived owing to wide foreign distribution in countries where the long arm of Stalin and Hoxha could not reach.

Following the death of Shehu, new editions of many of Hoxha's own ideological memoirs were produced, such as *The Khrushchevites* and *With Stalin*,[6] from which positive references to the deceased prime minister had been erased. Key Party texts, such as the *History of the Party of Labour of Albania*[7] were even more speedily edited and reissued, in keeping with their status as key ideological sources.

Taking the important example of the evolution of keystone Albanian myths before and after the death of Mehmet Shehu, I believe that we can begin to demythologise the role played by Enver Hoxha in the partisan campaign to liberate Tirana. In the post-1981 official texts Shehu's role as a wartime commander has been appropriated to Enver Hoxha, principally through omission.

If we examine the official history of the battle for Tirana, as it appeared in the English edition of *The History of Albania*[8] published in 1981, we find that:

[6]E. Hoxha, *The Khrushchevites: Memoirs*, Tirana: 8 Nëntori, 1980, and *ibid.*, *With Stalin: Memoirs*, Tirana: 8 Nëntori 1979.

[7]Cf. *History of the Party of Labour of Albania*, Tirana: Naim Frashëri, 1971 (1st English edition) to *ibid.*, Tirana: Naim Frashëri 1982 (2nd English edn).

[8]S. Pollo and A. Puto, *The History of Albania: From its Origin to the Present Day*. London: Routledge and Kegan Paul 1981.

The National Liberation Army which now had 70,000 soldiers in its ranks, undertook to liberate the remaining towns. The most important of these operations, conducted by General M. Shehu, Commander of the 1st Division, had the capital as its goal ... On 17 November Tiranë was freed.[9]

A similar version appears in the first edition of the *History of the Party of Labour of Albania* published in 1971, where we learn:

The operation was to be led by the Command of the 1st Army Corps. The fighting in the capital city and its surroundings was directed by the Commander of the 1st Storm Division Mehmet Shehu.[10]

However, by 1982 Shehu had disappeared from the official party myth surrounding the National Liberation War. Now we discover that:

Of these operations the most important was that for the liberation of Tirana. The order of the Commander-in-chief [Enver Hoxha] was to wipe out the enemy, to stop the plunder and destruction of the city by the Germans and to liberate Tirana at all costs. The operation was to be led by the Command of the 1st Army Corps.[11]

As we may observe, the 'personalisation' or attribution of military victory has been transferred from Mehmet Shehu to Enver Hoxha, who although presented in the pre-1981 texts as the inspiration behind the partisan war, now appears as the only explicitly named commander. The disgraced Shehu has simply been written out of the text.

I have chosen this specific example, because I believe that it illustrates well the often convoluted evolution of political and historical myth making. Once established, the basic story line remains unchanged, but the role played by individual characters changes according to political circumstances and expediency.

Enver Hoxha as the creator of a new Albania

Having offered insights into how Enver Hoxha's role as 'Liberator of Tirana' in Socialist Albanian historiography can be demythologised, I should now like to examine the way in which the historical Enver Hoxha became the key figure in what is effectively a modern creation myth—the construction of the New Albania. Creation myths are a common feature of most cultures. The myth which evolves generally

[9] *Ibid.*, p. 241.
[10] *History of the Party of Labour*, 1971, p. 221.
[11] *History of the Party of Labour*, 1982, p. 166.

as an oral tradition, becomes often codified in a written literary tradition (and is often jealously guarded and interpreted by a 'priestly' ruling class).

That there were various creation myths in circulation amongst Northern Albanian tribes is clear from the materials gathered by the British anthropologist Edith Durham (1863–1944). However, it may also be observed that there was no single, common creation myth—in contrast with, for example, the Japanese Shintoist myth, or the Judeo-Christian biblical accounts. In part, this may be attributed to the absence of a single national religious faith common to all Albanians, and perhaps in part to the relatively late development of a national consciousness during the early modern period.

I would suggest that Enver Hoxha consciously identified this absence of a nationwide myth. He took the chance to provide a new, and in its time, dynamic framework of national consciousness—'Albanianism', if you will. In the process of constructing his own myth, Hoxha syncretised Albanian history (selectively identifying those historical figures which would—like Old Testament prophets—provide validation for his claims). Thus a quasi-religious ideology was developed around the central figure of the Founder of a New Albania.

Hoxha even produced what might be considered his 'testament', a volume of memoirs entitled, appropriately for our purposes, *Laying the Foundations of the New Albania.*[12] This work contains much which relates to his own myth-making including highly selective historical narratives, long ideological monologues, demonisation of critics and opponents, and post hoc justification for controversial decisions (such as his contracts with the leaders of the Balli Kombëtar and with the Allied military missions.) Last, and perhaps most significant of all, it serves as a literary memorial through which his own personal version of the new creation myth would be handed down to future generations, guarded and interpreted faithfully by The Party.

Historically speaking, one may find many earlier examples of leaders actively manipulating history and myth. One thinks of the careers of Alexander the Great, Julius Caesar, Napoleon, Hitler, Stalin and Kim Il-Sung. We can see clear parallels between the classical model of the hero drawn from the Greco-Roman world and the roles played by the great dictators of the twentieth century. In this respect, Enver Hoxha played his role in the myth of the New Albania to its fullest extent.

[12]Hoxha, *Laying the Foundations*, 1984.

The hero of classical antiquity was required, above all, to be a military genius, a role Hoxha gradually expropriated for himself as both his colleagues and rivals died or were disgraced. The mythical hero was also required to enjoy the gift of semi-divine foresight (perhaps not a strong point of either Julius Caesar or Hitler) and wisdom. Above all, he (and, of course, such roles are pre-eminently patriarchal) must be possessed of a sense of grand mission usually to include conquest; reconstruction, and national consolidation.

All of these themes have been developed for Enver Hoxha within the parameters of his own myth and that of the New Albania. This is reflected in the party hagiography, of which the following is a representative example:

> Outstanding among the leaders is Comrade Enver Hoxha. He is the founder of the PLA [Party of Labour of Albania] and has led it through all the historical stages of the revolution. He has made the greatest contribution to working out its Marxist-Leninist revolutionary line. With his wisdom, determination, foresight and revolutionary courage, Comrade Enver Hoxha has ensured the consistent, revolutionary implementation of the Marxist-Leninist line and norms of the Party, has never allowed it to be diverted on to blind alleys and has brought it triumphant through all the difficult and complicated situations. In all his works, Comrade Enver Hoxha has made a Marxist-Leninist theoretical summing-up of the revolutionary experience of the PLA, thus making an invaluable contribution to the treasury of Marxism-Leninism.
>
> Enver Hoxha is the most beloved teacher and leader of the whole Albanian people, united in steel-like unity around the Party and its Central Committee.[13]

I have quoted this extract from the official *History of the Party of Labour of Albania* (2nd edition) at some length because I believe that this text contains most of the keystone myths which Hoxha himself promoted. All the essential aspects of the hero of classical myth have reappeared in a Marxist-Leninist context.

In this passage we find the pre-eminence of the leader-figure; a historic role as creator/founder of a movement; heroic attributes such as wisdom, leadership, foresight and courage; and semi-divine status conferred as 'teacher' and 'leader'. Other passages within the same text focus on Hoxha's alleged military genius, on his ability to unmask traitors, on his consuming love for Albania and its people,

[13] *History of the Party of Labour*, 1982, p. 617.

on his hatred for Albania's enemies, both within the country and outside, and many more similar themes.

Stripped of its Marxist-Leninist overlay, the passage quoted could have been applied in some measure by court hagiographers to any other dictator such as those listed above. The examination of such texts should be, the starting-point for the demythologising of those national myths created by Enver Hoxha and developed both during and after his death by the Party of Labour.

In particular, we also have a key text published under the name of Hoxha's successor as First Secretary, Ramiz Alia. In *Our Enver,*[14] Alia takes up the familiar themes of the myths developed during Hoxha's lifetime in chapters such as 'A great patriot and ardent internationalist' or 'Architect of the people's state power.'

Perhaps with greater insight than he himself realised, Alia touches upon key issues in the conclusion to his book:

> The epochs give birth to leaders such as Enver Hoxha and they have epoch-making dimensions. Just as historical epochs are never forgotten, so their heroes survive, are honored and respected for ever ... With his majestic work Enver Hoxha ... will always be present in the joys and worries of our society. The present and future generations will be guided by his teachings. Facing any major problem, facing any difficulty or obstacle, they will seek the advice of Enver.
>
> And Enver will help them. He will give them answers through his work.[15]

This is clearly not the language of mere politics. Here we have a virtual invocation to a secularised deity by the man chosen to succeed to the role of First Secretary. In an earlier age, Ramiz Alia would have taken the role of an apostle or cultic high priest.

Laying the foundations of a post-Enver Albania

The relevance of demythologising for Albania is that it is an essential part of the process of coming to terms with the past and re-evaluating history. The collapse of the Party of Labour regime and of Enver Hoxha's legacy in 1991 has shattered many Albanians' self-image while leaving no alternative unifying national vision of Albania or what it really means to be Albanian. Myths are vitally important to the process of self-understanding, in that they provide a framework

[14] R. Alia, *Our Enver*, Tirana: 8 Nëntori 1988.
[15] *Ibid.*, pp. 481–2.

for important shared experiences and a common vocabulary for national, ethnic or cultural groups.

Hoxha's principal myth, that of the construction of a New Albania, continues to have a particular resonance today in the light of current events in Kosovo. What is the Albanian nation? What role can Albania play in the modern world order? The enduring strength of Enver Hoxha's myths is that they would have provided an answer to those key questions. Perhaps not the right answer, but an answer nonetheless.

I believe that the process of re-evaluating the historical figure of Enver Hoxha and the role he played in the creation of modern Albania is critical. He cannot simply be ignored or demonised, nor can the myths in which he played such a key role in creating and developing. An important beginning was made in this process outside Albania by the late Arshi Pipa, who began analysing the roots of the Hoxha myth in those papers collected and published in 1990 as *Albanian Stalinism: Ideo-Political Aspects*.[16] However, it could be argued that Pipa's highly colourful and often bitter analysis has overshadowed his scholarship and in my view much vital work remains to be done.

Several year have passed since the collapse of the Party of Labour and it is never too late for non-partisan scholarship to take the lead in the vital task of demythologising and in restoring Albania's history to the entire nation. Enver Hoxha is neither a deity nor a demon, and his crucial role in Albanian history simply demands dispassionate re-evaluation.

[16]A. Pipa, *Albanian Stalinism: Ideo-Political Aspects*, Boulder, CO: East European Monographs 1990.

Part III

NATIONALIST HISTORIOGRAPHY— OR FRIENDS, FOES AND HEROES

THE MYTH OF ALI PASHA AND THE BEKTASHIS

THE CONSTRUCTION OF AN 'ALBANIAN BEKTASHI NATIONAL HISTORY'

Natalie Clayer

Where religion among the Albanians is concerned, we are confronted with many myths: superficiality of religion, exceptional religious tolerance, conversion to Islam to preserve the Albanian ethnic and national identity *vis-à-vis* the pressure exerted by Serbs or Greeks, etc. Some of these myths appeared at the end of the nineteenth century, others in the twentieth century, even within the last few years (such as the last example above). In this paper, I want to deal with the myth concerning the connections between Ali Pasha of Ioannina (or Tepelen) and the Bektashi order of dervishes at the beginning of the 19th century. I will try to show when, how and why this myth was built and perpetuated. Even if it is a myth of secondary importance now in Albanian national history, I think that studying it can throw light on certain phenomena, especially on the role of Westerners (historians, scholars and others), in the diffusion and amplification of some Balkan myths (even among the interested local groups).

In a wide selection of literature, Ali Pasha is believed to have been himself a Bektashi, initiated by the Shaykh Mimi (Shemimi) of Kruja, and to have been responsible for the diffusion of the Bektashi Order of dervishes among the Albanians. Evidence of these connections between the local governor and this very heterodox and syncretistic mystical brotherhood includes his tolerance towards Christians;[1] the fact that he would have founded several Bektashi establishments (*tekkes*); the representations of the pasha wearing a round cap on his

[1]Frederic William Hasluck, *Christianity and Islam under the Sultans*, Oxford: Clarendon Press 1929, pp. 71 and 590.

head, which some authors, like Birge,[2] have seen as a dervish cap, and more particularly a Bektashi cap–in the same way Hasluck has recognised a Bektashi *tadj* on the headstone of his tomb, according to an engraving.[3]

However, after a detailed examination of all these points through a re-reading of the writings of Ali's contemporaries (especially Ibrahim Manzour Effendi,[4] a French renegade, who adhered himself to one of the dervish brotherhoods) as well as through research done in the Ottoman archives, it appears that the history of the relationship between Ali Pasha and the dervishes has mostly to be seen apart from the Bektashi issue.

All the accounts of travellers, consuls and others from Ali Pasha's time testify to his liking for dervishes (an attitude which, by the way, was common to a lot of great Ottoman figures). However, the only reference to Bektashism was given by William Martin Leake when he wrote 'Trikalla has lately been adorned by the Pasha with a new Tekieh, or college of Bektashli dervishes, on the site of a former one,'[5] and further, 'At Aidinli, Ali Pasha is now building a Tekieh for his favourite Bektasis.'[6] I don't want to call this testimony into question because as we shall see, Ali Pasha has certainly helped some Bektashi *shaykhs*. But, there is a possibility that Leake, like many observers of the present day, attributed other kinds of dervishes to the Bektashis. He maintains that the head of the *tekke* was married to a woman from Ioannina, but marriage was not very common among the Bektashis of this zone, who belonged to the celibate branch of the Order. Some documents tell us that Ali Pasha founded a *tekke* for the Sa'di dervishes in Trikalla.[7] Did he found two establishments in the same town for two different *tarikats*? The question remains open.

However, in the most detailed account—that of Ibrahim Manzour—there is no confirmation of this peculiar relationship with the

[2]John Kinsley Birge, *The Bektashi order of Dervishes*, London: Luzac 1937, p. 72.

[3]Hasluck, *Christianity and Islam*, p. 588, fn. 2.

[4]Ibrahim-Manzour-efendi (Commandant du Génie, au service de ce vizir), *Mémoires sur la Grèce et l'Albanie pendant le gouvernement d'Ali-Pacha* (ouvrage pouvant servir de complément à celui de M. de Pouqueville), Paris: Ledoux 1827 (2nd edn). In the introductory part of the book, 'Notice géographique sur I'Albanie et sur les moeurs de ses habitants', 2, pp. i–xxxix, the author writes that he himself joined the Rifa 'i order of dervishes.

[5]William Martin Leake, *Travels in Northern Greece*, vol. IV, London: J. Rodwell 1835, p. 284–5.

[6]*Ibid.*, p. 413.

[7]Cf. Başbakanlık Arşivi (Istanbul), Cevdet Evkaf nos 7024, 1239 and 557.

Bektashi dervishes as presented by Leake. For example, the adventurer gives a list of *shaykhs* favoured by the pasha. He did not include the brotherhoods to which these *shaykhs* belonged. Nevertheless, several of them were of Arab origin (which is quite incompatible with a Bektashi connection)[8]. Besides, the Epirot Bektashis from the beginning of the 20th century, when conversing with Hasluck, 'did not recognize the names of the sheikhs enumerated by Ibrahim Manzour as belonging to their sect.'[9]

Research done in Istanbul's archives reveals that Ali Pasha favoured two particular *tarikats*: the Halvetiyye and the Sa'diyye. In fact, Ali Pasha seems to have been very close to the Sa'diyye, a dervish brotherhood of Syrian origin. In his own birthplace, that is to say in Tepelen, he built a *zaviye* for the Sa'di dervishes.[10] In Trikalla, where he occupied the function of *sandjak beyi*, he founded, as we have seen above, in the city quarter of the Big Mosque (*Djami-i kebîr mahallesi*), another *tekke* dedicated to the *sa'dî* dervishes.[11] According to the tradition, he would have contributed also to the opening of an establishment for this brotherhood in Köprülü/Veles (Macedonia) in 1207/1792–3.[12] Even in the Ottoman capital, he is said to have established, in 1191/1777 (i.e. very early), a *tekke* of the Sa'diyye, at Karagümrük, near the Edirne Gate.[13]

For the Halvetiyye he built a *tekke* in Ioannina, outside the city, on the road to Narda; another in the town of Preveza, where he built a mosque in 1806;[14] and a third in Petrela, a small town 20 km. south of Tirana. His favours to the dervishes of the Halvetiyye went also to already existing *tekkes* (in Gjirokastër and in the *kaza* of Tepelen).[15] He could have instigated the establishment of many more *halveti tekke* in this region, since we know, for example, that he built *tekkes* in some of the newly-converted villages of Labëri (like Kuç and

[8]Ibrahim-Manzour-efendi, *Mémoires*, pp. 273–80.

[9]Hasluck, *Christianity and Islam*, p. 588.

[10] Başbakanlık Arşivi (Istanbul), Cevdet Evkaf no. 23372.

[11]See footnote 7.

[12]Nehat Krasniqi, 'Dy dokumente gjenealogjike të rëndësishme', *Dituria Islame* (Prishtina), 59, June/July 1994, p. 13–19 (see p. 19).

[13]See Zakîr Şükri Efendi, *Die Istanbuler Derwisch-Konvente und ihre Scheiche Mecmu'a-i Tekaya*), Mehmet Serhan Tayşi and Klaus Kreiser (eds). Freiburg im Breisgau: Klaus Schwarz Verlag 1980, p. 70; and Özdamar, *Dersaâdet dergâhlari*, Istanbul: Kırk Kandil 1994, p. 94, where we learn that the tekke was called Ejder Tekyesi (*Tekke* of the great snake), from the name of its first *shaykh*, Ejder Şeyh Mehmed Sıdkî (d. 1244/1828–9).

[14]Ahmed Müfid [Libohova], *Tepedelenli Ali Pasha*, Istanbul, 1908, p. 109.

[15]See Nathalie Clayer, *Mystiques, état et société. Les Halvetis dans l'aire balkanique de la fin du XVe siècle à nos jours*, Leiden: E. J. Brill 1994, p. 206. Even Ali's son,

Nivica)[16] and that there, in the twentieth century, the existing *tekke* belonged to the Halvetiyye.[17]

The only archive document I have found that implicates Ali Pasha in the foundation of a Bektashi establishment concerns the *tekke* of Xhefaj Baba in Elbasan (central Albania). It would have been built in 1226/1811 'with his permission and with his rescript.'[18] This does not mean that he had not built or helped other Bektashi *tekkes*, like that of Melçan, near Korça, or that of Sadik Baba in the village of Koshtan (near Tepelen, founded in 1810, according to Hasluck).

Was Ali Pasha himself initiated to the Bektashiyye? Besides the fact that he seemed to have been closer to the Sadiyye, the Halvetiyye or even the Nakshibendiyye (the *tekke* of Parga was Nakshibendi,[19] as well as a well-kown *tekke* of Ioannina),[20] the evidence, such as the engravings depicting Ali Pasha and showing the headstone of his tomb wearing a twelve-sided cap or *tadj*, are not convincing at all. As far as the much-copied portrait, published in London in 1823, is concerned, I do not follow Birge who has seen a Bektashi cap.[21] Incidentally, Ibrahim Manzour, who knew perfectly what Sufi clothes were, did not allude at all to a dervish cap when he wrote about the pasha's head-dress:

> Il n'avait de simplicité que dans la coiffure: il ne portait de turban que deux fois par an, les deux fêtes de *Baïram* (fêtes mahométanes), et seulement pendant le temps qu'il était à la mosquée. [...] Le reste du temps il ne se coiffait jamais que d'une *choubarré*, bonnet de velours bleu ou violet, galonné en or, de la forme dont je l'ai représenté à la tête de ces Mémoires.[22]

And last but not least, Ali Pasha cannot be held responsible of the diffusion of the Bektashiyye among the (Southern) Albanians because

---

Mukhtar Pasha, is said to have built a *halveti tekke* in the vicinity of Tepelena (Ahmed Müfid, *Tepedelenli Ali Pasha*, p. 194, footnote).

[16] Müfid, *Tepedelenli Ali Pasha*, pp. 74–5.

[17] See Arkivi Qendror i Shtetit (Tiranë), F. 882, v. 1938, d. 17, fl. 38. In the two villages which resisted Ali Pasha for a while, Hormova and Kardhiqi, after his rule was instituted *tekkes* of the Halvetiyye were also founded.

[18] Başbakanlık Arşivi (Istanbul), Cevdet Evkaf no. 10764.

[19] Müfid, *Tepedelenli Ali Pasha*, p. 151; Ibrahim-Manzour-efendi, *Mémoires* ..., p. 212. The vizir appointed Seyyid Ahmed, a Moroccan dervish, who had been previously his diplomatic agent at the head of the new *tekke*.

[20] In his time, the *shaykh* Yusuf, head of the *tekke* of Arslan Pasha, in the fortress of Ioannina, had a great influence on Ali.

[21] Hasluck has not taken this evidence into account.

[22] Ibrahim-Manzour-efendi, *Mémoires* ..., p. 360.

a significant proportion of the Albanian Bektashi *tekkes* were founded in the last quarter of the 19th century or even at the beginning of the 20th century.[23]

It was in all probability during this period that the myth of Ali's Bektashi connections emerged. We will consider two groups of actors in the 'creation' and diffusion of the myths: Bektashi leaders, and Westerners who came into contact with them (above all Ippen, Degrand, Brailsford, F.W. Hasluck, and later Birge).[24] We have no Albanian Bektashi writings from this time which refer to the question, but the accounts of Westerners largely rely on oral tradition collected among Albanian Bektashis.[25]

If we analyse what is written by these scholars or consuls, we see that the emphasis on the relationship between the Bektashis and Ali Pasha is related to political considerations. Hasluck insisted that the pasha used this connection with the Bektashis for his own expansion and domination. Hasluck wrote that 'doctrines and organization [of the Bektashi sect in Albania] seem to have been used for political purposes by Ali Pasha of Yannina,' and that South Albania (Epirus) 'once bid fair to become an independent state under Ali Pasha of Yannina (d. 1822), who owed his power to his own astounding energy, but also to his alliance with the Bektashi.[26] According to Brailsford, Ali spread the Bektashi 'heresy' among the Albanian Muslims with the aim of dividing Albanians and Turks and creating the first national Albanian state.[27] As a consequence of this, Ali Pasha was considered to be 'responsible for the propagation of Bektashism' in Thessaly, in South Albania and in Kruja, because of the support he gave to its propagandists.[28]

So, clearly, the aim was to present Bektashism as a (or the) potential power in the creation of an 'Albanian identity' and an 'Albanian state'

[23]See Nathalie Clayer, *L'Albanie, pays des derviches*, Berlin-Wiesbaden: Otto Harrassowitz 1990.

[24]See Alexandre Degrand, *Souvenirs de la Haute-Albanie*, Paris: H. Welter 1901; H.N. Brailsford, *Macedonia: Its Races and their Future*, London: Methuen 1906; Theodor Ippen, *Skutari und die Nordalbanische Küstenebene*, Sarajevo: Daniel A. Kajon 1907; Hasluck, *Christianity ...*; Birge, *The Bektashi Order ...*

[25]In the edition of Hasluck's writings by his wife, a footnote (p. 537) explains: 'This idea was put forward long ago on the evidence of tradition, which is no safe guide, since a figure like Ali's bulks large in popular thought and is apt to absorb much that does not belong to it.'

[26]Hasluck, *Christianity and Islam*, pp. 377–8 and 439.

[27]Brailsford, *Macedonia*, p. 233.

[28]Hasluck, *Christianity and Islam*, pp. 439, 531 and 537.

independent of the 'Turks'.[29] In fact, the Bektashis had a special position in contesting the central (Sunni) authorities. As a religious group professing a heterodox Islam, they naturally opposed the Sunni-based policy of the Sultan Abdülhamid.[30] Subsequently, it was relatively easy to transform this religious opposition into a culturo-religious opposition and later into a politico-religious opposition. Indeed the Bektashis played a leading role after 1878 (and especially since the last decade of the nineteenth century) in the development of both cultural and political Albanianism in south and central Albania, introducing elements of this ideology in their religious doctrine.[31] In particular, the sultan was depicted as a 'Yezid' and the martyrdom of Qerbela, the suffering of the Albanians under his rule.

The use of a figure like Ali Pasha is due to the fact that he could more concretely embody this 'local resistance against the centre' through his policy, through the large autonomy which he managed to acquire, and through his punishment (1822) which, as it happens, was followed a few years later by the interdiction of the Bektashi order in the Ottoman Empire (1826). The large autonomy that the pasha gained, or the prefiguration of the first Albanian national state that Ali Pasha was supposed to have founded, corresponded to the aims or ideals of the Bektashi circles at the origin of the myth. That is why, in the process of creating a national history from the viewpoint of the Bektashis, Ali Pasha came to be presented as the second hero of the nation after Skanderbeg. And they both came to be presented as belonging to the Bektashi order. Having been educated at the Sultan's court, Skanderbeg is also believed to have been related to the Janissary corps and to have been a Bektashi. Baba Ali Tomori (Tyrabiu), in his history of the Bektashis published in Tirana in 1929, makes the fight of Skanderbeg, 'founder of an independent Albanian Principality', a part of the first struggle of the Bektashis against the Ottoman sultans.[32]

[29]See Ernest Raumsaur, *The Young Turks: Prelude to the Revolution of 1908*, Princeton University Press 1957.

[30]On this policy, see Selim Deringil, 'The struggle against shiisme in Hamidian Iraq', *Die Welt des Islams*, XXX/1990, pp. 45–62; 'Legitimacy structures in the Ottoman State: The reign of Abdülhamid II (1876–1909)', IJMES, 23 (1991), pp. 345–59, and *The Well-Protected Domains, Ideology and the Legitimation of Power in the Ottoman Empire 1976–1909*, London: I.B. Tauris 1998.

[31]Cf. N. Clayer, "Bektachisme et nationalisme albanais ,' in A. Popovic et G. Veinstein (eds.), *Bektachiyya. Etudes sur l'ordre mystique des Bektachis et les groupes relevant de Hadji Bektach*, Istanbul: Isis 1995, pp. 277–308.

[32][Ali Tyrabiu], *Historija e Bektashinjvet*, Tiranë: Mbrothësia 1929.

So the myth was clearly aimed at forming an Albanian national identity associated with the Bektashi religious identity, not only among the Bektashis but also among non-Bektashis who could be attracted to the ranks of the *tarikat* in order to contribute to the creation of an autonomous Albania. Like the myth of Kerbela, I think the myth of Ali Pasha remained more or less confined to Bektashi circles (and to the milieus of other mystical brotherhoods), except outside Albania, where it spread among the scientific community. The limited diffusion of the myth is certainly due to the fact that other religious communities had ways of their own of advertising the national identity.

In some circles, however, the myth was perpetuated, perhaps because of the 'protonational' character generally attributed to the pashaliks on the one hand, and on the other because of the necessity to diminish its pure Muslim character due to the strong denigration of Sunni Islam in the framework of the independent Albanian state, while the image of the Bektashis remained a liberal and nationalist one. It is perhaps for the same reason that King Zog or Ever Hoxha are sometimes believed to be of Bektashi origin.

The second group of diffusers of the myth are Westerners (historians, scholars and others) such as Hasluck, Brailsford and Ippen, but also their followers in the diffusion and amplification of the myth, even among the groups involved, i.e. the Albanian Bektashis, and the Albanians in general. First, the problem is that, as for other segments of Albanian history (or maybe more so), the necessary basic research has not been done, either in or outside Albania, and that the numerous syntheses simply reproduce clichés because it is hard not to do so.

Therefore, in the present case, the oral Bektashi tradition has never been checked properly. The Western fascination for these Muslims—considered in a sense as 'not completely Muslims' (and even 'crypto-Christians')—and more generally the lack of research on the Ottoman period using Ottoman sources, along with the lack of knowledge of Islamic matters contribute to the perpetuation of such myths, both within the scientific community and among the Albanians (especially when they themselves are involved in these myths). Indeed, for them, Western writings are very often used as a justification of their own sayings. There is actually a complex relationship between the local historiography and Western Albanology, which could be another very interesting topic to study.

PERCEPTIONS AND REALITY IN TWENTIETH-CENTURY ALBANIAN MILITARY PROWESS

Bernd J. Fischer

The poet Byron, in *Childe Harold's Pilgrimage*, presents perhaps the most–quoted romantic view of the military prowess of the Albanians, a view which did much to influence general Western attitudes: 'Fierce are Albania's children', Byron tells us; 'Where is the foe that ever saw their back? Who can so well the toil of war endure?'[1] While this appreciation of the fighting qualities of the Albanians dates from the age of romanticism, twentieth century foreign appreciations are no less romantic. Hitler, for example, considered Albania to be the last wild corner of Europe and the Albanians as a vital warrior mountain race—a perception which seems to combine Nazi racial theory with the fanciful novels of Karl May. While Hitler's perception was perhaps not as influential as Byron's, it was far from inconsequential. It was in fact an important element in explaining Nazi Germany's rather benign occupation policy in Albania during the Second World War.

Twentieth-century Albanian leaders have exploited this perception and have further embellished it for both foreign and domestic consumption. It is the purpose of this paper to briefly examine two pivotal military encounters between Albanian and foreign troops—the withdrawal of Italian troops from Vlora in 1920 and the withdrawal of German troops from Albania in 1944. These two episodes will be examined from the perspective of reality (or at least what I would call a reasonably objective view), perception, and finally the intended and actual consequences of that perception, with their positive as well as negative impact.

[1] *The Poetical Works of Lord Byron*, Oxford University Press 1923, p. 198.

The first encounter to be examined is the withdrawal of Italian troops from Albania in 1920. At the beginning of the First World War, the Italians took steps to safeguard their interests in the Balkans and their security in the Adriatic. On 30 October 1914, while still neutral, Italy occupied the island of Sazan, commanding the entrance to Vlora. On 16 December Italy took the harbour itself and gained allied acquiescence for the move in April 1915 through the secret treaty of London which brought Italy into the war and guaranteed to Italy 'full sovereignty over Valona, the island of Sazan and surrounding territory of sufficient extent to assure defense of these points.'[2] Near the end of the war the Italians moved into Albanian territory which had been occupied by Austria-Hungary, so that by late 1918 the Italians were in possession of most of the country. In 1919, fearing that Woodrow Wilson intended to block them from maintaining this advantageous position, the Italians signed a secret treaty with Greece, which assigned southern Albania to Greece but signaled Greek support for the maintenance of Italian sovereignty over Vlora and an Italian mandate over the remainder of Albania.[3] Wilson held firm against the official partition of Albania, indicating that Albania's fate would be decided by forces on the ground.

By 1920 these forces included a resurgent Albania, where several dozen leaders agreed at the Congress of Lushnije to begin to establish its authority over its territory by seeing to the removal of foreign troops.[4] But this task was accomplished for them, at least in the case of the Italians, principally by domestic Italian factors. The First World War had been more costly than anticipated for the Italians and they had received far less compensation than they had hoped for. Giovanni Giolitti and his liberals were much discredited and faced with all manner of social agitation. Communists and socialists organised railway and dock strikes which prevented the government from re-supplying Italian troops in Albania. Even soldiers in Italy went on strike and refused to board troopships at Bari and Brindisi. In the meantime in Albania, Italian troops were becoming susceptible to communist agitation and malaria. The Italian minister of war summed up the

[2]Joseph Swire, *Albania: the Rise of a Kingdom*, London: Geo. Allen and Unwin 1929, p. 254.

[3]For aspects of the Tittoni-Venizelos agreements see Stefanaq Pollo and Arben Puto, *The History of Albania: From its Origins to the Present Day*, London: Routledge and Kegan Paul 1981, p. 175.

[4]Michael Schmidt-Neke, *Entstehung und Ausbau der Königsdiktatur in Albanien (1912–1939)*, Munich: R. Oldenbourg 1987, p. 49 ff.

difficult situation by answering requests for reinforcement with the confession that 'internal conditions of country do not permit sending troops to Albania. Attempts to do so would provoke general strike, popular demonstrations gravely injurious to solidarity of Army, which must not be exposed to such hard tests.'[5] By May 1920 the Italians had evacuated all of Albania except Vlora, hoping to retain at least this last outpost to salvage something from the disaster of the First World War and thereby secure a favourable position in the Adriatic.

The new Albanian government of Suliman Delvina, with Ahmet Zogu as minister of the interior, demanded that the Italians continue their evacuation. When this demand was rejected the Albanian government, with Zogu taking an active role, clandestinely organised perhaps 4,000 Albanian irregulars who attacked Italian positions.[6] At the same time, many Albanian civilians in Vlora itself did what they could to harry the occupation forces. But the Italian force was well entrenched and formidable. The Italian commander, General Settimio Piacentini commanded over 15,000 troops supported by 200 guns, as well as elements of the Italian fleet.[7] While perhaps an exaggeration, there is still something to Joseph Swire's comment that 'had the Italians been determined to remain in the country, all the prowess and valor of the whole Albanian nation would not have prevented them from doing so.'[8] The Italians decided not to remain, and in exchange for the island of Sazan and the temporary occupation of points commanding the bay from the land, the Italians agreed to evacuate Vlora and renounce their 1917 self-proclaimed protectorate. The Italians also extended the new government official recognition within the frontiers delineated in 1913 and encouraged other states to do the same.[9] This was a turning point in the establishment of Albanian independence—while neighboring powers remained in Albania longer, the Italian withdrawal in a way put them on notice.

Perhaps in part because the Italian withdrawal was such an important development, it seemed to require more active Albanian involvement. Zogu, his publicists and others, did much to create the impression

[5]L.S. Stavrianos, *The Balkans since 1453*, London: Hurst 2000 (original edn 1958), p. 713.

[6]Ekrem Bey Vlora, *Lebenserinnerungen*, vol II. Munich: R. Oldenbourg 1973, p. 129.

[7]*Ibid.*, p. 128.

[8]Swire, *Albania: The Rise of a Kingdom*, p. 322.

[9]Herbert Monath, 'Die politisch-völkerrechtliche Entwicklung Albaniens 1913–1939', *Zeitschrift für Völkerrecht*, vol. 24, no. 3, (1940), p. 299.

that Albanian involvement was decisive. Christo Dako, who might be described as Zogu's official biographer, wrote in 1937 that Zogu, even before the final showdown at Vlora, had impressed both his Albanian opponents and the Italians to the point where they all recognised that resistance against his will was futile.[10] Representatives of the rival Albanian government in Durres, we are told, reported back to their leaders that there is 'no stopping this man, he is superior in every respect.'[11] The Italians, meanwhile, had withdrawn to Vlora without resisting Zogu because he had won some undefined psychological battle with the Italian commanders. They did not resist as it was useless and because they recognised that Zogu was inspired, and not, we are told repeatedly, an adventurer or a rebel. These same Italians were ultimately forced to surrender Vlora by the power of the official figure of 10,000 irregulars (who fought like lions) supported by a large number of citizens.

Much to the delight of Zogu, Italian opposition politicians supported this version of events. Benito Mussolini wrote in the *Popolo d'Italia* in August 1920: 'The real facts of the case will appear to the peoples of the Balkans and to others in this schematic but true aspect: a few thousand Albanian rebels have thrown a big power like Italy overboard.'[12] Albanian socialist historians tend to agree, one suggesting that 'the battle of Vlora constituted without a doubt one of the finest pages in the history of independent Albania: the patriotism and unity of a whole people, the heroism of the masses shine forth with exceptional brilliance.'[13]

So what were the consequences of this myth of unity, patriotism and heroism? There were some positive consequences generated by this fabrication for both Zogu and for Albania as a whole. Certainly, direct Albanian participation in clearing the country of foreigners was important for the creation of the Albanian national idea—and contributed to badly needed national unity. For Zogu—but also for Albania as a whole—the episode contributed to his own reputation, conferring on Zogu a political and national legitimacy which helped him come to power and assisted him in his goal of creating a modern nation-state.

[10]Christo Dako, *Zogu the First, King of the Albanians*, Tirana: Kristo Luarasi 1937, p. 89.

[11]*Ibid.*, p. 90.

[12]*Popolo d'Italia*, 5 August 1920.

[13]Pollo and Puto, *The History of Albania*, p. 179.

But there were also important negative consequences resulting from the creation of what can be described as a 'national myth'—consequences which were perhaps not immediately visible but in the long run may have overwhelmed the positive consequences. Once in power Zogu seems to have become mesmerised by his own propaganda—that a few thousand Albanians had overthrown a Great Power. And if that indeed was the case, need he be overly concerned with Italian intentions or potential? This consideration had a direct and decidedly negative impact on two important aspects of Zogu's regime. First, it encouraged Zogu not to take the Italians and their economic and political penetration too seriously. Zogu believed that in the final analysis, he would always be able to use the Italians for his own ends, but still control them—he saw himself as clever and the Italians as weak.[14] He was willing, therefore, to agree to an increasingly onerous series of pacts and agreements which restricted Albania's economic and political manoeuvrability. These included the SVEA (Società per lo Sviluppo Economico dell'Albania) and banking agreements of 1925, the Tirana Pacts of 1926–7, and the various overly generous loans which the Italians extended to Albania in the 1930s.[15] In exchange, the Italians were able to gain virtual control over the Albanian economy, veto power over any arrangements with foreign states, advisors attached to many Albanian ministries, and the role of quartermaster and trainer for Albanian security services.

This latter point constitutes the second aspect of Zogu's regime negatively impacted by the national myth of 1920. Although there are certainly many factors in Zogu's reluctance to establish a well-trained and well-disciplined army—including the cost of such an undertaking—Zogu's argument that the Italians in an emergency could easily be dealt with was a consideration as well. The result was the establishment of a small force—15,000 on paper, but probably closer to 8,000 in reality, a figure reduced to about 4,000 in winter—which was equipped and trained by the Italians.[16] Because Italian officers were assigned to virtually every unit, the Albanian army became as much, if not more, an instrument of Italian policy as it was an instrument of Zogu's policy. This is demonstrated during the April

[14]Bernd J. Fischer, *King Zog and the Struggle for Stability in Albania*, Boulder, CO: East European Monographs 1984, p. 100.

[15]For a discussion of the various agreements signed by Zogu see Fischer, *King Zog and the Struggle for Stability in Albania*.

[16]Bernd J. Fischer, *Albania at War*, 1939–1945, London: Hurst 1999, p. 22.

1939 Italian invasion of Albania, when the Albanian army proved itself of little use to either side. It could have made a difference. The Italian invasion, by some 22,000 troops supported by airforce and naval units, was poorly planned, poorly executed and succeeded only because there was so little resistance.[17] As Count Ciano's chief assistant Filippo Anfuso put it, 'if only the Albanians had possessed a well-armed fire brigade, they could have driven us into the Adriatic.'[18] Zogu's overestimation of the military effectiveness of Albanian irregulars in 1920 contributed to the loss of Albanian independence in 1939.

Albania's Second World War experience provides the second military encounter which leads to another false perception concerning the effectiveness of Albanian arms. Following the collapse of Italy in 1943, the Germans, essentially against their will, invaded and occupied Albania. The Germans could spare only about one third of the troops Italy had found it necessary to station in Albania—approximately 36,000 mostly garrison troops many of whom had been prisoners of war before being persuaded to join the German army.[19] Given these limitations, the Germans hoped to secure the coastline, the major towns and the major roads, leaving the rest of the country in the hands of what they hoped would be a relatively independent, neutral, yet friendly government with enough authority to create a stable political system and a reliable security force to control the growing resistance movements. The Germans were not altogether unsuccessful. Although the pacification of Albania through the construction of an independent regime with prestige and its own military authority largely eluded the Germans, they were able to hold the strategic points in Albania with a small number of troops, a number which steadily declined throughout the course of 1944. And the German army was able to withdraw, essentially unmolested with only moderate losses (about 2,400 with another 1,000 unaccounted for) over the period of the entire occupation.[20]

One of the keys to explaining Germany's relative success was its policy of seducing and then corrupting all of the non-communist elements of the resistance, including the nationalist Balli Kombëtar, the Zogists, and many of the independent chieftains. They all either

[17]United Kingdom, Foreign Office, FO371/23713 R/2953/1335/90, Rome, 13 April 1939.

[18]Denis Mack Smith, *Mussolini's Roman Empire*, London: Longman 1976, p. 153.

[19]Fischer, *Albania at War*, p. 262.

[20]*Ibid.*, p. 268.

collaborated outright—with some joining the puppet governments—or at least failed to actively resist the Germans hoping to use the Germans and the British to obtain an arsenal for fighting the communists once the Germans had gone. This strategy proved to be disastrous for the non-communists who lost their political credibility leaving the communists as the only group with long-term political prospects and short-term military significance.

But this military significance was limited, in part due the makeup of the partisans. Many of these people, at least in the early stages of the struggle, tended to be urban southerners who had little with which to resist, and little experience in terms of how to go about it. While British and German military reports on Albanian resistance capabilities tend to be pompous and racist, there is something to their analysis. After witnessing an attack by 800 partisans on a village in 1943, and the rapid dispersal of those partisans by some 300 Germans, a British observer complained that the partisans were little more than 'a thorough band of rascals with no fighting ability whatsoever.'[21] German evaluations of the nationalist and collaborationist forces were even less flattering. SS General Josef Fitzthun, charged with the creation of the regular army for the puppet regime of Rexhep Mitrovica, blamed his failure on the Albanian officer corps, which he complained was not only worthless but filled with pederasts.[22] General August Schmidthuber, the German commander of the SS Skanderbeg division, explained his failure by suggesting that the legend of Albanian military heroics was just a saga and that he personally could chase them all around the world with a light grenade–launcher.[23]

While these comments must be kept in the context of the source, the partisans did only very limited damage to the Germans. They were rarely able to hold fixed positions if the positions threatened German lines of communication, or German security in general. The large areas which the partisans controlled by late 1944 were generally areas in which the Germans had little interest. The largest battle took place in late October 1944 as the Germans had all but withdrawn from Albania. In the battle of Tirana, Enver Hoxha launched units of his now 40,000–strong partisan brigades at the capital, following a

[21] *Ibid.*, p. 205.

[22] Bernhard Kühmel, 'Deutschland und Albanien, 1943–1944. Die Auswirkungen der Besetzung und die innenpolitische Entwicklung des Landes', PhD diss., University of Bochum 1981, p. 205.

[23] *Ibid.*, p. 452.

significant lull in September, during which political considerations consumed much of Hoxha's time. This last assault on the Germans left the impression that Hoxha felt it necessary to get off a few shots before all the Germans had gone.

None of this should reflect badly on the Albanians—there were too many Germans and the partisans did not have the numbers, the training, the equipment, and in many areas, the popular backing needed to do much damage to the occupation forces. As a result, in the final analysis, the partisans proved to be little more than an annoyance to the Germans. Enver Hoxha, his lieutenants, and most Albanian socialist historians have of course created an entirely different perception. The withdrawal of German forces in 1944 was another defining moment for the re-establishment of Albanian independence and for the formation of the Stalinist state. The significance of this event required greater Albanian participation. Contemporary partisan accounts of the fighting tend to be stunning exaggerations which were even further embellished during the post-war period, particularly after 1978 and the beginning of Albania's total isolation. As an example, one socialist historian would have us believe that every partisan was 'a brilliant sharp-shooter.'[24] Just as the Albanian irregulars had expelled the Italians in 1920, so the partisans—while dispatching traitors in the process—expelled the Italians and the Germans in the Second World War. In a typical example of such rhetoric, Mehmet Shehu in his book *On the Experience of the National Liberation War and the Development of Our National Army* tells us that 'our National Liberation Army was able, relying only on its forces, to liberate the whole of the country from the Italian and German invaders and the rule of the exploiting classes which had placed themselves in the service of the foreign invaders.'[25]

Hoxha's motivation in pursuing this line of argument was, of course, similar to Zogu's, in part because much of the work for which Zogu was responsible—in terms of construction of a modern state—had been disrupted by the war. So Hoxha too found that the propagation of a military myth would facilitate unity. And it certainly did a great deal for his own legitimacy and that of his movement which was almost entirely alien to most Albanians. But as with Zogu, there were

[24]Lefter Kasneci, *Steeled in the Heat of Battle: A Brief Survey of the National Liberation War of the Albanian People*, 1941–1945, Tirana: Naim Frashëri 1966, p. 29.

[25]Mehmet Shehu, *On the Experience of the National Liberation War and the Development of Our National Army*, Tirana: 8 Nëntori 1978, p. 116.

important negative consequences from this embellishment of military achievement. One direct result was the stifling impact that the war of national liberation had on Albanian culture and parts of the educational system. The cult of the partisan war reached feverish proportions so that textbooks and traditional histories, literature for children, general literature, drama, film, and music, were all limited to variations on the same theme. Albania's wartime experience, although lasting only about five years, became one of the focal points of Albanian existence for the next half century.

But the propagation of the myth of the heroic partisan war contributed to more than just cultural sterility. It facilitated the excesses of the Hoxha regime. It contributed to the isolationist state-of-siege nationalism which helped to keep Hoxha in power—Albania against the world protected only by the glory of Albanian arms based on the principle of guerrilla war. Every Albanian was still a brilliant sharpshooter who could effectively defend the country from one of the hundreds of thousands of concrete bunkers which still scar the landscape. Obviously other factors, too, were responsible for the brutal regime of Enver Hoxha—but myths, in particular the myth of the partisan war—did much to legitimise Hoxha, allowing him to create a legacy from which Albania has yet to recover.

Thus these two episodes were important in the development of an Albanian national consciousness and a national idea, but their creation was not without cost. The 1920 myth at least contributed to the loss of Albanian independence in 1939, and the Second World War myth of a partisan victory contributed to the foundation, survival and basic nature of the Hoxha regime.

SMOKE WITHOUT FIRE?

ALBANIA, SOE AND THE COMMUNIST 'CONSPIRACY THEORY'

Roderick Bailey

One of the most controversial themes to emerge from British accounts of Albania's wartime history has been that of mismanagement at the overseas headquarters of the Special Operations Executive (SOE). Between April 1943 and November 1944, SOE sent over 100 officers and men to support Albanian guerrillas in fighting the occupying Italian and German forces. These British soldiers worked with both communist and nationalist groups until the German withdrawal and communist victory in late 1944. Yet claims would later be made that staff officers working inside SOE's headquarters in Bari had undermined the efforts of British officers working with the nationalists and so helped Enver Hoxha's communist 'partisans' to seize power. It was even suggested that agents of the NKVD operated within SOE's headquarters and that, had British policy favoured the nationalists, Albania would never have become a communist state. Today, the release of SOE's wartime records has allowed this picture to come under closer examination and this paper is an attempt at relating their contents to what has been termed the 'conspiracy theory'.[1] First of all, however, a short account of SOE's operations in Albania is necessary to place the theory in proper context.

SOE had been set up in 1940 to gather intelligence, carry out sabotage and support resistance movements inside Axis-occupied countries; in Winston Churchill's famous phrase: 'to set Europe ablaze'. In April 1943, acting on reports of growing local resistance to the

[1]Sir Reginald Hibbert, 'The War in Albania and the Conspiracy Theory', *Albanian Life* 57, 1995, p. 3–5.

occupying Italians and anxious to encourage it as a means of speeding Italy's collapse and diverting German resources away from the Eastern Front, SOE infiltrated a four-man mission into Albania. Code-named 'Concensus', the mission had orders to assess the potential of the Albanian resistance and, if they felt it worthwhile, to organise, train and arm it. In late June, the mission contacted Enver Hoxha and his 'Movement of National Liberation' (*Lëvizje Nacionalçlirimtare* or LNC); by the end of August an 800-strong brigade had been trained and armed with twenty tons of supplies dropped to the mission by the Royal Airforce. By the end of the year the LNC were receiving regular drops while a further fifty British personnel had been infiltrated to assist in locating and supporting other guerrilla bands.

The central problem encountered by SOE's officers in Albania was that, with no government in exile, many guerrilla leaders had taken up arms against the Axis with their eyes fixed on seizing or securing post-occupation power. SOE's attempts to encourage resistance were frequently frustrated by the reluctance or refusal of many Albanians to commit themselves to fighting the Italians. Political divisions between left and right were such that many were simply not prepared to risk reprisals or otherwise expend valuable material and energy that could be better spent later against domestic political opponents. This situation worsened following the Italian surrender and German invasion of Albania in September 1943 when the communist dominance of the national liberation movement became such that its nationalist members were driven out, many of them into the welcoming arms of the Germans.

British policy-making towards Albania thus became dominated by a fear that arming both nationalist and communist guerrillas encouraged the chances of wide-scale civil conflict, which in July 1944 would indeed break out. Until then, SOE was guided simply by Foreign Office and military directives to give 'financial and material assistance ... to all guerrilla bands, irrespective of their political allegiance, which are actively resisting the Germans or are genuinely prepared to do so.'[2] No break was made with any political or guerrilla movement for fear of alienating a potential source of future resistance. In accordance with this policy, SOE personnel in Albania were ordered to 'maintain contact with all guerrilla bands and individuals actively resisting the Germans, or who may be induced to assist the Allied war effort in

[2]Public Record Office (PRO), HS 5/11.

any material degree.'[3] In practice, this meant that SOE remained in touch with nationalist elements and kept working on them to fight the Germans even though, by the end of 1943, Hoxha's partisans were the only movement actually doing so and thereby receiving supplies.

In the spring of 1944 an attempt was then made by SOE and the Foreign Office to persuade certain nationalists to return to the LNC. This, it was hoped, would reduce the intensity of the civil war and counter the growth of Communism: few in London were attracted by the thought of a post-war Albania under communist rule, especially since a parallel situation had just been settled in Tito's favour in Yugoslavia. In April 1944, Lieut.-Col. Billy McLean and Major David Smiley, both members of the first mission sent into the country the previous year, were dropped into central Albania, together with Captain Julian Amery. Their mission, 'Concensus II', had orders to persuade the nationalist guerrillas to resume co-operation with the communists and fight the common enemy.

In 1948 Amery would publish the first detailed account of SOE's operations in Albania, as seen through the eyes of Concensus II.[4] He described how the mission's efforts had centred on Abas Kupi, a prominent tribal chieftain with an important following in northern Albania. A *gendarmerie* officer before the war, Kupi was a loyal supporter of the exiled King Zog and from the king's own region of Mati. Though he had never been a leading military or political figure, Kupi's resistance to the Italian invasion of April 1939, and, above all, his association with an earlier British effort against the Italians in 1941, had so enhanced his personal importance and reputation that he became one of the few non-communists on the liberation movement's central council. In late 1943 he had then split with Hoxha's movement and in the mountains of Mati established a pro-monarchy group, *Legaliteti* ('Legality'), and started talks with the anti-Zogist but fiercely anticommunist party, *Balli Kombëtar* (BK, 'National Front').

Throughout May and June 1944, Concensus II worked hard to persuade Kupi to fight the Germans. Foreign Office policy stated that no arms could be dropped to him beforehand: he had to attack the Germans first and thus commit himself to fighting. This commitment was also demanded of him by Hoxha's partisans, who refused to have

[3] *Ibid.*

[4] Julian Amery, *Sons of the Eagle*, London: Macmillan 1948

anything to do with any nationalist force until it showed evidence of open warfare against the Germans. Finally, in June, and after much prevarication, Kupi relented and agreed to carry out such an operation. On the night of 21 June 1944, David Smiley and a party of Kupi's men blew up Albania's third largest bridge at a spot called Gjoles on the road between Tirana and Shkodra. Concensus II were content that the operation fulfilled the demands for Kupi to fight and permitted him to receive arms from the Allies, arms he could use to open a wider campaign against the Germans and attract other nationalists to his side.

These supplies would never arrive. Within ten days the partisans had launched an offensive against the nationalist areas of northern Albania. Forced on the defensive, all the resources Kupi and other nationalists could muster were used against the northward advance of Hoxha's troops. A few, last-ditch attempts by nationalist forces to win arms and support from the Allies, in the form of two or three ambushes on German convoys in September 1944, were not enough to convince the Allied command that they warranted aid or even continued recognition. At the end of October 1944 Concensus II was withdrawn, and Kupi and all other nationalists were abandoned.

In his account of these events, Amery stressed the dismay of the officers of Concensus II at the way British policy had approached Albania and the reaction of their 'Headquarters' to the civil war. They were particularly shocked at Bari's weakness in restraining communist attacks on Kupi and stunned by the decision to resume supplying them after airdrops were initially suspended. Bari's refusal to evacuate Kupi when the mission was finally withdrawn had aroused further anger. Indeed, to Amery, the decision to abandon all nationalist guerrillas seemed not only 'dishonourable' but also reflective of a significant and unwarranted bias in Bari towards supporting the communist partisans. Amery spoke of 'a genuine enthusiasm' for Communism pervading SOE headquarters where officers 'revelled with indecent ... glee' at the fate of the nationalist forces.[5]

Amery's sentiments would be expressed with similar passion by a number of other officers in memoirs written after the war. Some suggested that British policy, by arming the communists and enabling them to seize power, had helped condemn Albania to fifty years of communist rule. Peter Kemp, writing in 1958, would describe Albania as 'a totally unnecessary sacrifice to Soviet imperialism. It was British

[5] *Ibid.*, p.334.

initiative, British arms and money that nurtured Albanian resistance in 1943; just as it was British policy in 1944 that surrendered to a hostile power, our influence, our honour and our friends.'[6] It was even speculated that British communists inside SOE's headquarters might have undermined the efforts of officers with the nationalists. Some writers told of a hostile reaction at the hands of headquarters staff after being evacuated from Albania to Bari, even being called 'fascists' by officers there for having worked with nationalist forces.[7] Kemp himself was the first to name one such officer, Captain John Eyre, whom he described as 'a serious young communist whose courteous manner could not altogether conceal his disapproval of my Albanian record.'[8] Other officers would allege that communist officers had manipulated British policy and been the crucial factor in the decision to drop more arms to Hoxha's communists and thus in bringing them to power. 'Loyal officers' like Abas Kupi, wrote Alexander Glen, were unnecessarily 'defeated and some ... betrayed. Kim Philby already had his colleagues well enough placed in some of the organisations concerned.'[9]

Though these memoirs all drew heavily on wartime diaries and mission signal logs, all suffered from the localised viewpoints their authors had occupied in 1943 and 1944 as well as from the inaccessibility of SOE's own records. With little first-hand knowledge of decision-making or the command structures in Bari, the claims they made were based only on suspicion and speculation: rumour and circumstantial evidence had to stand in for hard fact. The only direct exposure to SOE's Bari set-up that these officers had had was after they were evacuated, often disappointed and angry at the way Allied policy had developed. Finding staff at their own headquarters noticeably pro-partisan it was perhaps not surprising that some felt this attitude may have had an impact on policy-making, but nothing could be proved. Revelations during the 1950s and '60s of KGB penetration of British intelligence may explain the suggestions that it also occurred within SOE's Albanian Section, for no proof of Soviet infiltration of that unit has ever been produced. Nonetheless, for over thirty years these arguments were never seriously contested

[6]David Smiley, *Albanian Assignment*, London: Chatto and Windus 1984, p.152.

[7]*Ibid.*

[8]Peter Kemp, *No Colours or Crest*, London: Cassell 1958, p.231.

[9]Sir Alexander Glen, *Footholds against a Whirlwind*, London: Hutchinson 1975, p.157.

and the 'conspiracy theory' came to dominate the historiography of SOE in Albania.

With the release of most of Britain's wartime Foreign and War Office records in the 1970s, British policy-making was then allowed to come under closer scrutiny.[10] Claims that the key decisions had been made at the very highest levels and on military grounds gained weight; much of the earlier speculation was exposed as incorrect. Though the existence in SOE's Bari headquarters of ideological sympathy for Hoxha was not discounted, the 'conspiracy theory' was dismissed as a post-war invention aimed at disguising the failure of officers who had worked with the nationalists but were unable to get them to fight.

Locked inside SOE's own files, however, the precise workings of its headquarters remained obscure. Certainly, the debriefing reports of Concensus II now confirm that the opinions Kemp and others later expressed in print on which guerrillas deserved support had been genuinely held at the time. These officers had stressed the pressures at work on Kupi and other nationalists to stay neutral and the patience required of the British when trying to get them to fight; several also suggested the potential value of supporting nationalist groups thus countering the growth of Albanian Communism. However, such was the nature of their support and society that Kupi and others were best suited to a last-minute rising as the Germans withdrew, rather than the immediate, large-scale and sustained campaign demanded of them by British policy which would bring down on them severe German reprisals. They suggested that the situation of the partisans was different, because as a more mobile force with few fixed bases of support, the demoralising effect of German retaliation was rather less. It was felt this crucial distinction was not appreciated in Bari or London and that the nationalist position was being misunderstood. With more patience and encouragement on the part of the Allies, the nationalists could have fought and proven their worth.[11]

The files also suggest, however, that SOE's headquarters were indeed keen to see policy move away from supporting the likes of

[10]See, for example, Sir Reginald Hibbert, *Albania's National Liberation Struggle: The Bitter Victory*, London: Pinter 1991, *passim*; Elizabeth Barker, *British Policy in South East Europe in the Second World War*, London: Macmillan 1976, p.181; and David Stafford, *Britain and European Resistance 1940–1945: A Survey of the Special Operations Executive*, London: Macmillan 1983, pp.170–2.

[11]See, for example, PRO, HS 5/144 (Report of Major P.M.M. Kemp) and PRO, HS 5/123 (Report of Major G. Seymour).

Abas Kupi by the summer of 1944. Even before widespread civil war had broken out, staff officers in Bari submitted policy proposals urging the Foreign Office and military to abandon Kupi and give the partisans full support. Some of their other proposals spoke disparagingly of Kupi's potential. Julian Amery's estimate of Kupi's forces at 5,000 poorly armed men, for example, received in Bari at the end of May, was consistently dismissed by SOE there as illustrating Kupi's weakness, even though Amery felt that these forces were significant if only weapons could be found to arm them.[12] The destruction of the bridge by David Smiley and Kupi's men was also played down when it emerged that Kupi had refused to allow his name to be publicly linked with the operation.[13]

It is also possible that several reports sent out of Albania by Concensus II in June and July 1944 which spoke well of Kupi may have been suppressed at SOE's headquarters in Bari. All of these messages expressed the mission's growing belief in the possibility of fomenting a rising among the nationalists against the Germans as the latter withdrew from Albania. But rather then sending them on to policy-makers in London immediately by telegram as he had been specifically instructed to do, the head of the Albanian Section in Bari sent them instead by sea.[14] Correspondence between London and Bari, once the messages were eventually received, shows London's reaction to these delays was one of shock and anger at what could have caused them.[15]

The suggestion that the Section's head may have wanted to influence the flow of information to London is further supported by the debriefing report of Major George Seymour. By the time he was evacuated in July 1944, Seymour had spent almost a year in Albania working with both communists and nationalists and had developed similar opinions to McLean on which guerrillas deserved support. The conclusion to his report is quoted here in full:

> [When] I returned to Base at Bari ... I found the entire Albanian section biased to an unbelievable extent on behalf of the partisans. They were not even prepared to listen to the Nationalist case and views. I attempted to explain this case but when in the office I was called a Fascist I realised that the position was hopeless. I applied to be sent home to state my case there

[12]PRO, HS 5/11.
[13]PRO, HS 5/69.
[14]PRO, HS 5/69.
[15]PRO, HS 5/10.

and was informed by Major Watrous, the head of the Albanian section, that I would be sent home but not immediately, because at that time a policy was being decided in London and, if I went home then, it might alter the whole policy. A truly remarkable statement to be confronted with after one had spent eleven months working with and studying both partisans and nationalists. That we achieved but little is hardly surprising.[16]

Yet the new files also support the view that SOE's Bari headquarters were unlikely to have had much impact on the decision to abandon Kupi. The ability of SOE's staff officers to dictate the nature of Balkan operations had diminished steadily from late 1943, as changes in Allied command arrangements saw SOE's role increasingly subordinated to the regular military. By July 1944 both SOE (in Bari and in London) and even the Foreign Office were largely divorced from the decision-making process and the newly created Balkan Air Force, under the command of Air Vice-Marshal William Elliot, was largely in control of Albanian operations. Based in Bari, Elliot chaired a policy committee that included local representatives of the Foreign Office, the US State Department, Allied Forces Headquarters and SOE. SOE's Albanian Section did not sit on the committee and had virtually no direct input whatsoever.[17] But it was this committee that decided to recommend in September the withdrawal of Concensus II and, the following month, to order the physical abandonment of Kupi.

The Balkan Air Force's decision to give Hoxha's partisans exclusive support was made on the grounds that they simply had the best chance of inflicting substantial damage on the Germans. As the Germans started to withdraw through the Balkans in the summer of 1944, this military consideration carried all before it.[18] Constant anti-Axis activity was always a powerful reason for the Allies to support any Balkan guerrilla group. Hoxha's movement, in stark contrast to Kupi, had maintained a consistent record of action against the Germans throughout the spring and summer, even when he detached a brigade from the battle and launched it against Kupi in June 1944. By the middle of August, the fact that Hoxha's other forces were in action against the Germans, in trouble and in need of ammunition, saw Elliot and the Balkan Air Force Policy Committee agree to resume supplying them, even though, to all intents and purposes, a fresh civil war had broken out. Pulling out Concensus II was a logical extension of this

[16] PRO, HS 5/123.
[17] PRO, WO 204/8462.
[18] *Ibid.*

strict, military thinking. The presence of British soldiers with nationalist Albanians had always been damaging to Britain's relations with the partisans. Kupi and nationalists like him appeared unlikely to inflict much, if any, harm on the Germans, so that if the Albanian war effort was to be maximised, Concensus II should be withdrawn.

As far as explaining the behaviour of SOE's headquarters is concerned, George Seymour's reference to being called a 'fascist' must raise the question of whether ideology had anything to do with the Albanian Section's own opposition to Kupi. It does seem that some staff officers were leftwing and, in one case at least, considerably so. In a little-known memoir that concentrates mainly on his post-war spiritual development, John Eyre dwells fleetingly on his own wartime career and admits to having sympathised with the communists on ideological grounds:

> I came to accept the class basis of society during the war years, when I was working with Special Operations Executive, responsible for economic and political intelligence coming from our missions in occupied Albania ... On the staff of the Albanian country section I saw the Marxist-Leninist thesis working out under my very eyes. Julian Amery and [Billy] Maclean [*sic*], my colleagues in conspiracy, were battling against the winds of change while I and others, in our wisdom or ignorance, helped to stir up the hurricane.[19]

However, SOE records confirm that Eyre played only a junior role in the functioning of the Albanian Section. The twenty-three-year-old Elliott Watrous, head of the Section from the spring of 1944 and its solitary mouthpiece at local command level, was not nearly so left-wing as Eyre (who, it should be added, was responsible for the 'fascist' remarks aimed at Seymour and later at the officers of Concensus II).[20] Furthermore, comparisons between surviving signals and BLO debriefing reports show no evidence of Watrous exaggerating the strength of the partisans in any of his official correspondence of the period. Indeed, there is little reason to suggest that as the summer of 1944 wore on, the grounds on which Watrous (who alone was responsible for corresponding with SOE London) and other of the Section's officers opposed supporting the nationalists were very different to those of the Balkan Air Force Policy Committee.

[19]John Eyre, *The God Trip: The Story of a Mid-century Man*, London: Peter Owen 1976, pp.23–4.

[20]Correspondence and interviews undertaken by the author with former SOE and AFHQ staff.

It is significant that the growing opposition to Kupi came at a time when other British officers working with Hoxha were urging SOE headquarters for greater help in maximising the Albanian war effort. Debriefing reports and surviving cables indicate that many officers were convinced the partisans were better organised, more united and possessed the greater potential to hamper and harass the Germans than any other guerrilla group. Hoping to release this potential, these officers bombarded their headquarters during the early summer of 1944 with demands not only for arms but also for more exclusive support, since the continued presence of other British officers with the nationalists, though in accordance with British policy, was damaging their own relations with the communist partisans.

Several reports from British officers working with Hoxha's forces bear out the impatience with which they viewed the inactivity of the nationalist north. Major Brian Ensor, for example, who spent over nine months with Hoxha's partisans from February until September 1944, later wrote:

> My briefing before infiltration ... consisted of a statement that on all possible occasions I was to use British material and partisan manpower to kill Germans ... but I consider the support BLOs received to help them gain the full co-operation of the partisans, was criminal ... The partisans were, and would always be, the most effective fighting machine, provided they were not deprived of weapons and supplies to continue their fight against the Germans to the advantage of any doubtful resistance elements whose only claim to recognition consisted of empty promises and idle boastings ... My signals of April and May prove that I was always a staunch supporter of an immediate change of policy, because it was not possible to carry out my orders properly ... For a long time we were not trusted ... [and] held responsible [by the partisans] for a policy with which we did not agree and which was inhibiting partisan resistance to the Germans and preventing us from carrying out our briefing orders, i.e. harassing the Germans.[21]

Ensor's attitude was typical of many officers who served in southern Albania in the spring and summer of 1944.[22] What is more, many were evacuated to Bari during that period where they were able to voice their opinions in person, not only to SOE's Albanian Section but also to Elliot and his Policy Committee. Lieut.-Col. Alan Palmer, the senior British Liaison Officer with Hoxha's partisans for most of

[21]PRO, HS 5/136.

[22]See, for example, PRO, HS 5/127 (Report by Lt. Col. T.N.S. Wheeler), PRO, H.S. 5/128 (Report by Major H.V. Tilman) PRO, HS 5/129 (Report by Major W.V.G. Smith).

1944, dealt frequently with the military policy-makers throughout the summer and it is clear that his views in particular carried a good deal of weight. Palmer took two separate trips to Bari during this crucial period; by contrast, very few officers arrived in Bari between May and August with recent and first-hand knowledge of the nationalist position. It is perhaps not surprising to find that SOE Bari's policy suggestions of this period echo the arguments of Palmer, Ensor and officers like them both openly and consistently.

Whether giving exclusive support to Hoxha's partisans was the correct line for policy to take is not for discussion here. But it must be stressed that the key policy decisions in favour of the partisans were heavily influenced by the Balkan Air Force Command in Bari and not by the Albanian Section of SOE. Keen to minimise interference by the Foreign Office and SOE London, where minds were rather less 'pro-partisan,' attempts may have been made inside SOE Bari to suppress BLO support for the nationalists and there may have been some sympathy for the communist cause (and certainly for partisan efforts and losses). Yet the motives of these staff officers were unlikely to have been as 'sinister' as has been made out in the past or the outcome of their opposition so far reaching. Julian Amery, referring to SOE's Bari headquarters as 'an instrument of Enver Hodja [*sic*] in the British camp', goes too far.[23] Indeed, once the partisans had attacked him Kupi was effectively doomed to political defeat in any case, such were the strength and dynamism by then of Enver Hoxha's movement. SOE Bari's 'suppression' of reports, even if deliberate, came when partisan forces were already tearing into Kupi's men.[24] With the Balkan Air Force command in Bari heavily influential in policy-making and unshakeable in their concern for immediate action, it is unlikely that support from the field for a limited, last minute rising from Kupi would have had any impact on policy-making, even if it had arrived in London on time. What contributed to Allied thinking was a frustration with Kupi's inaction and lack of sympathy for his predicament, that quite possibly were born from a misunderstanding of the pressures at work on the nationalist desire to stay neutral. But it is hard to avoid concluding that the decision to abandon him in favour of the partisans simply reflected the widespread determination to realise this short-term military gain.

[23]Julian Amery, *Approach March: A Venture into Autobiography*, London: Hutchinson, 1973, p.405.

[24]PRO, HS 5/11 See also Hibbert, *Albania's National Liberation Struggle*, pp. 161–2.

Part IV

MYTHS AND CONTESTED BOUNDARIES

'*SHKOLLA SHQIPE*' AND NATIONHOOD

ALBANIANS IN PURSUIT OF EDUCATION IN THE NATIVE LANGUAGE IN INTERWAR (1918–41) AND POST-AUTONOMY (1989–98) KOSOVO

Denisa Kostovicova

The sense of nationhood of the Albanians in Kosovo was profoundly moulded by their quest for schools with Albanian as the language of instruction—*shkolla shqipe*—in the interwar period from 1918 to 1941 and in the post-autonomy period after 1989. The prohibition of Albanian secular schools in the interwar years and the curbing of self-rule of the Albanians in the sphere of education after the abolition of Kosovo's autonomy were aimed at arresting the rise of Albanian national consciousness. However, Kosovo Albanians embraced alternative schooling strategies and so nourished their sense of national distinctness during both periods. This paper looks at the ways Albanians in Kosovo furthered their sense of nationhood, because of, and in spite of, Serb-imposed restrictions on education in Albanian. It also examines symbolic pillars around which their sense of nationhood was constructed in the interwar and in the post-autonomy period.

Interwar defiance: The 'secret' schools of nationhood

The closure of Albanian-language schools that Austria-Hungary had opened and assisted during its occupation of Kosovo in the First World War[1] marked the return of Kosovo to Serbian control in 1918. Throughout the interwar period, secular schools with Albanian as the language of instruction were banned in the Serb-dominated Kingdom

[1]Cf. Jasar Redzepagic, *Razvoj prosvete i skolstva albanske narodnosti na teritoriji danasnje Jugoslavije*, Prishtina: Zajednica naucnih ustanova Kosova i Metohije 1968, pp. 299–315.

of Serbs, Croats and Slovenes, reconstituted as the Kingdom of Yugoslavia in 1929.[2] Instead, Serbian schools were set up in Kosovo and their doors opened to Albanians. However, even their geographic distribution had an ethnic bias. Schools were mainly opened in the areas populated by native Serbs of Kosovo and where Serbian settlers were moving in as part of Serbia's policy of boosting the Serb presence in the province.[3]

Education in the Serbian language was envisaged as a vehicle for the integration of Albanians into Serbia as loyal subjects. The curriculum, taught in the Serbian language was tailored to promote the common identity of Serbs, Croats and Slovenes in the new state.[4] Yet, what for Serbs was a policy of integration, for Albanians was a policy of denationalisation.[5] Albanian students attended a preparatory year in order to master Serbian, while religious instruction was provided separately for Serbian and Albanian students, taught by Orthodox priests and Muslim *mullahs* (teachers).[6]

The 1929 Law on People's Schools centralised and unified the state primary education system. It heralded greater state intervention in the now compulsory primary education and prescribed a uniform

[2]The benefits of the international legal obligations the Yugoslav state signed, like the Saint Germain Treaty on Protection of Minorities of 1919, or those of domestic legislation, like the Vidovdan Constitution of 1921 and the Law on People's Schools of 1929, all of which provided for primary education of minorities in their mother tongue, bypassed the Albanians, but not the Germans and Hungarians. See Svetozar Canovic, *Specificni problemi nastave u skolama Kosova i Metohije*, Belgrade: Zajednica naucnih ustanova Kosova i Metohije 1968, pp. 83–5; Noel Malcolm, *Kosovo: A Short History*, London: Macmillan 1998, p. 267; Ljubodrag Dimi, *Kulturna politika u Kraljevini Jugoslaviji*, vol. III, Belgrade: Stubovi kulture 1997, pp. 5–118.

[3]Miranda Vickers, *Between Serb and Albanian: A History of Kosovo*, London 1998, p. 105; Jasar Redzepagic, *Skolstvo i prosveta u Kosovskoj Mitrovici i okolini od druge polovine XIX stoleca do 1975. godine*, Prishtina: Akademia e shkencave dhe e arteve e Kosovës 1980, p. 31; Abdulla R. Vokrri, *Shkollat dhe arsimi në Kosovë ndërmjet dy Luftërave Botërore (1918–1941)*, Prishtina: Enti i Teksteve dhe i Mjeteve Mësimore i Kosovës 1990, pp. 27–8.

[4]On the cultural and educational policy in the interwar Yugoslavia centred on a common identity of the Kingdom's dominant Slav nations see: Andrew Baruch Wachtel, *Making a Nation, Breaking a Nation: Literature and Cultural Politics in Yugoslavia*, Stanford University Press 1998, pp. 67–127.

[5]Vokrri, *Shkollat dhe arsimi në Kosovë*, p. 22.

[6]Redzepagic, *Skolstvo i prosveta u Kosovskoj Mitrovici* ... 1980, p. 31; Vladeta Tesic et al., *Sto godina Prosvetnog saveta Srbije 1880–1980*, Belgrade: Zavod za udzbenike i nastavna sredstva 1980, pp. 111–35.

name for all schools: 'People's Schools.' However, Kosovo's schools were soon named after prominent Serbian figures.[7] Albanian and Serbian students were to learn together in mixed classes, so that children:

> ... would see that they are no strangers to each other, so that religious tolerance is furthered and enforced and a gap which is separating their parents still today, is gradually reduced through children.[8]

Religious instruction continued separately for Serbs and Albanians. Teachers were instructed not to force Albanian and Turkish students to take off their traditional headgear—*kece* (in Albanian *plis*) and *fes*—so as not to vex their ethnic and religious feelings. Nonetheless, these youngsters were to be made into citizens who 'with the passage of time, would never know of any other homeland outside the present homeland'[9].

A network of Serbian state schools in Kosovo remained underdeveloped in this period. Compared to Serbia (including Vojvodina but without Kosovo) with 8.96 classrooms per each 1,000 school-age children, in Kosovo there were 5.26. Only 30.2 per cent of school-age children of all nationalities in Kosovo went to school in 1939–40. In the Yugoslavia of that period, just Bosnia-Herzegovina had a worse record with 21 per cent.[10] Of those attending school in Kosovo, Serbs largely outnumbered Albanians. Some eleven thousand Albanians comprised about 30 per cent of all primary school children, while their number as compared to Serbs in secondary schools was negligible between 1940 and 41.[11]

While repressing Albanian secular schools, Serbian authorities condoned the work of private religious Muslim schools. This policy was driven by the same rationale as that of prohibiting secular schooling in Albanian—to undermine the feeling of Albanian national identity by stimulating the supremacy of collective identification based on religion. Albanians were to remain 'unenlightened and uncultured

[7]Vokrri, *Shkollat dhe arsimi në Kosovë* ..., pp. 12–13.

[8]Dimic, *Kulturna politika u Kraljevini Jugoslaviji*, vol. II, 1997, pp. 109–10 quoting A.J, (O.N.), f-87–91; A.J, CPB (38), f-63–69; A.J, 66 (pov), f-22 and 62.

[9]*Ibid.*, p. 110.

[10]Canovic, *Specificni problemi nastave u skolama Kosova i Metohije*, pp. 78–80; Dusan Kosanovic, 'Problem savremenog pedagoskog obrazovanja i permanentnog usavrsavanja nastavnog kadra i srednjih skola s posebnim osvrtom na specificne uslove u SAP Kosovu' (unpublished PhD manuscript), Prishtina: Univerzitet u Pristini 1980, p. 171.

[11]Canovic, *Specificni problemi nastave u skolama Kosova i Metohije*, p. 85.

for a long time to come.'[12] Ignorant of their national culture, it was reasoned, Albanians would be left without the symbolic 'arsenal' they needed to mount a nationalist challenge to the Yugoslav state. However, it was precisely these schools that contributed to the rise of Albanian national identity in the interwar period.

It was only well after the turn of the century that the conservative Muslim clergy in Kosovo, hitherto inimical to the national cultural movement, took up the cause of Albanian 'national' education.[13] The Turks' unrelenting opposition to education in Albanian, coupled with grass-roots efforts of Albanian nationalists to promote the national cultural revival, made a number of *mullahs*, (Muslim teachers) *hodjas* and *imams* (priests) in Kosovo embrace the cause of education in Albanian. Some got involved by coordinating the work of cultural clubs and appealing to patriots to take up teaching in Albanian, others by introducing Albanian instruction into religious schools.[14]

A *hodja* from the Lap region in the north of Kosovo described the relationship between national schooling and religion in the following terms:

> In the field of schooling, we find ourselves on the war front. In the conditions of war even the Koran permits eating not only of pork, but even of pig's ears and trotters, only the battlefield must not be abandoned![15]

Continued prohibition of Albanian secular schools in interwar Yugoslavia made the Muslim clergy in Kosovo follow up the trend of

[12]Muhamet Pirraku, 'Kulturno-prosvetni pokret Albanaca u Jugoslaviji (1919–1941)', *Jugoslovenski istorijski casopis* 1/4, 1978, pp. 356–70, here footnote 10, p. 358; Cf. Dimic, *Kulturna politika u Kraljevini Jugoslaviji*, vol. III, p. 123; Marco Dogo, 'National Truths and Disinformation in Albanian-Kosovar Historiography' in Ger Duijzings, Dusan Janjic and Shkelzën Maliqi (eds), *Kosovo-Kosova: Confrontation or Coexistence*, Peace Research Centre, University of Nijmegen, 1996, pp. 34–45, here pp. 38–9.

[13]On the opposition of conservative Muslim clergy from Kosovo to the adoption of the Latin alphabet for the Albanian language which Albanian national leaders advocated as a means of furthering Albanian national consciousness and unity and, instead, their insistence to hold on to the Arabic script of the Koran see: Stavro Skendi, 'The History of the Albanian Alphabet: A Case of Complex Cultural and Political Development', *Südost Forschungen XIX*, 1960, pp. 263–84, here p. 278

[14]Abdulla R. Vokrri, *Shkollat dhe arsimi në anën e Llapit brenda viteve 1878–1944*, Prishtina: Enti i Teksteve dhe i Mjeteve Mësimore i Kosovës 1995, pp. 11–14; Hysni Myzyri, *Arsimi kombëtar shqiptar (1908–1912)*, Prishtina: Enti i Teksteve dhe i Mjeteve Mësimore i Kosovës 1996, p. 201.

[15]Vokrri, *Shkollat dhe arsimi në anën e Llapit* ..., footnote 56, p. 29.

introducing the Albanian language in the religious schools that had been inaugurated in the last years of the Turkish rule. They began to abandon Turkish and Arabic language and script, partly or entirely, and to spread the knowledge of Albanian in their sermons and writings. They also began to give lessons in the Albanian language or distribute Albanian books, alongside religious instruction in *mektebs* (Muslim primary schools) and *medreses* (Muslim seminaries).[16]

The new national 'mission' of religious schools made Serbian educational authorities qualify *mektebs* as 'nationally harmful to the state.'[17] Similarly, *medresas* were portrayed 'as not serving our state in the least.'[18] Therefore, Serbo-Croat speaking Muslims from Bosnia, who spoke no Albanian, replaced Albanian *muftis* (senior Muslim clerics) and *imams*, who hardly spoke any Serbian. The policy was aimed at forestalling Albanian nationalist activity in religious institutions. However, Albanians gave precedence to their national language over common religious identification. Bosnian Muslim teachers faced fierce opposition and boycott by their Albanian co-religionists in Kosovo.[19]

The legalisation of religious schools in the 1930s entailed enhanced control of their curricula and a required fulfilment of often impossible conditions. Many *mektebs* and *medreses* were closed, but their spread was not hindered. By 1938–9 there were 296 *mejtepes* (i.e. *mektebs*) with 11,362 students, whilst nearly each town in Kosovo had a *medrese*. Ultimately, religious schools emerged as the biggest beneficiaries of the 1936 Law on the Islamic Community. It sanctioned the ultimate authority of *ullema-medzlis* in Skopje over the social and cultural life of Muslims. Albanians *de facto* obtained full religious-educational autonomy from the state.[20]

Clandestine efforts aimed at promoting the Albanian sense of nationhood in religious schools were paralleled by the institutional struggle for *shkolla shqipe*. Albanian members of the *Xhemijet*, the party representing Muslims in Sandjak, Kosovo and Macedonia demanded

[16]Vokrri, *Shkollat dhe arsimi në Kosovë*, pp. 303–14; Pirraku, 'Kulturno-prosvetni pokret Albanaca u Jugoslaviji ...,' pp. 360–1.

[17]Dimic, *Kulturna politika u Kraljevini Jugoslaviji*, vol. III, p. 130, quoting A.J, 66 (pov), f-22/a.j. 51; A.J, (pov), f-22/a.j. 55.

[18]*Ibid.*, p. 131 quoting A.J, 38 (CPB), f-64/169; A.J, 63, f-151/xv; AIJ, 63 (Versko odeljenje—Muslimanski odsek), f-137/x.

[19]Vokrri, *Shkollat dhe arsimi në anën e Llapit*, p. 78. Pirraku, 'Kulturno-prosvetni pokret Albanaca u Jugoslaviji,' p. 361.

[20]Dimic, *Kulturna politika u Kraljevini Jugoslaviji*, vol. III, pp. 131–2; Vokrri, *Shkollat dhe arsimi në Kosovë*, pp. 293–8.

Albanian-language schooling in the Parliament. However, they also developed an 'underground' activity and helped to revive Albanian secret schools,[21] of which there was already a tradition dating back to the time of the Ottoman prohibition of Albanian schools. While secular and religious teaching content was combined in religious schools, secret schools were entirely secular.

Since the end of the nineteenth century, secret schools sprang up in Albanian-populated areas in the Balkans, spreading from the south of Albania northwards to Kosovo, as a strategy to disseminate 'the knowledge of nationhood.' Secret classes that taught *shkrim/lexim*, reading and writing of Albanian, were set up in grocery stores and private houses, country inns and out in the open. Students of Albanian embraced Albanian primers, textbooks, newspapers and other patriotic publications that were smuggled into the Ottoman-controlled Albanian lands.[22]

Following the *Xhemijet*'s demise, the clandestine spread of Albanian lessons in interwar Kosovo continued, along with a secret distribution of Albanian books. Albanian nationalists from Kosovo staunchly opposed the education of Albanians in Serbian schools, for, as Hasan Prishtina said, 'they teach something else from what we wish our lads to learn.'[23] Hence, it was only the 'underground'—a secular or religious setting—that was conducive to furthering Albanian nationhood.

The educational policy of forcing Albanians into Serbian secular schools or leaving them to Muslim religious schools in interwar Kosovo failed. The education of Albanians in Serbian state schools came to be seen as 'training' Albanians for their national resistance to the Serbs,[24] as secular knowledge, albeit imparted in Serbian, stimulated the desire of Albanians for national self-awareness. At the same time, many Albanian *mullahs* began to stealthily teach 'national awakening' during religious classes, while Albanian students secretly circulated Albanian books in Serbian schools.[25]

[21]Ivo Banac, *The National Question in Yugoslavia: Origins, History, Politics*, Ithaca, NY: Cornell University Press 1984, pp. 377–8; Pirraku, 'Kulturno-prosvetni pokret Albanaca u Jugoslaviji,' p. 363–4; Malcolm, *Kosovo: A Short History*, pp. 269–72; Vokrri, *Shkollat dhe arsimi në Kosovë ...*, pp. 318–9.

[22]Hysni Myzyri, *Shkollat e para kombëtare shqipe* (1887–*korrik* 1908), Tirana: 8 Nëntori 1978, pp. 131–46; Edwin E. Jacques, *The Albanians. An Ethnic History from Prehistoric Times to the Present*, Jefferson: McFarland 1995, pp. 307–8.

[23]Vokrri, *Shkollat dhe arsimi në Kosovë*, p. 359.

[24]Pirraku, 'Kulturno-prosvetni pokret Albanaca u Jugoslaviji', p. 365; Vokrri, *Shkollat dhe arsimi në anën e Llapit*, pp. 58–9.

[25]Vokrri, *Shkollat dhe arsimi në Kosovë ...*, pp. 189–98.

Poignantly, it is the ban on secular education in Albanian, that turned Islamic institutions, *mektebs* and *medreses* of Kosovo's Sunni Muslim community but also *tekkes* (lodges) of its Sufi Orders, the ardent pioneers of the national cultural movement from the time of the Ottomans, into the hub of Albanian 'national' education in interwar Kosovo. As Pirraku argues, it is very difficult to accurately ascertain the impact of efforts aimed at enlightening the Kosovo Albanian youth in the national spirit due to their clandestine quality. He, however, adds that these efforts ought to be acknowledged for securing a continuity in a development of Albanian national culture,[26] and, hence, a sense of Albanian nationhood in Kosovo. Indeed, it was the battle for the opening of *shkolla shqipe*, rather than their existence that fed the Albanians' sense of nationhood in interwar Yugoslavia.

Post-autonomy 'shkolla shqipe': lessons in national freedom and martyrdom

The Serbian drive to revoke Kosovo's autonomy in the late 1980s stirred Albanian fears that with it, all their cultural rights would be revoked as well. Yet, Slobodan Milosevic, the then head of Serbia's Communist Party, assured them:

> Albanians indeed will not lose the right to their language, nor to their schools, nor to their cultural development. Nor will their work and creation and their entire life be threatened in any way because they are Albanians.[27]

However, a nationalist stigma had already been attached to education in the Albanian language in Kosovo.

Ever since the 1981 Albanian demonstrations in Kosovo, in the context of a dominant demand for the elevation of Kosovo's autonomous status in communist Yugoslavia to the status of a republic, the Albanian-language education system, and Prishtina University in particular, were identified as a 'hotbed of Albanian nationalism and separatism.' Despite purges of the educational content, the ban on imported textbooks from Albania, the expulsion of politically 'incorrect' educators and students, even their prosecution and imprisonment, and a ban on educational co-operation with Albania,[28] the Serbian

[26]Pirraku, 'Kulturno-prosvetni pokret Albanaca u Jugoslaviji', p. 369.

[27]*NIN*, 6 March 1989.

[28]Musa Limain *et al.*, *Studim. Gjendja dhe pozita e arsimit shqip në Kosovë në periudhën 1990–95 dhe mundësit e zhvillimit të mëtejmë*, Prishtina: Instituti Ekonomik

verdict on Albanian education in Kosovo remained unchanged. Therefore, the constitutional changes were to give Serbia jurisdiction over Kosovo's education, which would allow it: 'to decisively influence ... the educational content with the aim of developing the feeling of permanent membership in the SRS [Socialist Republic of Serbia] and the SFRY [Socialist Federal Republic of Yugoslavia]'.[29]

In spring 1990, the SRS Presidency announced the unification of Serbia's education,[30] ending Kosovo's self-rule in the area of education. Albanians lost the right to adopt a Kosovo curricula in line with the agreed ideological guidelines, which was the procedure applied since 1974.

The issue of primary and secondary curricula brought the Serbian-Albanian confrontation over education in Kosovo to a head. Albanians refused to accept the curricula compiled for them in Belgrade. Instead, they fully endorsed a decision to apply the curricula adopted by the Albanian members of the Education Council of Kosovo in August 1990.[31] In effect it marked the point of emergence of *shkolla shqipe* that would allow unconstrained expression to Albanian nationhood in Kosovo.

The demand for and opposition to Kosovo's constitutional reintegration into Serbia had made the nationalist mobilisation of Serbs and Albanians respectively a fact by the 1990s. In such an atmosphere, the issue of curricula lent itself to exclusive nationalist interpretation.[32] Albanians rejected the Serbian curricula for Kosovo not only

---

January 1996, pp. 17–23; Xhafer Xhaferi, 'Represioni serb ndaj Universitetit të Prishtinës', *Kosova: Revistë historike politike*, no. 5, 1997, pp. 23–7: p. 24.

[29]Danilo Z. Markovic, *Obrazovanje za buducnost*, Belgrade: Prosveta 1989, p. 128.

[30]*Jedinstvo*, 24 April 1990.

[31]*Shkëndija*, August 1990.

[32]The comparative analysis of the Kosovo and Serbian curricula for the so-called national subjects (Literature, History, Geography, Music ...) in primary and secondary schools carried out by the Serbian educational advisors and the response of the Albanian education officials indicate that the Serbian curricula planned the inclusion of the educational content that would allow the expression of Albanian national identity in Kosovo but reduced its volume. Therefore, the major difference between the Kosovo and Serbian curricula was in the inclusion into the Kosovo curricula of the content that was reduced in the Serbian ones envisaged for the use in Kosovo. Changes for the subject of Music in primary schools seem to be most radical to the extent that no or very few Albanian songs were encompassed in the Serbian curricula. The analysis and response are included in: Zecir Demi, 'Predmet: Pismena odbrana u svojstvu optuzenog za krivicno delo iz Clana 216 KZ Srbije', *Opstinski sud u Pristini*, Prishtina, 28 May 1998 (documents used in the trial).

as 'an attempt at a reduction of the Albanians' national identity',[33] but also as '*shkombëtarizmi* (denationalisation)' and 'an insult to Albanian national dignity.'[34] By contrast, Serbs assessed the Kosovo curricula as illegal and as a source of 'separatist indoctrination of pupils'.[35] Ironically, less than three years later a group of Yugoslav/Serbian experts under the auspices of then Prime Minister of the Federal Yugoslavia Milan Panic conducting negotiations with the Albanian delegation from Kosovo on education within the framework of the International Conference on the Former Yugoslavia in Geneva in 1992–3, assessed that 'there were no essential differences in the contents' of the 'disputed' curricula adopted by the Kosovo Education Council in August 1990 and those adopted by Serbia to be used in Kosovo.[36]

However, Serbia's educational unification also entailed Belgrade's control of student enrolment in Kosovo's schools and the university. Once the enrolment plans were drafted in Belgrade, thousands of Albanian youngsters were left without the possibility of continuing their education in Kosovo. Unlike non-transparent curricula, numbers clearly spoke for themselves.

Some 9,100 places for Albanian- and some 5,535 for Serbo-Croat-speaking students were envisaged in secondary schools for the 1991–2 school year, for some 32,000 pupils finishing primary schools in Albanian and about 4,000 pupils finishing school in Serbo-Croat in Kosovo. In other words, while 21,185 Albanian primary school graduates would remain without an opportunity to continue their education in Albanian, some 1,500 extra places were planned for the Serbo-Croat speakers in secondary schools.[37] At the same time, an equal number of places—1,580 for Serbo-Croat-and 1,580 Albanian-speaking students–was planned at the Prishtina University for the 1991/1992 academic year, for about 14,000 students graduating from secondary schools in the Albanian language and some 3,000 in Serbo-Croat in Kosovo.[38]

[33] *Bujku*, 12 Sept. 1991.

[34] *KOHA*, 13 Sept. 1995.

[35] *Bujku*, 4 June 1991.

[36] 'Kriticke primedbe vladine strane na skolske programe za osnovnu skolu', *Radna grupa za probleme obrazovanja na Kosmetu pri Zenevskoj konferenciji o bivsoj Jugoslaviji*, Belgrade, 8 Feb. 1993, p. 4 (official report compiled by the Yugoslav government working group); on the International Conference on the Former Yugoslavia, see, Stefan Troebst, 'Conflict in Kosovo: Failure of Prevention? An Analytical Documentation, 1992–1998', ECMI Working Paper, no. 1, May 1998, pp. 37–8.

[37] *Bujku*, 4 June 1991.

[38] *Zëri*, 15 June 1991; *Bujku*, 7 June 1991.

Serbian education policy in Kosovo was a nationalist remedy to the perceived 'Albanianisation', i.e. Albanian cultural and numerical dominance, of the educational system in the province. At a symbolic level, Belgrade now took control over how much 'national affirmation' it would allow Albanians in Kosovo. Also, equality, hitherto conceived as providing an opportunity to all to study in their native tongue, was now interpreted as a 1:1 ethnic parity in the overwhelmingly Albanian province.

The conflict over education culminated at the start of the new 1991–2 school year. On 1 September Serbian educators aided by Serbian police barred entrance to schools to all Albanian teachers and pupils who refused to submit to Serbia's control over the Albanian-language education.[39] Meanwhile, hundreds of Albanian university lecturers were dismissed by newly appointed Serbian faculty deans and education in the Albanian language at Prishtina University practically ceased.[40]

Serbian authorities remained intransigent towards the Albanians' demands to continue exercising their educational autonomy and return to their own educational facilities, for which they demonstrated in the autumn of 1991. The Kosovo Co-ordination Council for Education, the Albanian umbrella organisation of political parties and teachers' organisations, declared it was 'impossible' to start the new school year for all levels of education in the Albanian language.[41] For Albanians resistance to the imposition of Serbian educational policies was paramount to 'the defence ... of national identity.'[42]

Paradoxically, the unrestrained assertion of Albanian nationhood became feasible only after the creation of the so-called *arsimi paralel*—parallel education—the Albanian educational system in Kosovo mostly in private houses at the beginning of 1992. For the first time since Kosovo's inclusion into the Yugoslav state, Albanians administered Albanian-language education without any accountability to the Serbs.

Albanians' new *shtëpi shkolla*—house schools—became a symbolic embodiment of Albanian nationhood. Kosovo's education authorities approved a list of recommended school names for primary and secondary schools. They included prominent Albanian figures in

[39] *Zëri*, 7 Sept. 1991.

[40] *Bujku*, 1 Nov. 1991; Xhaferi, 'Represioni serb ndaj Universitetit të Prishtinës', pp. 25–7; Hajrullah Koliqi, *The Survival of the University of Prishtina, 1991–1996*, University of Prishtina 1997, pp. 38–9.

[41] *Bujku*, 20 Oct. 1991.

[42] *Zëri*, 31 Aug. 1991.

history, education, science and culture, many of whom were banned in Kosovo during Communism; geographical names such as *Drenica*, an area of Kosovo symbolic of Albanian resistance, and *Iliria*, territory inhabited by the ancient Illyrians; and historical events and dates such as the 'Prizren League' and '2nd July' (the day of Kosovo's independence[43]), as well as letters and nouns with a symbolic meaning: 'A' as the first letter of the alphabet, *Bashkimi* (unification), *Liria* (freedom), *Kombi* (nation), and *Martiri* (martyr).[44]

Alongside school names, changes in the curricula for primary and secondary schools, mainly in the so-called national courses—literature and language, history and geography[45]—gave meaning to Albanian nationhood. These curricula were initially 'deideologised.' The demise of Communism had resulted in the removal of 'ideological' subjects like Marxism.[46] Yet their 'deideologisation' also implied the assertion of the self-centred vision of Albanian nationhood.[47] The teaching of Serbo-Croat in Albanian schools was removed from the new Kosovo curricula.[48] At the same time, for example, the geography of former Yugoslavia was replaced by the geography of Kosovo in primary schools, and by the geography of Albanian lands in secondary schools.[49]

[43]On 2 July 1990, the Kosovo Assembly declared 'the constitutional declaration on Kosova as an independent and equal constituent unit within the framework of the Federation (Confederation) of Yugoslavia'. See Assembly of Kosova, Constitutional Declaration, 2 July 1990 in Marc Weller (ed.), *The Crisis in Kosovo 1989–1999: From the Dissolution of Yugoslavia to Rambouillet and the Outbreak of Hostilities*, vol. I, Cambridge: Documents and Analysis Publishing 1999, pp. 64–5; this document served as a basis for the declaration of Kosovo's independence. See Resolution of the Assembly of the Republic of Kosova on Independence, 22 September 1991, *ibid.*, p. 72.

[44]'Lista orientuese për emërtimin e enteve parashkollore, të shkollave fillore dhe të shkollave të mesme', *Pleqësia e Arsimit e Republikës së Kosovës*, Prishtina December 1991 (official document of the Kosovo Albanian education authority).

[45]*KOHA*, 1 June 1994.

[46]*Ibid.*

[47]Cf. *Shkëndija*, March 1998.

[48]Compulsory learning of the language of the other ethnic group was part of the educational policy during Communism in Kosovo of fostering interethnic tolerance between Serbs and Albanians. See Jasar Redzepagic, 'Ostvarivanje jezicke ravnopravnosti u oblasti obrazovanja u proslosti i danas', *Buletin*, Shkolla e lartë pedagogjike 'Skënderbeu' Gjilan, no. 1, 1987, pp. 7–21. The refusal of Serbo-Croat-speaking students in Kosovo in 1988–9 to learn Albanian was one of the harbingers of the conflict over the curricula.

[49]Zeqir Demi, *Roli i Pleqësisë së Arsimit të Republikës së Kosovës në pavarësimin e shkollës shqipe—Kushtet dhe rrethanat e jashtëzakonshme*, Prishtina: Pleqësisa e Arsimit e Republikës së Kosovës 1995, p. 48.

The changes in the curricula were carried out in accordance with the 'national goal.'[50] The principle of nationhood expressed at a political level in the form of Kosovo's independence was built into the curricula. It replaced 'symbolic engineering' of Albanian national identity along ideological lines characteristic of the Communist period when the curricula were aimed to foster Kosovo Albanians' sense of belonging to the Yugoslav political community while de-emphasising their sense of commonality and fraternity with Albanians in Albania proper. *Shkolla shqipe* nourished a Kosovo-centred sense of nationhood in the post-autonomy Kosovo. However, it also furthered a symbolic national unification of Albanians, which a former Kosovo Albanian official identified as an important role of an Albanian school.[51]

Following the agreement reached by the Education Ministry of Kosovo and the Education Ministry of Albania in August 1992, the first joint curricula for the subjects of Albanian Language and Literature, History, Geography, Music, Visual Arts and English in primary and secondary schools were compiled in 1994. The unification of curricula was the 'fulfilment of an old dream of the Albanian people of Kosovo for a spiritual and cultural integration with Albania.'[52] The publishing of joint school textbooks to be used in Kosovo and Albania followed it.[53] At the same time, as prescribed by Kosovo's education authorities, the portrait of Gjergj Kastrioti Skanderbeg, was hung in Albanian classrooms.[54] The choice of the great 15th century Albanian national hero evoked the sense of all-Albanian national unity.

Albanian 'parallel education' in the post-autonomy Kosovo was of particular importance as Albanians identified it as an 'attribute of (Kosovo's) statehood'.[55] The education system and education authorities were the only segment of Kosovo's autonomy that continued to function in the post-autonomy period in Kosovo.[56] In addition, they

[50]'Raporti i punës së Pleqësisë së arsimit të Kosovës për vitin 1991', Pleqësia e Arsimit e Republikës së Kosovës, Prishtina January 1992 (official report of the Kosovo Albanian education authority).

[51]Pajazit Nushi, 'Drejtimet strategjike të arsimit kombëtar dhe të shkollës shqipe' in N. Prifti (ed.), *Shekulli* 21, New York: Gjonlekaj Publishing Company 1996, pp. 9–15, here p. 10.

[52]Shqipe Gashi, *Shkollat e mesme të Prishtinës 1990/91–1996/97*, Prishtina: n.p. 1997, pp. 114–15.

[53]*KOHA*, 22 Nov. 1995.

[54]Demi, *Roli i Pleqësisë së Arsimit*, p. 45.

[55]*KOHA* (Shtojca), 7 June 1995.

[56]Demi, *Roli i Pleqësisë së Arsimit*, p. 5.

now exercised complete independence from Serbia. The idea of sovereign statehood was graphically imprinted on all school certificates and diplomas that bore the inscription of the 'Republic of Kosovo.'[57] As a 'functionalisation of the statehood of the Republic of Kosovo,' the survival of the 'parallel' Albanian educational system merited special effort, attention and sacrifice.[58]

Serbia's efforts aimed at imposing its vision on Albanian nationhood in the late 1980s produced the opposite result. Re-established mainly in private homes throughout Kosovo, the Albanian education system provided a hitherto unprecedented opportunity to symbolically tailor the Albanians' sense of national identity. Unlike the interwar period, the post-autonomy conception of Albanian nationhood was fully secular. The 'parallel system' in private schools was actually a secular state educational system in Albanian, whose qualitative and quantitative development in the post- Second World War Kosovo was remarkable.[59] Arguably, it was the very sense of Albanian nationhood that was elevated to the level of being sacred.

Post-autonomy graduates in Kosovo were the 'generations of the (Kosovo) Republic.'[60] They no longer studied the people's heroes who had fought for the 'brotherhood and unity' of Yugoslav nations and nationalities. Instead, they learnt about the declaration of Kosovo's independence, while prominent Albanian national figures were listed in their history textbooks, not as heroes, but with the word 'martyr, referring to people who fought for freedom and national independence ...'.[61]

[57]See the official certificates and documents reproduced in Gashi, *Shkollat e mesme të Prishtinës ...*, pp. 211–50.

[58]*Shkëndija*, April 1996.

[59]Cf. Dennison I. Rusinow, '*The Other Albania: Kosovo 1979*' part I: *Problems and Prospects*', American Universities Field Staff Reports, Europe, no. 5, 1980, pp. 1–17. For example, in the 1945/6 school year there were some 23,500 Albanian primary school and about 1,000 Albanian secondary school students in Kosovo. See Kosanovic, *Problem savremenog pedagoskog obrazovanja ...*, p. 183; Vojislav Okiljevic and Fazli Sulja, *Socijalisticki samoupravni preobrazaj obrazovanja i vaspitanja u SAP Kosovo*, Prishtina: Zavod za udzbenike i nastavna sredstva Socijalisticke Autonomne Pokrajine Kosova 1978, p. 16. In the 1989/90 school year, there were 304,836 Albanian primary and 66,361 Albanian secondary school pupils in Kosovo, see Limani, *Studim: Gjendja dhe pozita e arsimit shqip ...*, pp. 38 and 66. In 1988–89, there were 25,949 Albanians being educated at Prishtina University, established in 1970. See Destan Halimi (ed.), *Universiteti i Prishtinës 1970–1990*, Prishtina: Universitet i Prishtinës 1990, p. 56.

[60]*Zëri*, 23 Sept. 1995.

[61]*Zëri*, 15 April 1995.

The fact that Albanian students collected their school and university diplomas after years of studying in adapted rooms, shops, cellars, garages and attics was the most poignant lesson they learned about Serbs in the parallel schools of Kosovo. *Shkolla shqipe* in the post-autonomy Kosovo became the 'schools of resistance'[62] teaching the 'religion' of Kosovo's freedom.

A Serb-dictated educational policy, based on the principles of ethnic exclusion and control in the interwar and post-autonomy period in Kosovo directly fuelled the prospects of interethnic confrontation, rather than those of interethnic accommodation. The battle for an Albanian national school—*shkolla shqipe*—in Kosovo in both periods fuelled the Albanian national political movement. Alternative strategies that the Albanians were compelled to pursue to express and guard their sense of national identity seemed to vindicate the belief that a genuinely free *shkolla shqipe* could become a reality only once the national sovereignty in Kosovo had been achieved.

Contrary to intentions, the Serbian policy of prohibition and restriction on education in Albanian gave impetus to the sustained effort on the part of the Albanians to nourish their sense of nationhood. As a result, the Albanian national identity in Kosovo was clearly delineated in opposition to the Serbs as the ethnic 'Other.' Such a

[62]Shkëlzen Maliqi, *Kosova: Separate Worlds—Reflections and Analyses 1989–1998*, Peja: Dukagjini 1998, pp. 113–17. Notably, it was not only the education content that captures a dimension of resistance innate to *shkolla shqipe* in post-autonomy Kosovo. By and large, the Serbs turned a blind eye to the Albanians' flourishing parallel education system in Kosovo. However, acts of random violence exercised against Albanian pupils (like the breaking-up of classes or mistreatment of students and teachers, especially when caught with the diplomas with a 'Kosovo Republic' stamp) turned the schools into a genuine 'battlefield'. See '*The Frozen Smiles: Violence against Albanian Children in Kosova*', Democratic League of Kosova—Commission for Children's Rights of Women's Forum 1992 (Human Rights Report); 'Violations of Human Rights in Kosova 1995', Council for the Defence of Human Rights and Freedoms, paper written for the Commission on Human Rights, 52nd session, Geneva 1996; 'Kosovski Albanci II: Policijska represija', Izvestaj br. 16, February 1995, in *Pod lupom: Krsenje ljudskih prava na territoriji bivse Jugoslavije 1991–95, Fond za humanitarno pravo*, 1997, pp. 173–224 (Human Rights Report). Sacrifice for Albanian-language education was acknowledged in obituaries with the following words: 'We are proud to have had such a parent who did not even spare his life in the defence of *shkolla shqipe*' or 'With will and pride you gave [your life] for high Albanian national ideals, for sacredness of language, students and *shkolla shqipe*.' See Drita Halimi-Statovci, *Etnologjia Flet*, Prishtina: Instituti Albanologjik i Prishtinës 1998, p. 287.

symbolic mapping out of Albanian nationhood in Kosovo in terms of opposition, however, overshadowed important questions concerning the development of Albanian nationhood in Kosovo quite apart from the Serbs.

In the interwar period, the nascent sense of Albanian nationhood rested both on religious and secular foundations. The Muslim clergy embraced and furthered education in Albanian and so heralded ultimate superiority of national rather than religious identity in the Albanian community in Kosovo. But, their engagement, effectively, implied an interposition on nationhood of a strong sense of religious identity, rather than the demise of the latter. Such conceptualisation of nationhood around religion, starkly contrasted with efforts on the part of nationalists to construct the Albanians' sense of national identity in purely secular terms, creating possible tension between secular and religious visions of nationhood.

In the post-autonomy period, the secular vision of nationhood prevailed. However it also included a duality. A Kosovo-focused vision of nationhood with a political goal of Kosovo's independence as its political corollary, contrasted starkly with steps undertaken in the field of education to bring about the symbolic unification of all Albanians. Unification was not articulated as a political goal of an overwhelming majority of Albanians in Kosovo in the post-autonomy period but the symbolic unification of education could, arguably, spawn an analogous political demand for the political-cum-territorial unification of Kosovo and Albania.

Were this request to be articulated, the feeling of 'Albanianness'—Kosovo Albanians' sense of membership in a large Albanian community—would, inevitably be challenged by 'Kosovarness'—the Albanians' strong sense of Kosovar identity. It is the relationship between 'Kosovar' and 'all-Albanian' that the *shkolla shqipe* in Kosovo will have to resolve. Otherwise, it risks turning from a school that promoted the sense of Albanian national identity, despite the symbolic and institutional hurdles the Serbs had raised, into a school inconspicuously nourishing potential intra-Albanian tensions.

THE PERCEPTION OF THE ALBANIANS IN GREECE IN THE 1830s AND '40s

THE ROLE OF THE PRESS

Elias G. Skoulidas

The ideology of nationalism played a major role in the course of historical events in the Balkans in the nineteenth and the twentieth centuries.[1] In the ethnic states of the nineteenth century, the notion of the nation was related to a constant effort to form a common identity; this identity contributed, within the bounds of the feeling that people participated in the same community, to the social cohesion of the newly established states.[2]

The Greek ethnic state in the 1830s was very much interested in the formation of this ethnic identity and the consolidation of its existence as well.[3] The appearance of the 'Great Idea' and Greek irredentism in the early 1840s increased the interest in the Greek populations of the Ottoman empire, which was organised into *millets*, or

[1]For nationalism and its ideological conception in the Balkans see Paschalis M. Kitromilides, '"Imagined Communities" and the Origins of the National Question in the Balkan' *European History Quarterly* 19/2, (April 1989), pp. 149–92, where further bibliography is available. For the image of the Balkans in Europe see Elli Skopetea, *He Disi tis Anatolis. Ikones apo to telos tis Othomanikis Aftokratorias*, Athens: Themelio 1992; Maria Todorova, *Imagining the Balkans*, Oxford University Press 1997.

[2]Among others see Miroslav Hroch, *Social Preconditions of National Revival in Europe: A Comparative Analysis of the Social Composition of Patriotic Groups among the Smaller European Nations*, transl. Ben Fowkes, Cambridge University Press 1985; Eric J. Hobsbawm, *Nations and Nationalism since 1780: Programme, Myth, Reality*, Cambridge University Press 1990; Benedict Anderson, *Imagined Communities. Reflections on the Origin and Spread of Nationalism*, London: Verso 1991.

[3]See John Anthony Petropulos, *Politics and Statecraft in the Kingdom of Greece 1833–1843*, Princeton University Press 1968.

religious communities. There was much optimism about the territorial expansion of the Kingdom of Greece.[4]

The role of the press was significant in the cultivation of the Greek ethnic conception, dating back to the years preceding the War of Independence of 1821. During the period we will examine (1830–47), it is possible to confirm, directly or indirectly, that eighty-two Greek newspapers were published (seventy-eight written in Greek and four of them written in French). Some of the papers were bilingual (written in Greek and another foreign language) for a certain period of time and a great number of these publications were short-lived. Most of them did not publish on a daily basis. In terms of the geographical distribution of the papers fifty were published in Athens, fourteen in Nauplion, five in Patras, nine on the island of Syros, three on the island of Aegina and one in Trieste (a paper published by a Greek living in the Greek community there).[5]

During the reign of Otho the press in the Greek kingdom was the conveyor of the ideology supported by the three political parties then existing (the 'English' party, the 'Russian' party and the 'French' or national party) while there were also papers published which had close relations with some members of the Regency (1833–5). The political parties had their own specific orientations regarding foreign policy and domestic political issues, which derived, on the one hand, from the constant influence exerted on them by the representatives of the three 'Powers-Protectors' of the Greek state and on the other hand, from their connection with the royal court.[6] *Aiōn, Athēna, Sotēr, Elpis*, were regarded as some of the major papers of the day. Lacking adequate financing, these papers published reports from the European papers, while news from the Ottoman empire was conveyed by way of readers-subscriber's letters. In addition, papers of less importance

[4]Elli Skopetea, *To 'Protypo Vasilio' kai i Megali Idea. Opsis tou ethnikou provlimatos stin Ellada (1830–1880)*, Athens: Polytypo 1988, pp. 21–40; Sokratis Petmezas, 'Politikos Alytrotismos kai i ethniki enopiisi stin Ellada', *Histor*, 2/1990, pp. 95–107.

[5]See among others Kostas Mayer, *Historia tou ellinikou typou*, vol. 1 (1790–1900), Athens: A. Dimopoulos 1957, pp. 33–103; Sofia Antoniadou, 'O typos kata tin epanastasin kai kata tin vasilian tou Othonos', *Parnassos*, per. 2/13, 1971, pp. 403–18; Klimis Mastoridis, *Casting the Greek Newspaper: A study of the morphology of the ephemeris from its origins until the introduction of mechanical setting*, Thessaloniki: Hellenic Literary and Historical Archive 1999, pp.149–88.

[6]Gunnar Hering, *Die politischen Parteien in Griechenland 1821–1936*, vol.1, Munich: R. Oldenbourg 1992, pp. 53–286.

and even less well financed, usually reprinted the stories carried by the major papers.[7]

It seems that the attitude of the press towards Albanians was not affected by the different political ideologies the papers supported. The image of the Albanians was based on the ideology of the 'nation' and the expectations of a dominant group. The Albanians were conceived by the Greek press as part of the Ottoman empire, because, the great majority of them being Muslims, they were often used as organs of the mechanisms of the Ottoman administration. Although Orthodox Christian Albanians coexisted with Greeks, they were scarcely distinguished from the latter. References to Christian Albanians as a separate population, appeared only after 1839; in light of the impending reforms in the Ottoman empire and the Hatt-i Sherif of Gülhane.[8] Information about the Albanians in the south-western Balkans related to the feudal character of society and traditional social behaviour.

The Greek press of that period viewed the Albanians through a number of stereotypical perceptions. The Albanians were characterised as rebels because of their frequent revolts against the central authority. These rebellions formed the reaction of local *toparches* against the attempt of the Ottoman empire to lessen their power. The assassination of a great number of them in Monastir by Mehmed Reshid Pasha in 1830, the defection of Mustafa Pasha of Shkodra which resulted in his own extermination (1831),[9] in addition to the revolts led by numerous Albanian military leaders, like Zylyftar Poda and Tafil Buzi, throughout the decade of the 1830s, were some of the issues that concerned the Greek press.[10] Exaggerated rumours relevant to a revolt

[7] Andreas S. Skandames, 'Ho hellinikos typos kata tin periodon tis vasilias tou Othonos 1832–1862' in *Deltion tis Istorikis kai Ethnologikis Etaireias tis Ellados* 1967–1970 (ed. 1971), pp. 251–303; Sofia A. Antoniades, *Emmanuel Antoniades. Ho Agonistis, ho dimosiographos 1791–1863*, Athens: n.p. 1971.

[8] *Aiōn*, year of publication (y. p.)1, number of issue (n. i.)33, 18(30)/1/1839. The dates referring to the issues are given in both calendars (Julian-Gregorian), as the former was used in Greece at that period. We took into consideration all the available journals, even if they did not provide us with information.

[9] *Gēnike Ephimeris tis Hellados*, y.p. 6, n.i. 28, 11(23)/4/1831, n.i. 33, 6(18)/5/1831, n.i. 35, 13(25)/5/1831, n.i. 45, 17(29)/6/1831, n.i. 60, 8(20)/8/1831, n.i. 92, 28(10)/11(12)/1831.

[10] *Chronos*, y.p. 1, n.i. 13, 11(23)/6/1833, n.i. 32, 17(29)/8/1833, *Athēna*, y.p. 2, n.i. 130, 5(17)/8/1833, y.p. 3, n.i. 198, 21(3)/11(12)/1834, y.p. 4, n.i. 239, 11(23)/5/1835, *Sōter*, y.p. 1, n.i. 17, 11(23)/3/1834, n.i. 59, 12(24)/8/1833, n.i. 81, 18(30)/11/1834, y.p. 4, n.i. 54, 29(11)/4(5)/1837, *Ethnike*, n.i. 12, 18(30)/11/1834, *Mnimossini*, n.i. 20,

frequently spread, even though in some cases there was not the slightest suspicion or indication that such an event was about to occur. The fears of Greek journalists were driven by the potential oppression of the Orthodox Christians in the *sanjaks* of the western Balkans, like that of Ioannina, where they were considered as populations homogenous or friendly to the Greeks.

In their revolts, the Albanian leaders had the support of some of the Greek chieftains, who were lawless or dabbled in banditry. Tafil Buzi had a minor connection with Greek policymakers as well.[11] Greek journalists paid much attention to the relations between the leaders of these revolts and Mohammed Ali of Egypt. They suspected that the Pasha of Egypt in his attempt to disorientate the Sublime Port was involved in each rebellion. Consequently, the Ottomans would be forced to send military troops to put down Albanian rebellious acts in areas where they broke out, and not against him.[12] Rumours of unrest were constant, whether or not they conformed to reality.

During the 1840s, the Greek press was interested in the application of the *tanzimat* reforms and the reaction of Albanian landowners, which was very strong.[13] Greek journalists reported that much of the agitation was caused by Albanian objections to being recruited into the army of the Ottoman empire, and to the imposition of taxes.[14]

20(1)/7(8)/1835, *He Anagennithissa Hellas*, y.p. 1, n.i. 25, 5(17)/9/1836, *He Elpis*, y.p. 1, n.i. 52/53, 13(25)/5/1837, *Aiōn*, y.p. 1, n.i. 79, 9(21)/7/1839, Hellas, y.p. 1, n.i. 6, 2(14)/8/1839. For the reactions see Petrika Thëngjilli, *Kryengritjet popullore kundër osmane në Shqipëri 1833–1839*, Tirana: Akademia e Shkencave e RPSSH-Instituti i Historisë 1981.

[11] *Gēnike Ephimeris tis Hellados*, y.p. 7, n.i. 5, 20(1)/1(2)/1832, *Athēna*, n.i. 572, 29(10)/10(11)/1838.

[12] *Sotēr*, y.p. 1, n.i. 16, 8(20)/3/1834, n.i. 60, 16(28)/8/1834, n.i. 62, 23(4)/8(9)/1834, *Ēthnike*, n.i. 44, 22(3)/3(4)/1835, *Mnimossini*, n.i. 17/18, 6(18)/7/1835, n.i. 28, 13(25)/9/1835, *Aiōn*, n.i. 78, 5(17)/7/1839, n.i. 90, 16(28)/8/1839, *Athēna*, y.p. 8, n.i. 630, 5(17)/7/1839, n.i. 642, 19(31)/8/1839, n.i. 662, 21(2)/10(11)/1839. For the issue see Athanase G. Politis, *Le conflit turco-égyptien de 1838–1841 et les dernières années du règne de Mohamed Aly d'après les documents diplomatiques grecs*, Cairo: Imprimerie de l'Institut Français d'Archéologie Orientale du Caire pour la Société Royale de Géographie d'Égypte 1931.

[13] Ligor K. Mile, *Çështje të historisë agrare shqiptare (fundi i shek. XVIII-vitet 70 të shek. XIX)*, Tirana: Akademia e Shkencave e RPS të Shqipërisë-Instituti i Historisë 1984, pp. 105–76; Shukri Rahimi, 'Dokumentet angleze mbi ngjarjet të Shqiptarët (1844/45'), *Gjurmime Albanologjike, Seria e shkencave historike*, 13/1983 (ed. 1984), pp. 169–93.

[14] *Aiōn*, y.p. 2, n.i. 170, 12(24)/6/1840, n.i. 171, 16(28)/6/1840, y.p. 5, n.i. 453, 14(26)/7/1843, *Athēna*, y.p. 9, n.i. 726, 22(4)/6(7)/1840, y.p. 12, n.i. 1040, 7(19)/8/1843, n.i. 1054, 2(14)/10/1843.

They estimated that the Albanians were, as a racial group, different from the Ottomans. As a result, some thoughts relevant to cooperation between the Albanians and the Greeks existed. But at the same time, the press was very cautious, fearing that Greek relations with the Ottoman empire might be harmed.

Banditry in general was a worldwide phenomenon which occurred in various contexts, when rural populations were incorporated into ethnic-modern states. It played a considerable role to Greek political life; it was connected with problems related to the delineation of the Greek-Ottoman border, the tradition of Kleftes and Armatoli, the general disorder caused by both Greek irredentism and rebellions and finally, the endemic abnormality of political life in the Greek kingdom and the Ottoman empire.[15] Some of the Albanian chieftains were demoted from their former rank in the empire as border guards and guards at road crossings (*derbenciler*). They usually robbed in cooperation with Greek chieftains, especially on the frontier or the borderland zone. The lack of sufficient control on either side of the frontiers between the Ottoman empire and the Greek kingdom allowed them, when being chased by the officials of one, to take shelter in the territory just across the frontier.[16] They were also a scourge in the areas of the borderland and the *sanjaks* of Thessaly, where there was extensive agriculture, and in villages, like the ones of Zagori in the *kaza* of Ioannina, whose residents were wealthy.[17] Banditry also occurred in districts where Albanian populations were dominant.

Moreover, when a rebellion was suppressed, the remaining rebels turned to banditry. The Greek press criticised such acts and asked for sanctions. Whenever there was an agreement between the borderland Greek authorities and those of the Ottoman Empire,[18] the journals approved, even though, in the beginning, they adopted a quite suspicious attitude, assuming that the agreement would be declared null and

[15]See among others John S. Koliopoulos, *Listes. He kentriki Hellada sta mesa tou 19ou aiona*, Athens: Hermis 1979 (pp. 373–92 index including bandits); *ibid.*, *Brigands with a Cause: Brigandage and Irredentism in Modern Greece 1821–1912*, Oxford: Clarendon Press 1987; Riki van Boeschoten, 'Kleftarmatoloi, listes kai koinoniki listeia', *Mnimon* 13/1991, pp. 9–24; Nikos G. Kotaridis, *Paradosiaki epanastasi kai eikosiena*, Athens: Plethron 1993, pp. 241–302.

[16]*Sotēr*, n.i. 46, 24(6)/6(7)/1834, *Ēthnike*, n.i. 54, 14(26)/5/1835, *Athēna*, y.p. 4, n.i. 246, 5(17)/6/1835.

[17]*Ephimeris ton Angelion*, y.p. 1, n.i. 8, 8(20)/6/1835, *Ho Hellenikos Tachidromos*, y.p. 2, n.i. 15, 13(25)/7/1837, *Aiōn*, n.i. 17, 20(2)/11(12)/1838, *Athēna*, n.i. 630, 5(19)/7/1839, n.i. 639, 9(21)/8/1839, n.i. 671, 22(4)/11(12)/1839.

[18]*Aiōn*, y.p. 4, n.i. 335, 4(16)/3/1842, *Athēna*, y.p. 11, n.i. 916, 13(25)/5/1842.

void. As an indication of this attitude the press welcomed every action taken by Albanian leaders-guards as a positive one, when these persons imposed peace and quiet, especially in the case of Tahir Abasi and Çelo Picari (however, these chieftains' behaviour was not always approved of).[19]

For the Greek press of that period the notion of a 'bandit' was sometimes identified with 'Albanian' and this view dated back to the years before the War of Independence of 1821. We should bear in mind that the memories of the Albanian ravages at the end of the eighteenth century, after the Orlovs' defeat, were still vivid.

Greek journalists regarded Albanians as very important warriors, selected troops of the Empire, but they reproached them for two major vices: The first being that they were avaricious and always acted for money. Most frequently, they even took action without being well paid or nourished, since they lacked essential things for their survival. The incidents of Albanians coming from the mountainous north of Albania and joining the Ottoman army, were not rare; on the contrary, this area provided the Empire with many inexpensive soldiers, who were usually not paid regularly and often revolted.[20] Their second vice was their penchant for cruel and violent behaviour and the great damage they caused wherever they went. We should note that the Albanians as representatives of Ottoman authority, were differentiated from the Ottomans in order to highlight their cruelties which confirmed preconceived notions held by Greek journalists. Consequently, Greek papers reported the most distressing and terrifying images of the Albanian massacres.[21]

The needs of the Ottoman Empire for troops brought the Albanian Muslims to areas like Egypt, or Lebanon and Syria. In the Greek press, apart from references to their poverty and their bad situation in general, there were also extensive references to the transportation

[19]*Athēna*, n.i. 512, 2(14)/3/1838, n.i. 548, 6(18)/8/1838, *Sotēr*, y.p. 5, n.i. 13, 6(18)/3/1838, n.i. 42, 7(19)/7/1838, *Aiōn*, n.i. 14, 9(21)/11/1838, n.i. 17, 20(2)/11(12)/1838, n.i. 33, 18(30)/1/1839, n.i. 37, 1(13)/2/1839, n.i. 42, 22(6)/2(3)/1839, n.i. 46, 8(20)/3/1839, n.i. 55, 16(28)/4/1839.

[20]*Aiōn*, y.p. 2, n.i. 188, 14(26)/8/1840, y.p. 4, n.i. 376, 19(31)/8/1842, *Ho Achaikos Kirix*, y.p. 1, n.i. 24, 10(22)/12/1840, n.i. 47, 10(22)/6/1841, *Ephimeris ton Angelion kai Dikastikon*, y.p. 1, n.i. 27, 19(31)/4/1841, *He Tachipteros Fēme*, y.p. 5, n.i. 112, 14(26)/6/1841, *He Melissa*, y.p. 2 n.i. 50, 14(26)/6/1841.

[21]This was the case of Bulgaria and Lebanon, see *Aiōn*, y.p. 3, n.i. 213, 27(9)/11(12)/1840, n.i. 267, 14(26)/6/1841, *Ho Achaikos Kirix*, n.i. 40, 22(4)/4(5)/1841, *Athēna*, y.p. 10, n.i. 812, 3(15)/5/1841, n.i. 816, 17(29)/5/1841, *He Tachipteros Fēme*, y.p. 5, n.i. 110, 7(19)/6/1841.

of these Albanian troops. During the Eastern Crisis (1839–41) rumours spread in the district of Ioannina, that an expedition would be launched against Greece, not against Syria, to plunder the area.[22] The rumours were so extensive that Greek troops were sent to the border and the ambassadors of the five 'Great Powers' in Constantinople (Russia, Prussia, Britain, France, Austria-Hungary) intervened to defuse the crisis.[23] At times, the transport of Albanian troops was treated humorously in the Greek press, which reported stories of Albanian soldiers drowning or suffering from nausea when embarking from Preveza; some of them could not even reach the island of Lefkas.[24] However, it is worth mentioning that many Albanians in the service of the Pasha of Egypt fought very well, a fact that was commented on related to uprisings in 'Albania' proper. Additionally, irregular Albanian troops were sent to Crete.[25] The press described this movement thoroughly and was again mostly concerned with the fate of the Christians.

Demotion and dismissal was common, so soldiers often became bandits and bandits returned to being border guards. This often occurred in the Greek-Ottoman border area, since the 'wealth' of the Greek kingdom was a constant temptation for the poverty-stricken Albanian recruits.

Apart from the three characterisations discussed, the Greek press of the time indicates that Greek politicians accepted stereotypical notions about Albanians. They were seen as conveyors of a system of authority which thrived on conspiracies (Ali-Pashiotism). This notion was used in internal Greek politics with the principal target being Kolettes and his supporters, some of whom were members of Ali-Pasha's court in Ioannina. Most of the accusations were made by the journal *Ethnike*; this paper in 1835 reflected the policy of Armansberg, the arch-chancellor, and were directed against the paper *Sotēr*, which called Kolettes a disciple of Ali Pasha's court without intending to mock. Ali-Pashiotism was considered to be in opposition to the modernisation of the state.[26] Many other papers were involved in this

[22] *Aiōn*, y.p. 4, n.i. 336, 8(20)/3/1842.

[23] *Aiōn*, y.p. 4, n.i. 337, 10(22)/3/1842.

[24] *Aiōn*, y.p. 3, n.i. 275, 13(25)/7/1841.

[25] *Aiōn*, n.i. 252, 20(2)/4(5)/1841, n.i. 263, 31(12)/5(6)/1841, n.i. 265, 7(19)/6/1841, *He Melissa*, n.i. 54, 12(24)/7/1841.

[26] *Ethnike*, n.i. 19, 13(25)/12/1834, n.i. 45, 24(5)/3(4)/1835, n.i. 47, 15(27)/4/1835, *Athēna*, y.p. 4, n.i. 247, 8(20)/6/1835, n.i. 248, 12(24)/6/1835, n.i. 249, 15(27)/6/1835, *Aiōn*, y.p. 2, n.i. 140, 25(8)/2(3)/1840, y.p. 3, n.i. 307, 5(17)/11/1841, y.p. 4, n.i. 372, 5(17)/8/1842, *He Ethnike*, y.p. 1, n.i. 61, 30(12)/9(10)/1844.

conflict as well. The reproaches and the attacks became more intense during periods when Kolettes was prime minister or a minister.

The Arvanites, the Albanian subjects of the Greek kingdom, who were descendants of earlier settlers, dating back mainly from the thirteenth to the sixteenth centuries, were occasionally mentioned, particularly in the special section of the papers which dealt with court judgements. According to these references, Arvanites (the term '*Alvanoi*' was also used to describe the Arvanites) were bilingual, some of them spoke only Albanian and the majority were illiterate peasants and shepherds, who were taken to court for petty theft or cases involving the civil code.[27] They were not likely to be a group with ethnic identity. In a political analysis on the Eastern Question, reference was made to the fact that 'the Albanians formed one of the tribes contributing to the creation of the Greek nation'.[28] The 'national body' assimilated the linguistic minorities without any great difficulty. Relying on an event that took place in a municipality, Gavrio, in the north of the island of Andros concerning a magistrate's transfer, we learn that its residents spoke Albanian and Greek as well.[29] The Greek press was aware of the existence of Albanian populations living in the suburbs of the Greek capital, Athens, and Boeotia, but did not consider the language to be the most important element that differentiated the Christians, both Greek and Albanian. Similarly, these Albanian populations were used in the conflict which broke out in 1843 between the native and non-native Greek people with a view to maintaining the native Greeks' position. Albanians were also used in the municipal elections in Athens in 1840.[30]

In the early 1840s plans for the division of the Ottoman empire began to appear in the Greek press, some of them reprints from European journals. The territory, defined as Albania on the maps, although the borders were vague, was shown annexed to Greece. Furthermore, articles which included rumours of the existence of a secret Christian league in the northern Balkans, including 'northern Albania', which

[27] *He Anagennithissa Hellas*, y.p. 1, n.i. 27, 12(24)/9/1836, *Ephimeris ton Angelion*, y.p. 2, n.i. 86, 15(27)/10/1836, y.p. 3, n.i. 30, 29(10)/5(6)/1837, n.i. 51, 27(8)/7(8)/1837, *Athēna*, n.i. 392, 5(17)/12/1836.

[28] *Athēna*, y.p. 12, n.i. 981, 6(18)/1/1843.

[29] *Athēna*, y.p. 11, n.i. 923, 6(18)/6/1842, n.i. 929, 27(9)/6(7)/1842.

[30] *Aiōn*, y.p. 3, n.i. 204, 28(9)/10(11)/1840, n.i. 205, 30(11)/10(11)/1840. About the issue see Ioannis Dimakis, *He politiaki metaboli tou 1843 kai to zitima ton aftochthonon kai eterochthonon*, Athens: Themelio 1991 (especially about the reaction of the press, pp. 89–167).

would act in order to shake off the Ottomans, were republished.[31] As a result, there was a contradiction pitting the desire for the territorial expansion of Greece against the assumption that the Albanians were not desirable.

The Zenel Gjoleka Rebellion forced the Greek papers to make more political references to the Albanians. The great majority of the journals had this information but few commented on it. When they did, they included only the republication of the most important news and rumours. When speculating on the causes of the rebellion, their reports were usually contradictory. Another source of information was the Greek government, a fact that proves the great attention both the latter and the public opinion paid to the issue.[32] Greek papers, not being aware of the secret negotiations between Albanian leaders and Greek representatives, were mostly interested in the protection of the Christians. These negotiations were held under Kolettes' auspices.[33] The papers were usually in favour of the Ottoman troops and the reestablishment of peace. Moreover, they were concerned about the character of the 'rebellion' and suspected foreign involvement.

The role of policy was very important in the press's perception of Albanians. The assessments of the press regarding them during the period we have examined did not go far beyond the views which Greek society as a whole had formerly adopted. These views about the Albanians' behaviour reinforced similar views from the recent past. The political present or future of 'Albania' and 'Albanians' was seldom referred to.

Despite the different features, the attitude of the Greek press relied on the common experience of the coexistence of Greek and Albanian populations within the boundaries of common administrative forms

[31] *Athēna*, y.p. 10, n.i. 816, 17(29)/5/1841.

[32] *Elpis*, n.i. 410, 14(26)/8/1847, *Athēna*, n.i. 1431, 26(7)/7(8)/1847, *Aiōn*, y.p. 9, n.i. 795, 19(31)/7/1847.

[33] See also *Elpis*, n.i. 404, 17(29)/7/1847, n.i. 408, 2(14)/8/1847, *Athēna*, n.i. 1428, 13(25)/7/1847 to n.i. 1430, 20(1)/7(8)/1847, n.i. 1433, 3(15)/8/1847, *Aiōn*, y.p. 9, n.i. 796, 23(4)/7(8)/1847 to n.i. 799, 2(14)/8/1847, n.i. 804, 20(1)/8(9)/1847, n.i. 806, 27(8)/8(9)/1847, n.i. 809, 10(22)/9/1847, n.i. 811, 17(29)/9/1847, n.i. 812, 20(2)/9(10)/1847, n.i. 814, 9(21)/10/1847, n.i. 820, 29(10)/10(11)/1847, n.i. 835, 20(1)/12(1)/1847(8). As for the secret negotiations see Miltos 'M. Spyromilios, 'Hellas kai Albania. Ho Giolekas' *Ho Neos Kouvaras*, 3/1965, pp. 129–227; Mexhit Kokalari, "Besëlidhja Shqiptare' dhe kryengritja e madhe fshatare e vitit 1847", *Studime Historike*, 11(28)/2, 1974, pp. 131–61; Eleftheria I. Nikolaïdou, 'He stasi tis Tourkias apenanti stous Albanous se synartisi me ti diadosi tis Megalis Ideas stin Epiro (mesa 19ou aiona)', *Dodoni* 8/1979, pp. 81–109.

and explained attitudes at specific times and places. The Orthodox Christian Albanians were not often mentioned; the press focused mainly on the Muslim Albanians, adopting a critical point of view towards them. Various aspects of the coexistence and cooperation between the Greeks and the Albanians were considered too normal to be mentioned by the press. The secret negotiations between the Greeks and the Albanians (regardless of their religion), which took place during the entire nineteenth century, demonstrate the extensive contacts between the two communities and a sense of a common interest.[34]

[34]Miltos Spyromilios, 'Hellas kai Albania. Mia apopira prossegisseos Albanon kai Hellinon kata to 1877–1878', *Ho Neos Kouvaras* 2/1962, pp. 135–77; Shkëlzen Raça, *Marrëdhëniet Shqiptaro-Greke 1829–1881*, Prishtina: Instituti Albanologjik i Prishtinës 1990.

NORTH AMERICAN ALBANIAN IMMIGRATION

NARRATIVES OF POLITICAL MYTH

Annie Lafontaine

This chapter seeks to present a preliminary analysis of narratives held by Albanians about the transformation of their personal identity after migrating to North America in so far as it sheds light on some mythical images of Albanian and North American socio-political ideologies.

It does not present mythical narratives as such, but fragments of myths that can be found in the rhetoric of the definition of identity in relation to political ideologies. These fragments of myths belong to mythical narratives that are historically situated even if they carry themes that seem to be universal like the myth of origin. The point I want to focus on is the way individuals use those fragments to define themselves in relation to political ideologies, particularly in the migration situation.

The narrative analysis proposed thus focuses on two phenomena: the interpenetration of mythical images of an Albanian socio-political ideology with metaphors of a North American nationalism, as well as the relations maintained by Albanians living in North America towards the transition process of Albania as it pertains to the transformation of their individual identity.

The narratives

Let us begin with a summary of two narratives. The first comes from a person I interviewed in the Bronx, New York, in April 1999, to whom I had been referred because of his role in the Albanian-American community. The second narrative comes from a person who has taught me the Albanian language, and whom I therefore saw regularly after

September 1998. However, the narrative presented is based on one particular meeting.

PETRIT[1]

I met Petrit in his small office at an Albanian newspaper located in the Bronx, where he worked from 1992 to 1999. Although he told me he felt strange about the fact that he was becoming the subject of reports since the beginning of the war in Kosovo, since he had always been a reporter, he noted that he was glad to talk to me about the Albanian-American community and his own migration experience.

He considers the Bronx to be the nucleus of the Albanian-American community (which seems for him to include Kosovars and Albanians), and he feels his job at the newspaper placed him at the centre of the local Albanian community, or on the frontier between his community and American society in general. He thus feels privileged because he can see both American society and the Albanian community from a relatively external view point.

Petrit told me he came alone from Prishtina to the United States in 1992 at the age of thirty-one for political reasons. He did not explain these reasons in detail, but told me he had been implicated in student demonstrations in 1991 and was wanted by the Yugoslav authorities. He explained without any more detail that he received refugee status in Kosovo and later came to the United States. He later brought over his brother and parents. He now lives in New Jersey with his Albanian-American wife, who was born and raised in Buffalo, and their two children who were born in the United States.

Petrit considers himself part-Kosovo Albanian and part-American and does not intend to return to live in Kosovo. However, he told me this with hesitation. He knows that generally people who have left Kosovo want to go back there after its liberation. But Petrit focussed on the fact that he soon began to socialise and work like an American, being more and more assimilated, but at the same time he has kept his traditions, his culture and his Albanian language. American society, he suggested, is just as assimilating as it is liberal, and allows him to live a double identity. According to him, the respect for cultural differences which is very evident in the United States is one of the reasons why Albanians have feelings of loyalty towards the country. Most of his fellow-countrymen, he said, are just as 'pure' Americans as they are 'pure'

[1]Personal names used are ficticious.

Albanians. Petrit thinks it is important to live life in the context of both cultures, and he is thus passing on the values of both cultures to his children.

Although he emphasised that he would not go back to Kosovo, Petrit thinks that the 'occupation' of the Kosovo territory by Albanians is the mandatory condition for the perpetuation of the Albanian identity of people who have left the homeland. His Albanian identity, he specified, is based on the fact that Kosovo is still inhabited by ethnic Albanians. For him, it is impossible to think of the persistence of a Kosovo Albanian identity if there are no more Albanians in Kosovo. He told me that a part of himself, such as his family, must remain in Kosovo otherwise his identity is lost. According to him, even the people who are born in the United States share this feeling. The family, which Petrit asserts is considered by Albanians as the main conveyor of values, is a reminder of their love for Illyria—this divided country that they have never seen. This explains why so many of them have joined the ranks of the Kosovo Liberation Army. Every Albanian, according to Petrit, is of Illyrian origin and dreams of the realisation of a Greater Albania.

Regarding the Albanian-American community as such, Petrit explained to me that the war has brought together the Kosovars and the Albanians. They were not working together, according to him, because they did not feel the need, because they were divided for political and religious reasons, and because they did not have the same historical background. He asserted that the Kosovars, threatened by the Serbs, became nationalists, while the Albanians did not, enjoying the freedom of simply living as Albanians.

After the beginning of the war, according to Petrit, the Albanians from Albania realised that their fellow-countrymen needed their help. Their typical hospitality led to the creation of a new solidarity, a step forward towards the realisation of unification. He maintained that the journal where he worked played a significant role in unifying Kosovars and Albanians in the New York City area.

To explain the reasons why he thinks that ethnic pluralism is right for America and wrong for the Balkans, Petrit explained that in the Balkans people do not like living with other ethnic groups. Mixed communities in the Balkans might not be such a good idea because ethnic diversity there can lead to genocide. Yugoslavia was a forced union in which one of the parties, Serbia, did not respect the agreement. Consequently he thinks a divorce is needed. From his position in the United States, he has supported the realisation of this objective.

The suffering he endured as a result of his migration and adaptation experience seems to be expressed particularly by a strong rhetoric of unification and hybridisation: that of the Albanian/Kosovar-American community, that of Kosovo with Albania in the Balkans, and that of his own Kosovo Albanian identity with an American way of life.

The narrative of the other person will show that his suffering is expressed in a reverse rhetoric of exclusion and reclusion.

OLSI

Olsi is a thirty-year-old Albanian who arrived in Canada in 1995 after living in Greece. His parents still live in Tirana, but his sister lives in southern Italy. Olsi received refugee status when he arrived in Canada. He never had the dream of coming to live in America, but felt the need to leave his country only because he could not find work. He would rather have lived in Europe due to its geographical and cultural proximity with Albania. He now lives in Montreal with a young woman of Russian origin.

Olsi considers himself very nationalistic, but he insists that he has nothing against other people or religions. He believes that Albanians learn to become nationalists at a very young age. 'The true Albanian religion is simply being Albanian,' he argued. Not to be a nationalist means being a bastard. Nationalism is a question of individual and collective survival. He argued that this is something deeply rooted in the Albanian mentality.

According to Olsi, it is impossible to be two things at once. Consequently, he does not understand Albanians who are living the ethnic experience of the 'American dash.' He does not feel either North American or Canadian, although he has noticed that many aspects of his personality have changed. For example, he now considers himself to be more tolerant towards people of other ethnic backgrounds and cultures.

Olsi states that he has been forced to adapt himself rather quickly to the North American way of life but has taken the time to analyse the positive and negative aspects of assimilation, since he believes there is nothing worse than losing your culture: 'Without your culture, you have no one left with whom to identify'. According to this view, Albanian children born in America can, at a later stage of life, identify themselves as Americans. However, he maintained that it is the parents' responsibility to communicate the Albanian culture, especially the language, to their children.

Olsi distinguishes two types of Albanian people living in North America. First, there are those who came because they felt greatly attracted by North American culture. These people are very open-minded, but he feels that they are too deluded: they believe blindly in the 'American Dream.' These Albanians will rapidly lose their cultural roots and become assimilated into American society. Then there are those Albanians who do not identify themselves with North Americans but only with other Albanians. They try to keep their values, principles and traditions; most of them came to North America as refugees.

Although he does not say so, Olsi falls into a third category. He believes he is very open to other cultures; he speaks several European languages and he has friends from all parts of the world. Nevertheless, he does hold on to Albanian values, especially that of 'the family.' He does not understand why young Americans leave their family household so soon. The reason why he left his home early was because he had to. However, he would not go back to Albania to raise a family because of the poverty, violence, and corruption. Olsi feels that his homeland is losing its values, but he also doubts whether he would like to raise a family in North America, as he believes that the state is far too prominent in family affairs.

Olsi believes that Canadians are very tolerant, perhaps too tolerant because they do not sufficiently demand the respect of the people they are welcoming in. He feels that he can remain completely Albanian while holding a Canadian passport and benefiting from the freedom and all the economic advantages; he does not have to become someone else. For him Canada is a paradox, because it is the land of everyone and no one (at the same time); no one makes territorial claims as in the Balkans, and everyone is tolerated. By arguing in this manner, Olsi thus demonstrates that he is perhaps more assimilated into Canadian political ideology than he thinks.

He believes that cultural homogeneity, as in Albania during his childhood, is an ideal situation. In Albania, he claims, the family and the ethnic group are almost one and the same. However, he thinks that the savage transition to capitalism is causing changes in this mentality and the country's ideal cultural homogeneity is slowly disappearing. In Olsi's view Communism had until recently ensured the maintenance of some traditional Albanian values.

Although Olsi believes that the Albanian version of history is the more truthful and that it is important to defend the ethnic unity of the territory, he would never join the Kosovo Liberation Army. Although he believes that he is patriotic, he would not be willing to die for his country. Peace, he emphasised, is the most important thing, and it does not really matter whether Kosovo is or is not part of Albania because being Albanian is a question not of territorial boundaries but of culture and education. Thus one is always an Albanian whether one is in Albania, somewhere else in Europe, or America. Where one is makes no difference.

Interpretation

These two cases are presented in order to demonstrate two opposing views concerning the interpenetration of mythical images as they affect the identity transformation of the migrant. However, it would be unrealistic to assert that these views are fixed categories into which the migrants fall. But these examples can represent the complexity and the diversity of the experience of migration. Olsi, who came from a country closed for at least fifty years, has a narrative that focuses on the maintenance of his identity through conservatism and homogeneity. But he also holds a rhetoric that focuses on open-mindedness towards his adaptation in North America. Petrit, who came from Kosovo in Yugoslavia, a country more open to the outside but with ethnic tensions within, has a narrative that focuses on the perpetuation of his identity through hybridisation. But he also emphasises that every Kosovo Albanian must maintain part of his family in the homeland in order to perpetuate his identity. Both Olsi and Petrit thus seem to maintain contradictions in their identity and migration narratives. In examining these cases it is possible to see the impact of two different political myths and how the two men use fragments of these myths in different ways to reconstruct a coherent narrative.

In *Transnationalism from Below*[2] Luis Guarzino and Michael Smith observe that migrant individuals develop many political identities while reifying certain mythical images they hold. The two accounts were quite revealing on this point. For Petrit the migration process causes political identities to multiply, but his political loyalty to the homeland is still strong. But for Olsi the migration process leads to the reification of the Albanian political identity, while at the same time it causes a certain political disengagement from Albania and an open-mindedness to cultural diversity.

One of the main topics of conversation was the contrast between

[2]Michael Peter Smith and Luis Eduardo Guarnizo (eds), *Transnationalism from Below*, New Brunswick, NJ: Transaction Publishers 1998, p. 9.

the North American mythical images of liberal democracy, plurality, tolerance, equality and individual freedom, and the Albanian or Balkan mythical images of territorial socio-cultural homogeneity, which associates the country with the home and the nation with the family. Partly built around the *persona* of the immigrant founder-builder of a pluralist nation unified by liberal-democratic principles, the American political myth seems totally opposed to the Albanian one. For example, in the American setting, freedom is an individual right that allows people to have their own personal identity, whereas in the Albanian dimension it is a collective right to live together in the same way. This conception of the Albanian nation eliminates the possibility of pluralism, and negates all divisions based on membership in a clan or a religious community, as demonstrated in Stark Draper's text *The Conceptualisation of an Albanian Nation.*[3]

Petrit idealises his assimilation of these opposed mythical images, whereas, Olsi is constantly jeopardised by the assimilating American nationalist ideology; for him interpenetration is impossible. For Petrit the strength of his personal identity lies in its perfect duality. For Olsi it comes from his reasoned resistance to the assimilating process of the North American nationalist ideology on his lifestyle and principles. American liberal democracy, in his view, conveys acceptable principles, but they have certain drawbacks such as indifference, individualism and, as a result, social violence. He hopes to maintain the Albanian dream of an ethno-national society functioning in the image of perfect family life: mutual aid, respect for elders, homogeneity of thought and action, respect for honour and truth.

Olsi and Petrit differ in the way they use American and Albanian mythical images to redefine their personal identities. Petrit perfectly duplicates his identity—the American myth enables him to do just that—but he remains extremely attached to his ethnic origin, which is deeply rooted in a land where cultural homogeneity is considered the ideal. Proof of this attachment is the physical presence of part of his family in Kosovo. Olsi, on the other hand, completely refuses to be identified with North America; it is his way of staying loyal to his ethnic origin. The protection of his Albanian identity is guaranteed by the fact that he is so warmly disposed towards pre-transition Albania.

[3]Stark Draper, 'The Conceptualisation of an Albanian Nation,' *Ethnic and Racial Studies*, 20(1)/1997, pp. 123–44.

In conclusion, three questions must be posed. First, at which level—individual, familial, national or transnational—do we situate the analysis to explain the difference between the migrants who assimilate aspects of the political myths of their new country and those who do not? Is it at the point of junction between the individual and the institution? Secondly, is it possible to make a model out of the fragmentation process of political myths and the rearrangement of their fragments in the identity construction of migrant individuals? If so, what are the criteria? Finally, can we really speak of the interpenetration of mythical images as a specific phenomenon, or is this really the normal process of the creation and transformation of every myth?

'CULTURE' AND THE REINVENTION OF MYTH IN A BORDER AREA

Gilles de Rapper

Long-term ethnographic fieldwork allows the ethnographer to become familiar with what is called 'presentation of the self,' i.e., with what people say and do when they meet other people and have to create an image of themselves. A part of the presentation of the self has to do with collective identity, that is, with the presentation of the self as a member of a community, either national, local or religious, whose existence is justified on historical grounds. It is thus possible to have an idea of the impact of the myths, created and used in the nation's claim for existence, on society, especially on local communities which are not directly involved in the process of myth-making. Here we shall examine what happens to those myths in the southern Albanian district of Devoll, on the border with Greece. The argument is that although national myths are widely spread in this peripheral area through school and media, they are shaped to a specific form by the international border and the way it influences social organisation and local perceptions of the self and the other.

National myths and their local forms

Nationwide myths created and transmitted by political and intellectual élites differ from local ones in so far as they are based on wider knowledge of society and history, while local myths are usually rooted in local society and history, even when they pertain to the whole nation. People tend to see the nation according to the organisation and contradictions of their own local society. It is thus impossible to talk of 'local myths' on one side and of 'national myths' on the other:

both are national in that they offer an explanation of the existence and characteristics of the nation. Moreover, constant interactions exist between the two levels, through books, school and newspapers.

As usual with national identity[1] and with myth in general,[2] the same myths can be heard in quite different forms from different people and in different contexts. This is the case with four national myths that appear in our local society in complete contradiction with their official form, i.e. with the variant which is transmitted through schools, research institutions, state media and national politics. These four myths have to do with religion, independence, traditions and national unity.

It is common in Albania to say that all Albanians, whether Christian or Muslim, are brothers, and that their only religion is their common Albanian nationality.[3] The dogma of national unity as against religious differentiation is at the core of the most widely-spread Albanian national rhetoric. However, this rhetoric is challenged when local society is underpinned by, and conceptualised in terms of, religious differentiation. This is the case in mixed areas where Muslims and Christians live in separate villages (or in separate neighbourhoods), and both have strong identities as religious communities—as in Devoll. In this specific context, religion cannot consist of just being Albanian. On the contrary, people are very well aware of belonging to a specific religious community, and national identity is rarely thought of outside the basic opposition between Muslims and Christians. For instance, both Muslims and Christians claim a Christian origin for the whole nation, and Christians enjoy a higher prestige as representatives of the 'real' or 'authentic' Albanian nation. Although many declare that religion does not matter, the way people talk and behave within local society clearly shows that they have to be Christian or Muslim in order to be Albanian, and that it is better to be Christian than Muslim.

Independence and isolation is another basis of national rhetoric, since it strengthens the feeling of the nation's uniqueness and autono-

[1]Cf. Andras Zempleni, 'Les manques de la nation. Sur quelques propriétés de la "patrie" et de la "nation" en Hongrie contemporaine' in Daniel Fabre (ed.), *L'Europe entre cultures et nations*, Paris: Éditions de la MSH 1996, pp. 121–55.

[2]Cf. Claude Lévi-Strauss, *Anthropologie structurale deux*, Paris: Plon 1973, pp. 175–233.

[3]Repetition of such statements can be both a source of amusement and exasperation among visiting foreigners. See for instance François Maspéro, *Balkans-Transit*, Paris: Seuil 1997.

mous existence. However, when local society is shaped by a long tradition of emigration abroad, the official variant is again challenged. This is the case in the Devoll and, to a certain extent, in southeastern Albania, whence many people migrated to America during the first half of the twentieth century.[4] Today the area claims a cultural superiority over all other Albanian regions due to its long and continuous links with the West. Its relative wealth and the better education of its inhabitants are expressly connected to the influence of emigration to Western countries. Remote and isolated areas are never seen as the cradle and sanctuary of authentic Albanian values, but rather as backward, poor and dangerous places. Contact with the outside world through knowledge of foreign languages, travel or emigration is explicitly sought out and acts as a source of social prestige.

In the same way, local people do not seem to value tradition as a marker of national identity. On the contrary, loyalty to traditions such as ritual 'hospitality' or 'manliness' and 'heroism' is often stigmatised as 'fanaticism,' i.e. as an extremist from of behaviour that has a negative influence on the image people give of themselves. People contrast what they see as modern and educated behaviour—they call it 'culture' (*kulturë*)—with what they call fanaticism. When they feel that they are not acting 'heroically' (e.g. because they are afraid of every manifestation of authority), they typically reply 'We are not brave, but we have got culture' (*në s'jemi trimë, por jemi me kulturë*). Heroism and traditions are used here not to assert national identity, but rather, by being denigrated, to give local society a distinctive image of modernity.

The difference between the North and the South in Albania—the distinction between Ghegs and Tosks—is usually seen as historic, linguistic and ethnic. However, in local society the words *geg* and *tosk* are never heard, and the relevant distinction is simply between 'north' and 'south'. There is no actual territorial border between north and south: the difference lies in distinctive representations of the 'self' and the 'other' rather than on geography or society. This is obvious in the conception of space. From the local point of view, the north is sometimes seen as an entirely mountainous area inhabited by backward and dirty shepherds. With no roads or contact with the outside, it is a closed space. Local society, said to be representative of the south, is then characterised by its agriculture and its links with the world. However, at different times, due to its own mountains, local society pretends

[4]Emigration to America is itself inscribed in a context of mobility which was first limited to the Ottoman Empire (Istanbul, Egypt).

to be higher, in terms of both altitude and moral value. The north is then seen as a composite of lowlands and valleys open to bad influences and filled with a filthy atmosphere. The difference between north and south thus appears as a local and contextual realisation of underlying symbolic oppositions between high and low, open and closed, dirty and clean, and is not historicised or ethnicised as a distinctive feature of the nation.[5]

Once again, these variations should not be understood as an opposition between a local conception and a national one. In fact, when asked openly, people usually tend to answer by the official form of those myths, which is known nation-wide. The local forms appear in everyday and informal conversation as a reaction to events or to the behaviour of other people. The difference is thus rather between a constructed and idealised form of national identity and a second form, rooted in everyday life and in local social relationships. Both can be seen as discourses of a society on itself, but their production and destination are different.

Moreover, in local conceptions all these myths have to do with the concept of 'culture.' The opposition between Muslims and Christians is conceived in terms of the cultural superiority of the latter, as with the opposition of north versus south, tradition versus modernity, and isolation versus links with the outside world. The concept of culture thus appears as a key to the understanding of these myths and of their impact on society.

The concept of culture

First of all, it is important to note that the concept of culture is both a popular category which is not consciously elaborated, and an over-elaborated concept in Western philosophy and social science that has had considerable influence on the Albanian national movement. Among local populations people talk about culture and are able to apply the two categories of 'with culture' (*me kulturë*) and 'without culture' (*pa kulturë*) to both individuals and communities, but no one is able to give an extensive definition of what culture is. The dictionary definition, on the other hand, does not fit with the local conception. The definition that follows is thus based on the present writer's own

[5]On the local forms of national identity in the Devoll, see Gilles de Rapper, 'La Frontière albanaise. Famille, société et identité collective en Albanie du sud', unpublished doctoral dissertation, University of Paris X-Nanterre 1998.

elaboration of various applications of the word in everyday situations.

'Culture' can be defined by a series of four components on the one hand, and by its functioning on the other. The four components are as follows:

Language. 'To have culture' means first to speak one's own language correctly, i.e., in the standard form rather than using a local dialect. It also means speaking at least one of the most valued foreign languages (English, French, Italian). For instance, during the electoral campaign of 1996, all the candidates of the Devoll were presented in meetings as speaking several foreign languages. Almost certainly most of them were far from actually speaking so many different languages, but the very fact that they were said to speak them has such high cultural value that no one in the audience would think of questioning this ability. Someone who is said to speak one or more than one foreign language 'has culture' and thus cannot be a cheater.

We are very close here to the Gellnerian model of the nation, with its need for a unified national language. Culture here means 'national culture' as opposed to the remains of local diversity, and people from the Devoll feel proud that the way they speak is very close to standard Albanian.

Knowledge. Any kind of knowledge is valued, especially if it has been learned at school or university, or by travelling abroad. The villages which are said to be 'with culture' are those where the first Albanian schools opened early in the twentieth century, as well as those from which people emigrated to the West. Once again, the insistence on schools and education reminds us of the Gellnerian model of the nation.

The outside world. 'Culture' also means contacts with the outside world through emigration or travel, or even through television or personal contacts with visiting foreigners. Once again some foreign countries are more valued than others, and it is better, in terms of 'culture', to have family in the United States rather than in Greece, or to watch French rather than Turkish television.

Technology. 'Culture' also has a material dimension, related to the modernisation of village life. Villages with paved streets, water, electricity and two-storied stone houses 'have more culture' than those that have a more rural aspect. Inside the house the use of a table and chairs instead of *sofër* (the low round table) and rugs is said to be a sign of 'higher culture.' Today TV sets, refrigerators, video recorders and cameras tend to be considered both as signs of culture (they connect people to the outside world and to modernity) and as a source of social prestige. Indeed, because 'culture' is not spread equally among the population, it also brings prestige to the individuals who are credited 'with culture.' With these two last points, 'culture' appears as a form of modernity, but more precisely as a way of learning modernity from abroad, by way of imitation.

As can be seen, the local conception of culture is not far from the definition used in social anthropology, but it differs, first, by the importance of relations with the outside world, and, second, by its normative dimension. Clearly, from the local point of view there is only one form of 'culture,' or at least one good form of it. Some people have 'culture,' others do not, and those who have acquired it first are superior. This also means that 'culture' is not attached to a particular group or community, but can be transmitted from one group to another. For instance, it is usually assumed that the West has more 'culture,' and thus people in Albania should learn from foreigners how to behave and live. 'Culture' is also a historic process, which is not given at one time to everyone. 'History' is, so to speak, the history of how 'culture' comes to villages and individuals all over the country.

If the local conception of 'culture' appears to be in contradiction with the anthropological one due to its historic and normative character, it is nonetheless very close to another classical definition of it in Western tradition. Two traditions can indeed be distinguished in the definition of 'culture' in Western thought. The first one dates back to the eighteenth century and the Enlightenment. 'Culture' is seen as a distinctive feature of all human societies and is opposed to 'nature'; it is to be understood as 'high culture' and is related to an unbroken tradition from classical antiquity. In that sense, it is considered superior: 'culture' is a kind of behaviour, knowledge and judgement to which everyone should aspire in order to be a human being and not a 'barbarian'. The second and contrary perspective relates to the nineteenth century and Romanticism. 'Culture' is no longer universal and normative, but plural and peculiar: there are different 'cultures,' each the achievement of one particular people or social, national, or religious group. 'It' is thus defined as the integrated beliefs, practices and social forms that give the group its coherence and specificity.[6]

The fact that the local Albanian conception is closer to the classical universalist definition does not mean that Albania was more

[6]Adam Kuper, 'Culture, Identity and the Project of a Cosmopolitan Anthropology' in *Man*, vol. 29, no. 3, (1994), pp. 537–54, here p. 539; and Ernest Gellner, *Nations and Nationalism*, London: Basil Blackwell 1983, chapter 7.

influenced by the French Enlightenment than by German Romanticism. It should rather make us question the anthropological and sociological basis of these two traditions. Both can indeed be seen as different ways of talking about identity and especially of tracing the border between the group and the outside. The relativist definition relies on the idea that each group receives its characteristics from nature, or at least from a given and unquestionable order from which all borders were drawn from the beginning. This conception will be called 'primordialist,' since 'it focuses on gender and generation, kinship, ethnicity and race, for constructing and reinforcing the boundary between inside and outside'.[7] The universalist definition, on the other hand, ranks the members of the group and the outsiders on a scale of 'culture,' i.e. according to their relative proximity with an absolute value, 'culture.' It will be called 'sacred' as it relates 'the collectivity to an unchanging and eternal realm of the sacred and the sublime—be it defined as God or Reason, Progress or Rationality'.[8] Both conceptions must be understood as ideal types: they are not exclusive and can be found together, though not having equal importance, in the same national identity.

The concept of culture appears to be central to the construction of the Albanian national identity for two reasons: first, the tracing of the border between 'we' and the 'other' relies on the idea that 'culture' should be the distinctive attribute of insiders while outsiders (and especially neighbours) are seen as barbarians, and second, 'culture' is present in all symbolic oppositions on which national myths are constructed. 'Culture' is thus not only one myth among many. As a structuring principle of local society and as a frame for every discourse of society on itself, the concept of culture appears to be at the basis of all the national myths and to constitute the myth *par excellence.*

Once again, this definition of culture should not be seen as a local form as opposed to a nation or state-centred form. It is rather the local interpretation of a concept that has been widely used and spread through Albanian history, from the beginning of the national movement until today. Indeed, apart from political independence, all national movements in Southeastern Europe also aimed at the modernisation of society through contact with Western culture and technology, creation of a national unified language, and organisation of a national

[7]Shmuel Eisenstadt and Bernhard Giesen, 'The Construction of Collective Identity', *Archives Européennes de Sociologie*, XXXVI, 1/ 1995, pp. 72–102, here p. 77.

[8]*Ibid.*, p. 82.

educational system. However, we can look at the way culture has come to be so central in the definition of collective identities in this border area.

Culture vs. non-culture

First, some of the internal divisions of local society are conceived in terms of 'culture.' This is mainly the case for the opposition between Muslims and Christians, which forms one of the main features of social organisation in this area. Christians form a minority in this area, as they do in Albania as a whole. Although they do not live in a separate territory, they are not entirely mixed with Muslims. They live in different villages and, in the few instances where they live in the same village, they still live in separate neighbourhoods. Moreover, a spatial differentiation exists between the two communities: Christians live in the mountains, Muslims in the lowlands (see table):

SPACE AND RELIGION IN THE 43 VILLAGES OF THE DEVOLL

	Lowland villages	*Mountain villages*
Orthodox Christians	3	6
Muslims	25	9

As elsewhere in the Mediterranean, the mountains are strongly associated with backwardness, poverty and violence, as stated earlier regarding the difference between north and south, while lowlands are associated with agriculture and hence wealth and the possibility of sustaining a larger population. Muslim villages are always bigger than Christian mountain villages. This spatial difference thus relates to a social differentiation which has to do with occupation (Muslims are peasants, Christians are craftsmen) and prosperity (life is easier in the plain than in the mountains). It also has a historical dimension; because of Ottoman political and administrative organisation, the ownership of agricultural lands would be easier for Muslims than for Christians, who would be driven up into the mountains which were of no special interest to the Muslims. The association of Muslims with land and prosperity is thus a result of their privileged relationship with the state, and of the authority they exercise over Christians.

The situation described above belongs to an idealised and partly imagined past, as both emigration and Communism have engendered deep social and economic changes. Emigration to the West, mainly to the United States, until the Second World War was more a Christian phenomenon in the Devoll partly because of their more desperate economic situation. Mostly, however, the émigrés would maintain strong links with their village of origin, either coming back every few years or sending money both for the family and the village as a community, and to working for improved conditions for all villagers by funding road works, mills or water adduction. By thus remaining members of their original community, they would contribute to social change, introducing new habits and artefacts still classified as 'modern,' which in local conceptions cannot be expressed other than as part of 'culture.' The role of Communism was similar since by fighting traditional land ownership and religious practice, it was a strong factor in modernisation. The development of schools was also responsible for the spreading of the idea of culture. As noted earlier, villagers are still proud of the long existence of schools in their villages and of the number of children they send to high school and university: it is a sign of their high level of culture compared to neighbouring villages.

Moreover, as most religious practices and beliefs were attacked by Communism, the way people identify with their religious communities had more to do with 'culture' than with religion as much, which was also partly the case earlier, since religious communities in Ottoman society were also social groups, acting for the socialisation of their members. The opposition between religious communities is not concerned with theological differences. Nothing is done to attack the beliefs and practices of members of the other community. Rather, the way religion is experienced is partly syncretistic, with popular religion also of great importance. What is involved in the relations between the two communities is rather the construction of an image of the other, which is used to mirror one's own identity. For instance, Muslims present themselves as 'loyal' and 'generous,' while Christians are 'disloyal' and 'selfish.' Christians on the other hand see themselves as 'intelligent' and 'thrifty' and Muslims as 'stupid' and overly 'liberal.' These crossed representations are important as they trace borders inside local society and are at the basis of most feelings of identity.

However, although each community tries to give an image of 'culture' and is prompt to stigmatise its absence in the behaviour of members of the other community, there is a general acknowledgement of the higher culture of Christians. This is best expressed by the Muslims themselves claiming Christian origin and presenting their conversion to Islam as accidental. Christians are also generally credited with better education and closer links with the outside world. Through emigration and education they are given credit for most of the social changes of the last decades, from clothes (Christians dress *allafranga*) to wedding rituals and food habits. Here lies the most important difference between the local conception of the nation and the national one. Both nationalist thinkers of the nineteenth century and communists tried to place 'culture' (meaning modernity and progress) above religion and to use it as a way to minimise religious differentiation in the new nation. However, in local conceptions, 'culture' is a part of religion—or in other words, religious affiliation is access to 'culture' or to a higher level of 'culture.' Thus the two communities are not equal in this—even if they are explicitly declared to be equal where personal salvation is concerned: one of them gives its members better access to 'culture.' For historical and social reasons, dating mostly from the end of the nineteenth century and the twentieth century, Christians as a community are given this privilege in the Devoll, in the same way as they and other minorities such as the Jews and Armenians were in other parts of the Ottoman Empire.

The cultural differentiation between Christians and Muslims probably started in the last days of the Ottoman empire. It was given a strong emphasis under Communism, as 'culture' became one of the symbols of the country's modernisation. The cultural difference between Muslims and Christians today results from a more recent phenomenon: the opening of the border with Greece and a large emigration to that country. In this border area Greece appears as the nearest example of a modern and prosperous state, and although the Greeks are usually criticised by both Muslims and Christians as 'disloyal' and 'selfish,' the Greek way of life is idealised as the embodiment of 'culture.' Here Christians are again privileged due to the identification of all Christians with Greeks, which is common in this part of the Balkans.

Local myths of origin leave no room for the Illyrians. These myths are essentially summed up in statements such as 'Muslims descend from Christians' or 'Our ancestors were Christians.' What local people look for is not evidence of single autochthous nation, for which purpose the Illyrians might be cited, but rather the confirmation that they belong to the realm of 'culture.' Similarly, the way local people talk about the difference between north and south has nothing to do with the nation's historical genesis. Local people use an imagined north as a mirror for their own weaknesses in such a way as to contrast north and south as 'without culture' (poor, backward, violent, traditional) and 'with culture' (rich, developed, well-educated, modern). Once again, they get confirmation that they are on the good side, while others are not.

This chapter has sought to explain what happens to national myths once they have been created and propagated inside a society. There is no fundamental opposition between national myths as expressed by the centre of the state or the élites on one hand, and by local population on the other. However, local myths are shaped by specific conditions and interests which are not homogeneous throughout the country. Such combinations and transformations are common to most systems of myths. Indeed the material used in these myths, such as symbolic juxtapositions, the concept of culture and representations of space, is common to the greater part of Albanian national mythology. In this particular case national myths are mediated by the concept of 'culture', which is itself the main means by which local people talk about themselves and others. This concept takes its meaning mainly from the specific social organisation of local society. We are thus reminded that the study of myths and representations should always be articulated in conjunction with the study of social structure.

Part V

MYTHS OF DEMOCRACY, DEVELOPMENT AND THE FUTURE

MYTHS AND NEW FORMS OF GOVERNANCE IN CONTEMPORARY ALBANIA

Mariella Pandolfi

Though geographically connected to Europe and the Mediterranean, the Balkans have been culturally constructed as a space of alterity. The region has been thought of and described in a way that both effaced and exemplified Europe's contradictions and conflicts.[1] Throughout the twentieth century a 'Voltaireian and Hegelian' logic represented Albania as an unknown and mysterious land. Travellers and journalists visiting it at the beginning of the century claimed that the Sahara or Tibet were far more familiar in European imagery; Albania was, according to Bismarck, a geographical abstraction and an anomaly of history. Throughout the Cold War Hoxha's regime (whose propaganda was also broadcast in Italian by Radio Tirana) remained a black hole, evoking from time to time frightful images of a ferocious Communism. It was also idealised as the last bulwark in Europe of pure Communism, having switched its international allegiance from the Soviet bloc to the Chinese.

Many remember how at the end of the 1960s the conversations of Western tourists crossing the Adriatic between Corfu and Brindisi on Greek or Italian ferries evoked the dangers posed by Albania's proximity. The distance separating Kanoni Point in Corfu from Butrint in Albania being only a few hundred metres, each time the ferries approached the channel, an iron silence would fall on the passengers, and there would be whispers of guns, missiles and rifles trained on the Western world.

[1]Maria Todorova, *Imagining the Balkans*, Oxford University Press 1997.

Orientalism

These travellers' conversations embodied an Orientalist logic,[2] though one that did not evoke the sensuality and the spicy aromas of the Orient but rather viewed the Balkans as violent and fragmented as well as being mysterious. The fear of that Orient contained various views of Communism across a spectrum, with the cruel and isolated 'barbaric' ideal-type at one end and the aloof, self-sufficient ideal-type at the other end: two poles where history ended and stood still. It was the beginning of the 1970s, and to the '68' generation the Greek Mediterranean, with its countless islands, represented an alternative to the mystical passage to India; it offered Oriental aromas without necessitating a journey to India. That forbidden territory just across from the Club Mediterranée in Corfu was as attractive to the younger generation as it was repellent to their elders. As the ferry continued on its course, that 'forbidden' land slowly drifted away and became again an opaque screen at a safe distance from the West.

Throughout the Cold War, the idea of a small, mysterious and poor world prefaced both the demonising propaganda of anti-Communism and the idealisation of Communism. The Cold War ended in 1989, and by 1991 media narratives were suggesting that the antithetical imageries of freedom and hell could well inhabit the same reality. It was a paradoxical representation fuelled by the explosion of the Albanian refugee crisis.

The multitudes crowding the ferries, clinging to their bulkheads and mooring-lines and confined inside Italian football stadiums did not appear as a sum-total of individual suffering, nor were they seen as one of the many possible aspects of a complex society. As with a picture by Hieronymus Bosch, to think of those countless faces and their entangled limbs as belonging to full-fledged individual political and social actors with their own personal histories, emotions and life projects was all but impossible.

The refusal to recognise that such territorial and cultural reality was the product of complex events showed how tenacious were the essentialist representations through which the West perceived the region. To peer behind this essentialist screen one would have to engage in the centuries-long violent dialogue between Eastern and Western temporal power. Both of these forms of domination crystallised Catholicism, Orthodox Christianity and Islam into firm ethnic iden-

[2]Edward Said, *Orientalism*, New York: Random House 1979.

tities, precluding the emergence of hybrid forms. These essentialisms were strengthened by the myth that a standardised package of interventions can evangelise and convert a population.

Ironically, this has been the logic of Western interventions in Albania, which has deployed its own standardised package under the guise of 'usefulness,' thereby strengthening both essentialist social forms and the stereotypes that still inform such interventions. From diplomatic representatives to international institutions, from military personnel to journalists and the vast array of experts and volunteers, all in their own ways have sustained and strengthened stereotyping discourses and practices that had developed since 1945.

Folklorisation

The story, told by many Western military experts in Albania, of 600,000 bunkers scattered throughout the land from the mountains on the sea based on a paranoid project devoid of any military logic, and the re-discovery of customary laws that suddenly returned to be enforced in the mountain regions and in the suburbs of Tirana, became the centrepiece of an exotic scenario. This scenario enchanted European law experts who had a passion for 'cultural archaeology' and researchers who invested in cultural heritage and for whom exoticising and folklorising was a professional practice. Thus blinded to the reality before them, they used the scenario to justify the violence waged by the people against their material existence and the hierarchical logic of their local institutions.

One only needs to mention the numerous abridged and edited versions of the *kanun* published throughout Europe in the 1990s[3] to understand how Albanian customary law became the master template for understanding the emergence of anti-state parallel power structures, the naïve cruelty of financial pyramids, the widespread local violence and other criminal activities. The *kanun* became the background to an essentialist strategy where alterity and guilt combined to generate stereotypes so resilient that they have survived, despite the continuous contacts, through commercial, political and cultural exchanges that have involved all Albanian social actors with the outside world since

[3]Cf. Padre Paolo Dodaj (translator), *Il Kanun. Le basi morali giuridiche della società albanese,* Lecce: Verba Mundi, *besa* 2, 1996; Shtjefen Gjeçov (translated, with an introduction, by Leonard Fox), *The Code of Leke Dukagjini*, New York: Gjonlekaj 1989; Patricia Resta (ed.), *Il Kanun di Lek Dukagjini*, Lecce: Besa 1996.

the fall of Communism. Albanians have attempted to reinvent a politics of memory free of all official ideology as a strategy for re-appropriating continuity with their past. However even this has been trivialised by the international media and numerous foreign 'witnesses' who entered their territory. Hence, reports by all kinds of governmental, non-governmental or diplomatic agencies have produced both an 'unofficial' discourse, legitimated by an 'I-was-there-I-saw' rhetoric, as well as an 'official' discourse comprising protocols and international agreements. However, both discourses reproduced a rigid and pre-constituted identity for the Albanian transition. In this international context, 'the Albanians' has became a category within which the only permitted discourses and practices are those that confirm the '*grand recit*' that allows Europe's multiple identitarian strategies to be reunited through a project of mass evangelisation on its last frontier. Putting into practice the gospel of the market economy, democracy and the universal value of human rights has produced a stage where the whole world can witness how institution-building and the establishment of a free market economy can be generated by the application of an 'exact' set of rules.

Reality has of course turned out to be different and far more complicated. The process of transition that took place in Albania over the 1990s was like a journey through a labyrinth.[4] The invocation of 'transition' is often a stratagem for avoiding the ambiguities and contradictions that all transitions from dictatorship towards a gradual modernisation entail, and Albania has been no exception. Transitions construct a constellation of often contradictory practices and meanings around the social actors involved: hence, the perception of being lost in a labyrinth which, after the collapse of a political utopia characterised by total social control, may well generate anxiety. From the point of view of a radical democratisation of society, the central period of Albanian 'transition' reveals some complex and interesting aspects. First, an unavoidable urbanisation process that has led to new forms of marginality; secondly, the emergence of a new generation gap, resulting in a conflict between cohorts divided by different memories and life projects; and thirdly, the transformation of élites and the conflict between rural and urban and between political-bureaucratic and intellectual élites.[5] The result has been the emergence of almost

[4]Ivan Ditchev, 'D'oncle Enver à oncle Sam. Les ruines de l'utopie' in *Outrement. Albanie utopie*, no 90/1996, pp. 28–40, p. 32.

[5]Mohamed Kullashi, *Humanisme et haine. Les intellectuels et le nationalisme en ex-Yougoslavie*, Paris: L'Harmattan 1998, p. 148.

xenophobic and nationalistic traits, and a class of sophisticated and polyglot intellectuals who combine a familiarity with the international scene with a critical stance towards the developments of Albanian civil society and the international community. Their opinions often have little currency outside their international audience, and at best enjoy an extremely restricted local audience. These intellectuals operate in a transnational medium far more complex than the world inhabited by the majority of Albanian social and political actors.

Which Albania?

In the course of this essentialising process, a large number of the experts involved—relief workers, diplomats, politicians, international bureaucrats, soldiers and many others—have argued for the need to place Albania under international tutelage. These diverse arguments all fail to take into account the actual needs of Albanian society, being largely the expression of internal politics in the countries involved in the 'westernising discipline' of Albania. To take care of Albania, to 'place it under tutelage,' is a strategy for hiding the tensions and conflicts that exist among EU members and between US and European geopolitical strategies *vis-à-vis* the post-communist project in the Balkans. Most important, Western involvement in Albania has become a media spectacle whereby the 'modernising' proposals to be implemented privilege electoral politics within each country (Greece or Italy, for example) rather than the real priorities and needs of Albania itself.

Throughout the 1990s this process gave rise to two different rhetorical expressions. One claimed that the 'modernising' project was directed towards a state of nature whose violent, savage, and primitive regression resulted from the collapse of the previous repressive regime. The other used the rhetoric of the New Humanism to underscore that suffering, extreme poverty and isolation called for immediate intervention and rapid social change. This change was proposed, when not imposed, through a package of predetermined interventions developed according to the logic of Western governmentality. If it is important to reflect on the legitimacy of humanitarian aid, it is even more important to reflect on how such aid is carried out by the political and social actors on the ground.

Standardised practices and rhetoric accompany aid packages devised by experts and hard-working bureaucrats with little knowledge of the local reality. Sitting in their distant offices, sometimes after a brief stay in Albania, they have produced documents, reports and strategic studies on institution building in the country. Whether informed by positive or negative rhetoric, the production of these political-military-humanitarian interventions has certainly reduced, when it has not effaced, the zone of autonomous action and negotiation available to Albanian social actors. Consequently local political actors have become 'humanitarian hostages' of the supra-colonial pedagogy. The rhetoric of 'civilisation' and 'accountability' has been enforced through a dense and constant international presence whose objective has been to justify and supervise the 'progress' of the transition and the goodwill of Albanian society and institutions. Living in the two most prestigious hotels in the capital, the Tirana and the Rogner (the first a metaphor of the previous regime's planned modernisation, the second of its post-communist version), experts, project directors or mission directors, together with a constellation of religious emissaries and transnational officials, have produced reports, strategic studies, and documents on every aspect of Albanian society tailored to the parameters of Brussels, Washington, Paris, Rome or Athens. This avalanche of paper has become a self-fulfilling prophecy, creating the society it envisages through humanitarian interventions.

That many Western interventions in Albania are still informed by such stereotypes attests to the robustness of essentialist representations—despite the fact that many civilian and military experts who have worked or directly interacted with sectors of Albanian society have been impressed by the high level of schooling, and the familiarity with foreign languages of the younger generation of Albanians who gained easy access to scholarships to study abroad. However, this realisation has not resulted in a more sophisticated approach, and seems to have been utterly ignored by the numerous reports and documents arguing in favour of humanitarian intervention. One only needs to look at TV and newspaper reports and at North American and European websites to conclude that 'Western' as a category is much more than a mere essentialisation of historical and cultural diversity.

Despite the difference in rhetorical motives and strategies, the West has produced documents informed by similar political strategies. Consequently, different institutions and governments that placed Albania under their 'tutelage' by setting priorities have thinned its social complexity, making it sociologically opaque. In the process they have projected their own ghosts on to this territory, rationalising this action as 'universal responsibility' or using the failure of local policies to legitimise the strengthening of the humanitarian industry.

Even though the military-humanitarian industry is a non-partisan parallel system within which often antagonistic strategies and responses emerge, there is a macro-level of production of discourses, reports and actions which are very similar in their impact on the ground.

Is Italy Albanian or is Albania Italian?

Italian intervention throughout the Albanian transition phase is a clear example of how this 'postcommunist' territory has been the target of contradictory strategies. The resulting short-circuit has strengthened the supra-colonial character of humanitarian intervention. For almost five years following the changes of 1991, the attitudes of the Italian media and civil society were constructed out of an imaginary Albania modelled on the peculiar experience of the Italian deep south, the Mezzogiorno. Indeed, Albanians have become a litmus test for the new socio-cultural models that have shaped recent north-south conflicts in Italy.[6] The politics of memory in Italy used the Albanian transition to work through the 'problem' of Italy's south, with its history of migration and underdevelopment from early in the twentieth century to the economic miracle of the 1960s.

The Albanian question was thus approached in Italy as another southern question. Albania was conceived as a primitive and violent south, riddled by criminality and clientelist politics. No attempt was made to develop a more refined analysis of this territory whose historical connection to Italy was limited to the brief period of Fascist colonisation. Hence, a double image of Albania: as a 'south' to be demonised, or as a courageous brother deserving of help because he had managed to free himself from the communist regime. Both opposing images were completely instrumental to the different phases of Italian electoral politics. These two different rhetorical strategies were the product of the ever-present conflict between the northern and southern regions of Italy. To be sure, it is hard to find a discursive production capable of offering a reading that does justice to the complexity of post-communist Albania. Concerns rooted in the logic of Italian politics have furnished a ready model for developing and executing the vast and contradictory array of military-humanitarian interventions in Albania.

These transplanted strategies rooted in local concerns have emphasised Albanian identity to further parochial political projects.

[6]Fabio Martelli, *Capire l'Albania*, Bologna: Il Mulino 1998, p. 85.

From this point of view accepting Albanians has arisen from the need of the Italians to re-legitimise a past they had relegated to oblivion. It rests on a reading of their history as a long evolutionary process of national identity-building which has been afraid of its own past and its relationship with Europe.[7] For Italy to accept its mission as the main bridge between Europe and the post-communist Balkans has implied coming to terms with the ghosts of its own past. The double bind message of Italian media and politicians has polarised civil society between two rhetorical tropes. One invokes invasion—the poor, the wretched and the lawless overrunning Italy—while the other invokes brotherhood and solidarity towards the victims of Communism, which has often meant the legitimisation of free market adventurers.

Most recently, a third trope has emerged whose political relevance is more complex though far from adequate. This has developed as an attempt to contrast the isolation and diffidence resulting from the tensions of Italy's relationship with its European partners. According to this last configuration, Italy is able, because of Albania, to negotiate the complexities of globalised geopolitics, and intervention there opens the possibility of a strengthened negotiating autonomy *vis-à-vis* its European partners. The Albanian identity this third discourse constructs is therefore entangled in Italian fragility within the European Union with the emergent project of a Southern Europe identity which, originating in Albania, would find in Italy its most accomplished expression. Once more, the same model of identity underpinning the two countries is separated only by a different rate of social growth.[8]

[7] *Ibid.*, p. 92.

[8] 'If one looks at the map of Europe, one can easily see that Italy is the juncture and at the crossroads of three European dimensions. Italy is part of the European Union, it is close to Central and Eastern Europe, and it is a Mediterranean country. Yesterday these three European dimensions were separated, today they are interconnected and complement each other. This must inform Italian foreign policy ... these are three axes that are also connected to a fourth dimension: a global foreign policy able to defend Italian interests all over the globalised world of today. It is through its expansion in Central Europe that the European Union will be able to build a new identity capable of bridging over the historical differences and to make the best out of the unification process ... a true Italian ostpolitik that will allow Italy to become a gateway to the Orient of the European Union and to develop a political bridge between this gateway and the other European nations.' (Pietro Fassino, 'Che cosa significa Ostpolitik' in *Limes. Il triangolo dei Balcani*, no. 3/1998, pp. 263–74; translated by the author from Italian).

Humanitarian industry

Though different in style, the strategies of individuals, parties and Western governments, all reflect a military-humanitarian logic that generates forms and procedures leading to supra-colonial practices. From 1991 until the crucial months of the war, the international presence in Kosovo resembled a spider's web in which the spider is difficult to discern. Although Western governments have been actively present at various institutional levels, the true agents of military-economic-humanitarian action have been the various international organisations, agencies, foundations and NGOs, which we can define as 'mobile sovereignties'. The power they wield is real enough and is superimposed on to bureaucratic procedures and lengthy intergovernmental negotiations. Their power controls and generates its own communication networks shaped by the temporality of emergency. This complex array of humanitarian actions, which is neither neutral nor open to negotiation, generates in these territories-in-transition a new form of cultural domination: the culture of urgency, with rapid and efficient interventions on a specific territory occupied by the humanitarian industry. Indeed, urgency in itself implies a social deregulation that calls for immediate action without any long-range planning. It also precludes collective renegotiation of the timing of the intervention between all the social actors involved, in this case Albania and international agencies. Whenever this does not happen, we enter an area of intervention we can only define as supra-colonialism, a new form of domination which overrides all pre-existing forms of governance in the name of humanitarian action. This supra-colonialism produces constant erosions of democracy, collective participation and political negotiation. As Laïdi notes,[9] the strength of all urgent action resides in its appeal to 'emotion' rather than to 'reason'. Indeed, how could one contest the legitimacy of an action that seeks to rescue victims of massacres and other human rights violations? Moreover, the feeling of urgency produced by this new scenario tends to generate a profound distrust towards all institutions, which are perceived as slow, constrained by bureaucracies and lacking the will to act. Consequently, according to this logic any behaviour

[9]Zaidi Laïdi, 'Le temps mondial comme évènement planétaire' in Laïdi *et al.* (eds), *Le temps mondial, editions complexes*, Bruxelles: Éditions Complexe, pp. 11–52, here p. 46.

that aims to develop a plan of action rather than an immediate response is certain to meet with failure.

Mobile sovereignties and supra-colonialism

The new military humanism recently discussed by Chomsky[10] thus covered this small country with its protective umbrella of international NGOs and UN agencies operating alongside Italian military-economical-humanitarian operations such as *Pellicano*, *Alba* and *Arcobaleno*. Over the years the Western presence was diverse and numerous: MAPE (European police), AFOR (Albanian Force) made up of nineteen national contingents, more than 7,000 NATO soldiers, four groups of international observers including those constituted by personnel of the Organisation for Security and Cooperation in Europe, and a dozen missions from Western governments. During the Kosovo conflict 180 international Non-Governmental Organisations were present in Albania. Since the mid-1990s Albania has turned into a laboratory where all the confused strategies devised by the West to work out its new political agenda *via-à-vis* post-Communism could be observed as if under a magnifying glass. The Kosovo crisis and the ensuing conflict have not only made explicit the existence of the complex network developed by humanitarian agencies since the end of the cold war; they have also revealed the vitality of the charity business. The victimisation, reconciliation and atonement industry is fuelled by huge amounts of dollars most of which have been spent to construct, feed and celebrate the intervention scenario. The humanitarian industry has been gradually superimposed on to political territoriality. As a result all local institutions have been either forced into tutelage or deprived of any decision-making capability at every operative juncture.

Although the humanitarian industry has a long history, in Albania and Kosovo a new albeit confused project has gradually begun to emerge. This is a different form of humanitarian intervention—one that reveals increasingly close ties between the humanitarian industry and military presence. In fact, the ambiguous difficult neutrality claimed by the founding charters of all humanitarian organisations has paradoxically increased their dependent status *vis-à-vis* military

[10]Noam Chomsky, *The New Military Humanism: Lessons from Kosovo*, Vancouver: New Star Books 1999, p. 38.

logistics. Helicopters, armoured vehicles and transport offered by NATO have created in advance the alibi legitimising a similar extension of the role of this military alliance in humanitarian crises to come. Albania and Kosovo have thus become territorial perimeters, in which international organisations have gradually generated two levels of citizenship. One has close ties with urgent operations, and interacts with the international presence and with Albanians working as 'local staff.' The other is made up of all those invisible citizens who are excluded from the 'humanitarian' circuit. Close examination of the political-economical-military network of humanitarian operations over the 1990s shows clearly the increasing role of transnational 'mobile sovereignty[11] legitimised by the media and by a view of universal human rights that takes no account of the local context. It is a process which, while superimposing itself on to the whole of Albanian society, does not contemplate negotiations with any of its members, be they political or institutional actors.

What range of negotiation is available to Albanian social actors in this context? How can they negotiate an organisation of memory, oblivion and reconciliation of their own which is not constructed by transnational bureaucrats? How, based on historical and cultural strategies of their own, can they be allowed to appropriate the different phases of their history with its myths, pain and loathing? How, can they reconcile this with the need for urgent action and transnational interference with their own values, truth and ready-made institutional paradigms?

The spider's web of supra-colonialism, embodied in the packaged democratisation and modernisation imposed by these mobile sovereignties on the territories experiencing the post-communist transition, increasingly resembles a compulsive strategy. This action is the product of the textual discourse of feasibility studies and universal human values that ignore local reality within this perspective, the principle of causality is abandoned for the sake of urgent action. Retracing the causal chain of events after the fact is useless and almost impossible. Urgent action and interference only bolster discourses that reinforce transnational myths and efface local ones. Only with great difficulty do they accept that, by opening international activity

[11] Arjun Appadurai, 'Sovereignty without Territoriality. Notes for a Postnational Geography' in Patricia Yager (ed), *Geography of Identity*, Ann Arbor: University of Michigan Press 1996, pp. 40–58, here p. 45.

on Albanian soil to all Albanian social actors, a reasonable compromise between local needs and universal values might emerge. The inability of the humanitarian industry to elaborate a project in which urgency-interference is not supreme reduces the dissemination of transnational operative standards within Albanian society to its mere operationalist enforcement, and makes negative effects unavoidable. The logic and politics of humanitarianism are superimposed on the local context and generate a sort of mimicry, which is first exacerbated by the urgency scenario and then legitimised as autonomous practices and evidence of the 'good conduct' of modernisation. At the local level, mobile sovereignties constitute new forms of domination that operate through a powerful network of alliances that monopolise legitimacy and authority. Consequently, local institutions and the government only acquire legitimacy insofar as they are located within this circuit. Yet they are marginalised and often play the passive role of 'accountants' of mobile sovereignties acting in the name of the universal values of aid, reconciliation and economic welfare. Hence, these local agents have no decision-making power on what actions to perform and when to perform them.

What are the procedures that allow mobile sovereignties, whose strategies and origins are transnational, to acquire local power? Their strength derives from their nomadism that allows them to structure global and local institutional practice into a novel and productive network, and is the result of the humanist ideological umbrella that allows them to mobilise and disseminate increasingly powerful élites from developed countries on the one side, and to recruit local élites on the other. Such new forms of domination merely replace one outside power with another. They both override and absorb the remnants of pre-existing local or global power structures in an ever-changing articulation of the urgent action discourse.

YOUTH NGOs IN ALBANIA

CIVIL SOCIETY DEVELOPMENT, LOCAL CULTURAL CONSTRUCTIONS OF DEMOCRACY, AND STRATEGIES OF SURVIVAL AT WORK

Nicola Mai

In the summer of 1998 I became the co-ordinator of a development project aimed at strengthening local civil society through the establishment of a network of eleven youth centres in the main urban areas of Albania. Because the project was based on a partnership agreement with a local youth NGO, I was able to immerse myself in the daily experience of Albanian young people and in the complexity of the cultural constellation in which they find themselves experimenting with their identities.

This chapter analyses the opposing and competing discourses and cultural constructions of democracy that guide the 'survival strategies'[1] developed by Albanian youth associations. This occurs within the context of social, cultural, political and economic change which followed the collapse of the communist state and the sudden introduction of a free market economy. It begins within an ethnographic perspective: how are foreign ideas and practices appropriated and transformed in the light of locally available social, cultural and economic resources, and to serve newly emerging local needs and priorities?

Civil society vs. civilised society: whose idea of (civil) society?

This question has particular pertinence when one is considering the phase of transformation through which many former communist

[1]Sue Bridger and Frances Pine, 'Introduction: Transitions to Post-Socialism and Cultures of Survival' in Sue Bridger and Frances Pine (eds), *Surviving Post-Socialism: Local Strategies and Regional Responses in Eastern Europe and the Former Soviet Union*, London: Routledge 1998, pp. 1–15, here p. 11.

East European countries are still passing. Development agencies and international institutions trying to introduce and foster civil society are very visible and powerful actors. Under Communism the nations of Eastern Europe never had a 'civil society,' which exists when individuals or groups are free to associate and form organisations that are both independent from the state and able to mediate in different ways between citizens and the state. Because the lack of civil society was an essential part of the totalitarian communist state, creating such a society through programs aimed at the establishment and support of Non-Governmental Organisations has become a major objective in the process of democratisation of former communist countries.[2] This is often based on the assumption that the more NGOs exist in a country, the more democratic it is. This, together with the fact that democracy building and civil society development are implemented as projects which provide local populations legitimate access to cultural and economic resources and to social advancement, has led to a 'proliferation of competing NGOs often with a small nucleus, stiff competition for the attention of foreign donors, and difficulties in joining forces in umbrella organisations, sharing information and resources'.[3]

Today Albania, like all other Eastern European countries, has experienced both the phase of Communism, when the West was either an ideal or an enemy, and that of post-Communism, when it was associated with the 'shock of the new.' It now finds itself at the beginning of the next phase, which Steven Sampson defines as, post-post-Communism. This is a phase in which the West, 'enters in full force ... it poses demands, it creates barriers, it offers opportunities, it facilitates or frustrates personal projects and strategies'. Whereas post-Communism is a phase in which the West 'subsumes the East through globalisation, commodities, symbols and western aid projects, post-Communism is a stage in which the West structures everyday life.'[4]

A new privileged social class has emerged locally in conjunction with the world of democracy-building projects. Albanian people

[2]J.R. Wedel (1994) quoted in Chris Hann and Elizabelh Dunn (eds), *Civil Society: Challenging Western Models*, London: Routledge 1996, p. 1.

[3]Steven Sampson, 'Exporting Democracy, Preventing Mafia: Rebirth of Eastern Europe in the Era of Post-post-Communism' in Klas-Göran Karlsson, Bo Petersson and Barbara Törnquist-Plewa (eds), *Collective Identities in an Era of Transformations: Analyzing Developments in East and Central Europe and the Former Soviet Union*, Lund University Press 1998, pp. 151–86, here p. 172.

[4]*Ibid.*, pp. 155–6.

who work for international development agencies not only can generally enjoy higher living standards than the rest of the population, but also have access to resources which have become highly strategic in the post-communist period: they can travel abroad, buy Western consumer goods, and send their children to the West to complete their education.

Local cultural constructions of 'democracy', 'society' and 'civil society'

There are two aspects of Albanian Communism which have important implications for Albanian young people's cultural construction of democracy and how this has influenced the process of establishment of civil society in Albania: lack of contact with the outside world and the subversive meaning which consumption acquired in the Enverist state.

As for the lack of contact with the outside world, bureaucratic, social and border controls were very efficient in making it impossible for Albanians to leave their own country, either physically or metaphorically, for forty-five years.[5] An efficient system of social surveillance made it extremely dangerous for any Albanian to transgress the regime's rules and prescriptions, which concerned many aspects of private life and individual freedom. All this assisted the regime's claims that Albania was close to paradise on earth, because it prevented its people from accessing any other source of information about the outside world apart from unauthorised viewing of Italian television, which played a major part in providing information about an alternative way of life from the mid-1970s.

As for consumption, in Albania as in other socialist regimes it came to acquire a central role within the emergence of a political opposition. By insisting that under Socialism actual material living standards would improve, and by failing to meet these expectations, socialist regimes ended up arousing the desire to consume and keeping it alive by deprivation. This, combined with growing resistance to the regimes and their rules, its laws and values, led people to build their social identities specifically through consumption.[6] A political alternative to totalitarianism was elaborated within an individualised

[5]See Miranda Vickers, *The Albanians: a Modern History*, London: I. B. Tauris, 1995, pp. 185–209, and Derek Hall, *Albania and the Albanians*, London: Pinter 1994, pp. 55–102.

[6]Katherine Verdery, quoted in Caroline Humphrey, 'A culture of disillusionment' in Daniel Miller (ed.), *Worlds Apart: Modernity through the Prism of the Local*, London: Routledge 1995, pp. 43–68, here pp. 55–6.

private dimension associated with consumption, where leisure and private desires were free from the need to be publicly acknowledged as ethic.[7]

As a consequence of all of these dynamics, democracy in Albania at first, came to be understood in terms of both a higher level of material wealth associated with the possibility to purchase Western commodities, and a condition of absence of rules and laws restricting individual will. In particular, the representation of Italian society by Italian television, by referring predominantly to dynamics of consumption, has emphasised practices and discourses of social inclusion, linked to access to Western consumer goods; it underplays the existence within capitalist societies of a system of rules restricting the entitlement to rights, regulating the use of force, and limiting the access to resources. Because of the lack of knowledge of the contradictions and actual functioning of capitalist democracies, these came to be conceived in the first post-communist years primarily in terms of a utopian and amoral world of unrestricted fulfilment of the individual consumerist's imagination, without any collective, political and ethical dimension. Here one can easily trace the projection on to the West and its capitalist democracies of the communist utopia of a world free of material hardship, social inequality, discrimination and exploitation—the historical promise Enver Hoxha never fulfilled.

The most striking aspect of contemporary Albanian culture for our purposes is its cultural and social fragmentation, seen by Artan Fuga as resulting from the conflict between contradictory systems of thought: homogeneous and heterogeneous.[8] Homogeneous thinking can be defined as a cognitive approach based on a principle of subordinating all conceptual space to one of the categorial poles involved in the process of intellectual confrontation (i.e. the debate about individual agency and social structure). While heterogeneous thinking starts from an acknowledgement of the value of difference and the attempt to synthesise the arguments produced by all of the categorial poles around which the debate is structured. The former tends to legitimise authoritarian power, the latter democracy. Artan Fuga contends that within Albanian culture a logic based on homo-

[7]Oleg Kharkhordin, 'The Soviet Individual: Genealogy of a Dissimulating Animal' in Mike Featherstone *et al.* (eds), *Global Modernities*, London: Sage 1995, pp. 209–27, here pp. 214–15.

[8]Artan Fuga, *L'Albanie entre la pensée totalitaire et la raison fragmentaire*, Paris: L'Harmattan 1998, p. 28.

geneous thought has been, and still is, dominant over aspects based on heterogeneous thought and categories:

> The intellectual education of citizens and of the elite has taken place under the influence of concepts emanating from a homogeneous logic structure: yes or no, good or bad, white or black, patriots or traitors. Meanwhile political institutions have been founded on concepts emanating from a heterogeneous logic structure. A contradiction, which undermines all social structures, has been created. The hegemonic mentality refuses the different, the other, the competitor, while the parliamentary institutions of a democratic state have been founded on the basis of the acknowledgement of the other, of the opponent, who has been denied by the dominant mentality.[9]

In this perspective, the condition of instability and fragmentation in contemporary Albania can be seen as a consequence of the difficult process of transformation from a cognitive system based on homogeneous thought, that has historically legitimised authoritarianism, to one in which new concepts and categories referring to heterogeneous thought have been introduced. This situation has brought about a widespread coexistence of practices and concepts which stem from historical, social and cultural experiences referring to two opposed cognitive orders, and producing conflicting values systems, social practices and interpretations of power relations.

If this is true of the Albanian people as a whole it is particularly true of young people and most of all, those involved in youth organisations. They have not only been more exposed, being young, to the influence of foreign media and thus to models of personhood and society that are potentially expressions of heterogeneous thought, but also because they are directly involved in the process of introducing and deploying of a new cognitive order—its founding concepts, roles and models—tending towards the democratisation of society. The fact that the latter has been first encountered in the absence of direct experience of the social, cultural and economic environment that produced them historically means that democratic concepts and practices have often been used strategically rather than understood in their full cultural, political and emancipatory relevance. Democracy has been associated more with a specific set of consumer goods, phrases, technologies, resources and practices, rather than with an unfinished political project based on the acknowledgement of difference as the main resource.

[9] *Ibid.*, p. 133.

The micro-physics of Albanian civil society

Some of these dynamics can be explained through a series of examples referring to the daily life of Albanian youth NGOs. In the first months of the project, work with the young members of the partner organisation was monopolised by endless negotiations on every single piece of furniture and equipment needed to set up the youth centres. When I heard remarks like 'We need neon lights and nice green carpets in here, we can not possibly have old-fashioned glass bulbs for lights and wooden tables—everybody will think we are a bunch of communists!', I was reminded that there was something more than furnishing going on. Then eventually it came clear that at the real core of this apparently marginal discussion were two politically different conceptions and models of democracy, translating into opposite understandings of both civil society and its aims, functions, and spaces. My attempt to introduce and advocate an alternative model of civil society which would be critical in relation to the predicaments of liberal democracy clashed against an uncritical, consumerist and materialist understanding of democracy, which had been internalised through the offerings of Italian television.[10] Moreover this depoliticised and fixed interpretation of democracy had been confirmed by the encounter with the high-tech and high-investment model of civil society offered by the many international foundations and organisations already present in the country since the first post-communist years. As a result of this encounter, civil society-building had been understood and experienced as a depoliticised agglomerate of fixed jargon expressions, and standardised working environments, material resources and working opportunities, rather than as an attempt to introduce a new social and cultural order based on new forms of thought.

This brought deeply contradictory forms of thought and practice to the chaotic world of youth NGOs. This is particularly evident in the way roles and functions are actually structured. In theory, work is organised according to rules and instruments corresponding to concepts such as public accountability, transparency and the sharing of information and responsibilities, which are expression of a democratic and heterogeneous logical framework. There is usually an executive manager, a board nominating the executive figures and verifying

[10]Arjun Appadurai, 'Disjuncture and Difference in the Global Cultural Economy' in Mike Featherstone (ed.), *Global Culture*, London: Sage 1990, p. 296.

the quality and effectiveness of the various activities, and a president mediating between these two functions. In practice, every function, from the recruitment of personnel to financial management and public relations, still tends 'naturally' to be dealt with directly by a central figure—usually the NGO's 'president' in whose absence activities are often blocked since no one else can take responsibility for action. Here one can easily detect the persistence, alongside the adopted democratic model, of a hegemonic and culturally sanctioned model of social organisation based on a homogeneous mode of thought and tending to be authoritarian, centralising and all-encompassing.

Another aspect of the life of youth NGOs in which the coexistence of conflicting modes of thought is visible is the management of diversity of opinion, conflict, and disagreement, which tends very quickly to be interpreted as a conspiracy either of local people working within funding institutions or of staff members supposedly influenced by competing NGOs. Homogeneous thought necessarily produces a paranoid vision of the world polarised between personal friends and enemies. Within such a cognitive environment the most difficult task is managing dissent, competition, and difference democratically, which implies introducing the possibility of being 'friends' and still disagreeing and vice versa. Typically every attempt to introduce a more complex and potentially more useful reading of events tends to be dismissed on the basis that as a foreigner one cannot understand how things function with Albanian people working in local or international institutions. Paradoxically, these tend to be criticised harshly for supposedly operating according to the same personalistic, manipulative and conspiratorial logic according to which social dynamics and relations are interpreted in the first place.

It is over access to resources managed by international organisations and local partner associations that strategic discourses of identity and otherness come more clearly into play. In the course of the everyday work of development, through the many confrontations and misunderstandings that constantly arise, conflicts emerge 'in which various kinds of identity marking mechanisms are at work ... in which discourses and practices of filiation, difference, essentialisation and stereotyping make themselves felt.'[11] It is through these dynamics of self-definition in relation to the mighty and overwhelming presence of the formerly idealised other, the West, that new local identities take shape on both sides of the confrontation. Western development

[11]Sampson, 'Exporting Democracy, Preventing Mafia', pp. 151—2.

agencies typically generalise about their local partners describing 'them' as manipulative, intellectually passive, and focused on the pursuit of individual goals, while their Albanian counterparts accuse the Western partners of being patronising and authoritative, and denying them access to strategic information or to the actual resources of the projects in which they are jointly involved.

Indeed some international organisations or institutions come to Albania with a non-negotiable, predigested and simplified definition of democratic cooperation, and require local associations to assimilate it; resources are made dependent on the willingness of the latter to cooperate on a situation where there is often no political, ideological or spiritual basis for cooperation. If it is true that, in the current situation, the collision between authoritarian-homogeneous conceptual frameworks and democratic-heterogeneous ones generates fragmentation and competition and that this hinders the development of a democratic political culture, it is also true that democratisation is about negotiating new ways of interpreting reality rather than forcing them on people, regardless of their culture and history.

In March 1999 for instance the Council of Europe promoted a week-long seminar aimed at the diffusion of information about existing EU youth policies, funding and training possibilities and, ultimately, the democratisation of the youth NGO sector in Albania. The event was organised through a series of small workshops and plenary sessions in which the representatives of the main Albanian youth organisations participated. Small group sessions using role play games and group dynamics for the introduction of methods and practices aimed at the sharing of information and responsibilities were useful and fruitful, but the method of direct confrontation between the representatives of competing youth associations was totally unsuccessful.

The dynamics of interaction that shaped the plenary sessions were of great interest and at the same time revealed much about the conditions in which civil society is sometimes being constructed in Albania. The representatives of the single NGOs involved in the discussion were practically forced to find common ground on which to cooperate in the future, since substantial funding possibilities offered by the Council of Europe for the development of youth policies in Albania were at stake. While the leaders of the two main local organisations involved in this process of mediation spent most of the time professing their intention to cooperate 'democratically' in the future, what was really going on was a fierce duel, rather than a debate, between two enemies in the eyes of a referee, in this case an international institution, on the grounds of the supposed democratic credentials of the associations involved.

Here was a clash between the two different ways of realising the objectives of the meeting in relation to the parties' agendas and priorities. The Council of Europe people wanted to enforce cooperation between two associations which did not share a common attitude on the future of Albanian society and the role of youth in it; they wanted to be seen as promoting a democratic and collaborative attitude within the world of youth associations even in the absence of the basic precondition to cooperate, namely the will to do so. They downplayed strategically relevant and meaningful differences which should have been democratically acknowledged and respected. On the other hand each of the two Albanian youth NGOs strategically and mimetically used these already instrumentalised criteria and policies of democratic legitimacy, supposedly independence from political power and the ability to respect and acknowledge the value of different ideas and initiatives, in order to have for itself exclusive access to funding and legitimisation from a very prestigious international institution. While pretending to acknowledge the acceptability of the positions of the interlocutors, the leaders of the two main youth associations involved were in fact subtly accusing each other of having compromised themselves through hidden links with political power, with the evident aim of excluding the competitor completely from access to funding and legitimation. This revealed how phrases, concepts and criteria used in projects to build democracy can be used insincerely and strategically within a substantially non-democratic conception of social relations and society as a whole. It also highlights the possibility of the persistence within international and local organisations alike of a largely authoritarian homogeneous mode of thought in the face of the introduction of a new conceptual framework.

In considering Albanian young people's cultural construction of democracy and the way it influences the actual building of civil society, it is important to highlight the fact that democracy has been understood primarily in terms of a concrete improvement of material living conditions. This means that the process of construction of civil society has been mainly experienced and conceived of as a set of strategic practices, concrete resources and opportunities linked to the access to those conditions. The current materialistic and neoliberal interpretation of democracy and civil society in Albania must be related on the one hand to the fact that these concepts have been historically introduced in the absence of any possibility for young Albanians to gain unmediated access to the actual economic, social and cultural context that shaped them. On the other hand, it is also the consequence of the active introduction into the country of a politicised model of society from the network of international organisations and institutions. The convergence of the introduction of a neoliberal model of society with a local cultural construction of democracy in terms of better material living conditions, which is not immediately associated with production and work, has important consequences for the way civil society is being built in Albania. Such a disempowering interpretation of democracy is consistent with the creation of a civil society which is economically dependent, on and potentially politically subject to, foreign investment without any prospect of change. The fact that the field within which civil society is organising itself is dominated by international funding institutions through direct financial support of local initiatives and activities means that Albanian civil society completely depends on political agendas and policies that originate elsewhere and that refer to a model of development which does not necessarily envisage the empowerment of local resources for local uses. Moreover, the convergence of a materialistic interpretation of democracy and the introduction of a neoliberal model of civil society brings with it the danger of reinvigorating an already established dynamic of reductive simplification.

The youth NGO project for which I have been working began by analysing emerging social needs and local cultural constructions of democracy, in order to introduce and negotiate a potentially more empowering model of interpretation and implementation of civil society. This begins with identifying the emancipatory elements within both local and foreign systems of knowledge, beyond any reductive and disempowering internalisation of Occidentalist vs. Orientalist discourses[12] and against any utopian comprehensive ready-to-apply recipe for constructing of a democratic society. This has been carried out through the gradual and negotiated introduction of common and shared moments of identification and open discussion of responsibilities, roles and initiatives, of ideation of new projects and activities, and the evaluation of work done. After much confrontation and discussion, an organisational framework now coexists with regular meetings of

[12]Cf. Sampson, 'Exporting Democracy, Preventing Mafia ...'

the staff in which initiatives are discussed, tasks are assigned and information shared; these are considered fundamental instruments and moments for the functioning of the organisation. In fact, the most ambitious aim of the project has been to make youth centres financially, administratively, politically, and culturally self-sustaining and independent and thus to enable young Albanian to identify priorities and organise activities according to their own political and ideological prerogatives and their own understanding and reading of their society, its history and its future.

CONSPIRACY THEORIES IN ALBANIAN POLITICS AND MEDIA

Fabian Schmidt

Conspiracy theories are a specific type of myth. They involve complex perceptions of a particular 'truth.' They pretend to be 'true', and thus they are well presented and can create a dynamic of self-fulfilling prophecy. Once an author has successfully presented a conspiracy theory and convinced parts of his audience, he will find believers. They in turn begin to promote the theory.

Through the mass media this can have a significant effect. Propaganda and agitation are based on such a communicative mechanism. Communication Studies have shown that people read selectively—usually those things that reinforce the beliefs they have already. Average individuals do not read or listen in order to change their views but rather to reconfirm them. They do this even if the content of what they receive contradicts their beliefs. As with other myths, the conspiracy theory becomes an authentic part of collective existence.

In this chapter some examples are presented to illustrate how such conspiracy theories have been used and presented in the Albanian media during recent times. The country's political life is harshly polarised. After the end of Communism the political scene was divided into two large camps, one around the Democratic Party led by Sali Berisha and the other around the Socialist Party, reformed heirs to the communists, led by Fatos Nano. Soon after the end of Communism, the Democrats and Socialists developed similarly moderate political programs following the models of West European conservative and social-democratic parties respectively. The two camps were divided less by programmatic or formulated ideological differences than by a polarisation between the two party leaderships and their own constituencies that seemed to be more concerned with patronage and clientelism than with political orientation and practicalities. It was reinforced by the fact that the 'truths' of the two sides were, and largely still are, mutually exclusive: indeed, their belief systems strongly shaped the developing political conflict.

Berisha, who won the 1992 elections and ended the rule of the last communist President, Ramiz Alia, came under increasing criticism during the first four years of his term. Some of his former allies, who split off from what had once been a large anti-communist movement, and the opposition Socialists charged him with conducting an increasingly authoritarian policy. The conflict escalated in the May 1996 parliamentary elections, when the opposition charged the Democrats with manipulating the electoral process. This was reflected in the media before and during the elections. During the campaign the political actors used conspiracy theories to discredit their respective political enemies. While conspiracy theories may have been used by the media on all sides, the most striking examples were to be found in the daily *Albania*, a nominally independent paper that made no attempt to disguise its sympathy for the Democrats.

The Democrats at the time accused the Socialist Party of trying to reintroduce Communism and nationalise the economy, and their sympathisers gave substance to that theory with numerous articles in the party daily *Rilindja Demokratike* and other friendly publications, in particular in *Albania*. The effect was considerable. A student from Shkodra, who was a supporter of the Democrats, told me in all sincerity before the elections of her belief that if the Socialists won, they would re-introduce Communism and nationalise the economy, a policy in clear contradiction to the party's program after its reform. It was clear after the Socialists took power in 1997, that they did not do this; still, this 'truth' was strong at the time in that part of Albania's divided political spectrum.

Thus the Democratic Party and Berisha's government were trying to discredit the opposition through the media. At the time *Albania* also promoted the theory that the Socialist Party daily *Zëri i Popullit* was financed by the Russian and Yugoslav secret services along with the opposition daily *Koha Jone*.[1] None of these charges was ever substantiated, but they enabled the government to prepare the ground for a crackdown against these organs. A few days after the accusations were published, police impounded delivery trucks carrying stocks

[1] *Albania*, 24 January 1996.

of *Koha Jone* and held them until well after the election. Also there were many acts of violence against the opposition and opposition media. Thus the conspiracy theories, as well as presenting the opposition as a threat to democracy, also apparently served to legitimise violence.

At the end of the election campaign, *Koha Jone* had heavy debts, and because it was the last powerful independent publication in Albania at the time, the Media Development Loan Fund in Prague decided to lend it money. This gave the rival publication *Albania* another opportunity to publish a highly polemical article, claiming that a co-sponsor of the fund, George Soros—whom *Albania* referred to as 'the Jew'—was trying to build up a media monopoly in the country by buying up the press.[2] Thus it added another foreign actor to its conspiracy theory. The article concluded:

> Soros may have been driven out of Belgrade, he will also not be allowed into China or Cuba. This has no great consequence for the Albanians. It is important that Soros takes care of his own business and leaves the Albanian media alone so that they can take care of their own business.[3]

Subsequently *Albania* published a series of articles about Soros, 'discovering' other alleged conspiracies in his foundations in other countries. That particular conspiracy theory about the rich Jew from the United States who invests in Albania to establish his media monopoly at the expense of Albanians, and who is sympathetic to the 'communist' opposition, adds a dimension of xenophobia, a common ingredient of conspiracy theory.

After the unrest that shook the country in the spring of 1997 after the collapse of the fraudulent 'pyramid' investment schemes, *Albania* developed a new complex conspiracy theory that centred on Greece and several key politicians in the Socialist-led coalition government of Fatos Nano. *Albania* published numerous articles claiming that Nano, his foreign minister and other cabinet members had an anti-Albanian orientation. The implication was that they were selling the country to the Greeks. The paper pointed out that 94 per cent of the members of the new government were from southern Albania, and claimed that Nano had referred to that region as 'Northern Epirus' rather than as 'Southern Albania.'[4] It thus tried to prove that 'Nano

[2] *Albania*, 25 July 1996.

[3] *Ibid.*

[4] *Albania*—email edition, 27 July 1997, received through the circular distribution of Albanews: http://listserv.acsu.buffalo.edu/archives/albanews.html.

is [a] "Greek" politician, who has accepted [the term] "North Epirus" politically'[5], meaning that he recognised Greek nationalist claims to large parts of southern Albania. The article went on:

> Nano is the closest friend of the PASOK Finance Minister, Papadopoulos, the author of the book on 'North-Epirus' and ardent defender of the thesis of its unification with Greece. Upon his mediation, the son of Fatos Nano is receiving education in Thessaloniki on a rich scholarship.

It concluded that Nano was committing 'national treachery'.[6]

The article was in line with statements by the Democratic Party such as: 'The composition of the government is discriminating against the Catholic community in Albania'.[7] Pushing Nano into a Greek corner also had the intention of undermining his political legitimacy after the elections. At the centre of the strategy was an attempt to show that the Greek secret service was involved in the spring unrest in Albania and had followed this by positioning its loyalists, including Nano and Foreign Minister Paskal Milo, in the government. '*Albania*' wrote:

> During the election campaign of 1997 the Greek soldiers in the south of Albania began campaigning openly ... for the deputies of the Greek minority. In Vlora and Permet, trucks of aid supplies for the pro-Greek deputies were accompanied by Alba soldiers. ... It became evident that Greece, though a modest contributor [of humanitarian aid], was a big profiteer. It managed to subdue Italy almost in an unscrupulous way in its domination of south-western and central Albania, and what is most important it won over the new Tirana leaders.[8]

Another article in the same paper claimed:

> The Greek secret service turned southern Albania into a training field and took full control of all the destroyed military units and the left-over logistics. In the end they began dismantling the ground-to-air missiles to avoid any potential danger from a disintegrated army in the south.[9]

The alleged aim of this strategy was 'a question of pure economic, political and historical Greek interests. ... Greece must win all the

[5] *Ibid.*, 29 July 1997.

[6] *Ibid.*

[7] Declaration of the Democratic Party of Albania, in *Albania*, 29 July 1997.

[8] *Albania*—email edition, 30 July 1997, received through the circular distribution of Albanews: http://listserv.acsu.buffalo.edu/archives/albanews.html.

[9] *Ibid.*

tenders of the European Union in Albania, to exploit cheap Albanian labour.'[10] From this follows an alleged capitulation by Albania. Thus the paper argued that when Albania signed an agreement for the deployment of 200 Greek troops in Albania to guard military barracks and a military hospital, it 'signed its own capitulation'.[11]

In the summer of 1997 while the government had not yet been appointed, another author elaborated on what other favours Greece expected from Nano:

> Fatos Nano is being forced [by Papadopoulos] to appoint one of the most suspicious and exposed anti-Albanian figures to the post of Foreign Minister, i.e. Paskal Milo, descendant of one of the darkest representatives of Greek chauvinism on Albania. [The article does not elaborate on this.] Meanwhile, the post of Culture Minister is ready to go to the Union Party for Human Rights, representing [the] Greek-Vlach minority, while similar projects are under way to transfer the Parliament Presidency and the Interior Ministry to people reared in foreign embassies in Tirana. Thus, in effect, the Socialists lose control of the Albanian government and it is transferred to those who brought them to power by setting Albania ablaze.[12]

In exchange, the Socialists allegedly received favours from the Greeks, thus making the conspiracy theory complete:

> The bandits coming to terms with the [Interior] Minister [Neritan] Ceka, proving that they are obeying him in the same way as when they killed, and set fire to plundered southern Albania. But the Albanian criminals who are leaving Albania quietly with Greek and American visas are a new potential danger for the countries where they are going.[13]

However, the conspracy thory did not only involve the Greeks. As early as May 1997 *Albania* ran an article claiming that officials from the US Central Intelligence Agency (CIA) were involved in southern Albania on behalf of the Greek-Albanian Socialist network.[14]

In subsequent debates, such as one over the drafting of a new constitution in the fall of 1998, the pro-Democratic Party press tried to present the Socialist government as 'anti-national',[15] arguing that this was demonstrated by an article in the constitution that allowed Albanian citizens freely to change their ethnicity and religion. Berisha

[10] *Ibid.*, 6 August 1997.
[11] *Ibid.*, 18 December 1997.
[12] *Ibid.*, 15 July 1997,.
[13] *Ibid.*, 15 August 1997.
[14] *Albania*, 21 May 1997.
[15] *Albania*—email edition, 10 November 1998.

then argued that many Albanians would declare themselves to Greek in order to stand a better chance of emigrating, and claimed that Greece was promoting 'ethnic cleansing',[16] while the Council of Europe considered this provision as rather liberal. The pro-Democratic Party media returned to polemics over an article in the constitution allowing the government to nationalise property in exceptional cases, for example if it wanted to build important infrastructured projects such as highways. The journalists again claimed that the Socialists were trying to use communist methods.

This small selection shows that a conspiracy theory is a mosaic of many parts. Similar conspiracies can also be found in other parts of the Albanian political spectrum. The key reason for their potency is the weakness of open political discourse, democratic culture, transparency and civil society. The more developed the democratic culture, the less likely it is that an audience will accept the axioms of the conspiracy theories because they are not credible. Absence of a broad social consensus on the authority and credibility of independent institutions, especially the judiciary, provides a fertile breeding-ground for conspiracy theories, and the continuing weakness of the judiciary and law enforcement have added a further dimension to the development of conspiracy theories, because many apparently political crimes remain unsolved. The killing of the Democratic Party legislator Azem Hajdari is a case in point; the inability of the prosecutors to solve it reinforces conspiracy theories.

There can be little doubt that the long reign of Communism in Albania encouraged such theories, partly because the political leadership used alleged conspiracies to explain changes in power and purges. The Kosovo conflict also encouraged conspiracy theorists. The existence of conspiracies in Albania is still widely accepted, as visitors to the country, especially journalists, usually discover. This is to a great extent a legacy of the communist-era secret service (*Sigurimi*). Even today locals often suspect foreigners of being spies, especially if they know the Albanian language. Many outsiders consider this as part of Albania's recent historic heritage and dismiss it with a smile, but Albania's civil society badly needs to emancipate itself from such explanation patterns especially where social and other broader problems are concerned. Conspiracy theories often serve as an excuse to avoid taking responsibility; therefore civil society needs to become more self-confident and build transparent institutions and procedures.

[16] Press statement by the Democratic Party of Albania, Tirana, 10 November 1998.

INDEX